Praise for *Where Yellow Flowers Bloom*

Cantin writes gracefully and honestly about unimaginable loss. Her courage and perseverance to find her son are a testament to her family. Her brave voice will have you grabbing your hankies in this gripping memoir.
— Leslie Zemeckis, actress, filmmaker, and author of *Feuding Fan Dancers* and *Goddess of Love Incarnate*

Kim Cantin tells the terrifying story of what happened when she and her family were engulfed in the 2018 mudslide in Montecito that tore their house apart, destroyed a community, and brought tragic consequences. She explores in vivid detail that horrific night and how she gathered strength, physically and emotionally, to undertake a years-long search for the remains of her teenage son while processing her own trauma and that of her surviving daughter. Kim is a mama bear who refuses to give up—even in the face of opposition. *Where Yellow Flowers Bloom* is brave, insightful—and harrowing.
— Catherine Saillant, Southern California journalist

Where Yellow Flowers Bloom is more than a portrait of a family disaster. It's a riveting account of the love and perseverance that carry a mother and daughter into a new life where kindness becomes intrinsically entwined with survival.
— D. Donovan, Sr. Reviewer, Midwest Book Review

Kim invites us to traverse the debris fields of devastation, grief, and loss as she tenaciously and heroically searches for her son's body. Although the mudslide demolished her family and life, guided by her heart and her gut she expanded and transformed darkness into light, loss into hope, and faith into homecoming. Readers will be in awe at how the unseen forces of kindness, intuition, synchronicities, and cutting-edge science come together and affirm that even when it seems darkest, light can find us all and shine.
— Catherine Weissenberg, author of *Beyond Ever After*

A gripping story of determination and resilience. Kim's journey reveals the fullness of the human experience. She takes you from agonizing loss to true growth thanks to the blessings of human kindness and the soul's gifts of strength, insights, and eternal love. — Suzanne Giesemann, author of *Still Right Here* and *Messages of Hope*

Inspiration rises from this heart-wrenching story like treasured possessions and cherished memories painfully extracted from the Montecito mud.... Kim Cantin shares a message of courageous resilience, dauntless determination, and undying hope. Her fascinating search through the enormous wreckage of her home, her town, and her life uncovers the power of human kindness, astonishing synchronicities from beyond our physical plane, and a deep "knowing" that love is eternal. For anyone enduring great loss, this book may be a touchstone for navigating the journey of healing and rebirth.
— Don Fergusson, author of *Salmon to Siddhartha*

Grief transforms into connections in Kim Cantin's memoir that centers on the 2018 Southern California mudflows.... Moved along by gathered memories, this is a vulnerable text. Cantin's language is raw.... The mudslide that is the book's impetus lasted only a few minutes, but its effects linger. Written by one of its survivors, *Where Yellow Flowers Bloom* pays homage to the community members and family members who rallied to search for those who went missing. — S.A. Ehle, *Foreword Reviews*

Survivors with similar stories, as well as anyone with curiosity about the event or about a woman with limitless strength, will find this book enthralling.
— *Blue Ink Review*

This is an unbelievable story of triumph over tragedy. It takes the catastrophic experience of a natural disaster and provides a highly charged, emotionally riveting account of survival and healing. Kim Cantin, the author, is a wife and mother who lost her husband and son in a crushing mudslide and found the courage and strength to walk with her daughter through this deep, dark valley of the shadow of death. — Dr. Gayle D. Beebe, President, Westmont College

WHERE YELLOW FLOWERS BLOOM

WHERE YELLOW FLOWERS BLOOM

A True Story of Hope through Unimaginable Loss

KIM CANTIN

PRECOCITY PRESS

Copyright © 2023 by Kim Cantin

All rights reserved. No part of this book may be used or reproduced in any manner without written permission from the author and publisher.

Editors: Leslie Wells, Lydia Martinez, and Julie Simpson
Creative Director and Cover Designer: Susan Shankin
Cover and Interior Illustrations: Luisa J. Millicent
Book Design and Layout: Andrea Reider
Precocity Press, Los Angeles, CA

This book contains material protected under International and Federal Copyright Laws and Treaties. No part of this publication may be reproduced, distributed, or transmitted in any form or by any means, including photocopying, recording, or other electronic or mechanical methods, without the prior written permission of the author, except in the case of brief quotations embodied in critical reviews and certain other noncommercial uses permitted by copyright law. For permission requests, email the publisher at: susan@precocitypress.com.

Trademarks that appear in the text of this book are used for purpose of identification only. No endorsement or sponsorship of this book by the trademark owners is claimed or implied.

Hardcover ISBN: 979-8-9877766-4-3
Trade paperback ISBN: 979-8-9873501-6-4
eBook ISBN: 979-8-9873501-7-1

Library of Congress Control Number: 2023902778
First edition printed in the United States of America

Author's Note: This book is a memoir based on the author's recollection of experiences over time, and quotations are sometimes reconstructed from the author's memory. While the book is a work of non-fiction, some names and identifying details have been changed, and some events have been compressed. The author recognizes that the recollections of friends, family members, practitioners and other participants in the events described here may differ from her own, but every effort has been made to evoke what the author saw and heard with the greatest possible accuracy.

To Dave, Jack, and Lauren —
My greatest teachers, for whom my love forever shines

In deep gratitude for all the helpers along the journey

CONTENTS

PART 1
RESCUE   1

Chapter 1   A Cry for Help   3

PART 2
WEEKS BEFORE   9

Chapter 2   November 2017   11
Chapter 3   The Thomas Fire   14
Chapter 4   A New Year: The First Week of January 2018   36

PART 3
TRAGEDY   47

Chapter 5   The Night of the Unimaginable   49
Chapter 6   We've Got a Victim Up Here   55
Chapter 7   Entombed   61
Chapter 8   Hospital, Hammond's, and Notoriety   67
Chapter 9   Two Memorials and a Chumash Ritual   80
Chapter 10   The Magnitude of Loss and Our Survival   90
Chapter 11   Steep Incline   94
Chapter 12   Musical Healing   99

PART 4
THE SEARCH   109

Chapter 13   Facing the Rubble   111
Chapter 14   The Crooked House   116
Chapter 15   The Sacred Search Team   130
Chapter 16   New Traditions   140
Chapter 17   Stairs and a View   144

Chapter 18	Paint-Covered Hands	152
Chapter 19	A Teacup, a Falcon, and a Superhero	158
Chapter 20	Search Dogs, Creek Walls, and Treasures Returned	170
Chapter 21	Photos and Baby Booties	175
Chapter 22	A Message of Hope	179
Chapter 23	A Community Search	184
Chapter 24	Valentine's Day, 2019	189
Chapter 25	"Look at Me"	193
Chapter 26	Boomerang	196
Chapter 27	Burled Tree, Drains, and Reuben	198
Chapter 28	Gifts Returned and Kintsugi	206
Chapter 29	A Surprise, a Heartthrob, and a Baseball Jersey	211
Chapter 30	A Birthday Celebrated	215
Chapter 31	Anthropology and Liposuction	217
Chapter 32	Consistently Clear Messages and COVID Lockdown	227
Chapter 33	Memorial Days	233
Chapter 34	Miraculous	251

PART 5
CRACKED OPEN 255

Chapter 35	Whispers	257
Chapter 36	Grief: An "And" Conversation	264
Chapter 37	Why Me?	269
Chapter 38	Finding Jack, Pieces of Love	273

PART 6
EPILOGUE 277

Years Later	279
Acknowledgments	285
Credits	291
About the Author	293

PART 1
RESCUE

"Do You Hear What I Hear?"
— BING CROSBY

CHAPTER 1

A CRY FOR HELP

IN SUMMER 2019, the daunting task of college applications descended upon us. It felt as if we were participants in a long, hard marathon designed in a complicated maze pattern. At times, I wondered if Lauren would make it to the finish line in one, sane piece. This was certainly not the type of summer activity from my youth. Back in the eighties, I worked a part-time job, and when not working, I relaxed with friends by a pool, covered with a thin smear of SPF 6, gingerly holding my hand-held radio with an earphone covering one ear. But for Lauren, this was the summer of a part-time job and writing multiple college applications, as well as securing recommendation letters.

On a sweltering Tuesday, Andy, one of Lauren's firefighter rescuers, sent over his recommendation letter. As I read it, sorrow swelled in my chest, along with a sense of profound gratitude that she'd survived and was now able to write college applications. I realized what a rock my then 14-year-old daughter had been under incredible duress. But, this Tuesday, eighteen months after the unimaginable occurred, was the first time that I learned about her rescuer's experience. His letter told me even more about the horror she had endured.

The first time I heard 14-year-old Lauren Cantin, she was fighting for her life. It was January 9, 2018; I was on duty as a Firefighter Paramedic with the Montecito Fire Department. The historic Thomas Fire had burned through Montecito, a small seaside town, a month before, and left multiple feet of ash and hydrophobic dirt sitting precariously on the mountainside. An "atmospheric river" rainstorm event caused the material to break loose, resulting in a devastating debris flow.

It was dark and bitterly cold. The rain continued to come down; everywhere I turned, there was a challenging hazard to be navigated. A massive mudslide had wiped out parts of Montecito, and I was one of many on a rescue mission. As I climbed off a debris pile, my co-worker Ben asked if I heard someone calling for help. I could not, due to a deafening nearby broken natural gas main. So, I stopped to listen more closely, and I heard a very faint scream for help. I pointed toward a damaged white house about 100 yards away, where I thought I heard the scream coming from, but Ben pointed to the debris pile I had just jumped off. There was no way a survivor could be in that pile, which was approximately 50 feet long by 20 feet wide and 20 feet tall. There were two crushed vehicles on top of it, along with part of an electrical pole and transformer, a refrigerator, a truck toolbox, part of a roof, and multiple large trees entwined together with mud that filled every gap of space.

I wondered whether a person could end up in the middle of this pile without being crushed; however, I was certain no one could breathe with the amount of mud caked into every crevice.

Since Ben was certain he heard the scream coming from the debris pile, I took a closer listen to the pile. And then I heard it, a very faint yell for help. This was the first time I heard Lauren Cantin.

Ben and I began to dig as we put in a call for extra help. Over the next two hours, we carefully removed debris from the pile, with help from our team and the Long Beach Firefighters — one piece at a time; we worked to create an escape route for what sounded like a young girl. While we could not see her and she could not see us, we were able to talk to her during her rescue. Lauren miraculously had a pocket of air the size of a volleyball, from which she was able to breathe, and had survived alone in the dark, cold, wet, treacherous mud for hours before we heard her cry for help. We discovered that her body was folded in half awkwardly, so her head was looking down at her feet.

She questioned us, asking, "What happened? Where is my family? Am I still in my home?"

We asked her what her name was, and she told us her name was Lauren Cantin. "Where is my family?" she asked. "We found your mother and we have not found the boys yet, but we are looking," I responded.

As we worked to get her out, she told us where she lived, where each of her family members were when a wall of water and boulders slammed into her home. When we asked about her body orientation and whether she had any injuries, she described that her head was looking toward her feet, and she felt scrapes on her legs from being pinned by debris. Lauren was bent over in an awkward position like a starfish, with head and torso faced down and arms and legs bent in unnatural positions. Her head was pulled down into the mud by the weight of her long brown hair, now caked in heavy mud. My partner brought over scissors, and we asked if we could cut her hair to relieve this discomfort. "Not today!" Lauren replied. We were impressed at how helpful, brave, and calm she was while we worked to get her out from the debris pile. We knew she was getting hypothermic. My partner went in to ask for her arm and proceeded to insert a needle to begin providing Lauren some medication. After two long hours, we used the jaws of life to cut the last tree branch, and finally we were able to free Lauren, a 14-year-old girl covered in mud, from the abyss where she had been trapped.

Incredibly, she was able to climb out of the debris pile with our help. She was in shock and once out of her hole, she looked down at her muddy pajama bottoms. Twisting her torso slightly to look at her behind, she said,

Lauren's early morning rescue
Photo credit Tom Piozet

"Oh, I should have worn different pants!" What? It was clear she was in shock, and she was referring to the gaping ripped hole she had in the backside of her favorite pajama bottoms. The TV crews captured this moment for the world to see. I assured her no one could tell, as she and the pajama bottoms were the same color of brown, thick, stinky mud.

We asked Lauren if she wanted to be carried to the ambulance. As Lauren looked out of her entombment, now free for the first time, an expression on her face was a stunning image of shock and disbelief as she looked at what seemed like a decimated war zone filled with mud, boulders, and no home in sight. "I'll walk," Lauren said as she looked at the ambulance. Using our arms to steady her, we let her walk toward the ambulance, and everyone was in awe that she was doing this. We later learned that in addition to the cuts on her face, she had a cracked rib, bruised pelvis, and numerous cuts on her body. Ben, the rest of the team, and I, were incredulous that she had survived.

When we looked around, we noticed TV videographers capturing the moment of Lauren's rescue; later we learned the footage was aired around the world.

PART 2
WEEKS BEFORE

"Better Together"
—Jack Johnson

CHAPTER 2

NOVEMBER 2017

THANKSGIVING WAS a week away. This year, we were planning a quiet day with just the four of us. Based on the hectic pace of the year, a low-key, easy day was the perfect tonic. As I organized the work papers on my desk, I had an overwhelming sense that I needed to have a family portrait taken. One picture would be for the cover of our annual Christmas card; the others I'd keep just for us. In recent years, we'd been too busy to slow down enough to take family pictures, but now I wanted them done.

I called a friend in town who is a great photographer, and asked if she'd help us. We met near the Peter Bakewell Trail, an open walking space about four hundred yards from our home. The trail is a beautiful area that locals go to when they want to walk in nature.

My friend led us into an open space, looking for the perfect location. After ten minutes, she stopped. We stood next to a grouping of uneven boulders, on which she wanted us to sit. Next, she walked us toward a downed tree trunk, where she assembled us for another group shot. After rearranging us, asking us to smile, and taking many

Cantin family picture taken weeks before the tragedy
Photo credit Medeighnia Westwick

camera clicks, she had what she needed. Then, we remembered that Lauren needed headshots for her vocal contest submission. So, she led Lauren to a wooden pedestrian bridge that crossed over the creek, and finished the shoot.

It was a lovely afternoon. I felt happy and relieved that we had a set of new family pictures. Time was short, since Jack would be off to college in a couple of years. Lauren was transforming from our adorable, chatty girl, into a beautiful and kind woman. Dave and I felt fortunate that we were not showing too much gray, and were still in love.

Once back at home, I still could not relax. Feeling restless, I realized that I wanted professional pictures of our Irish Setter, Chester. His coat was starting to gray, now that he was seven years old. He was such a handsome dog. I didn't want to spend more money on pictures

Chester and Kim, December 2017
Photo credit Kristen Smith of Veils & Tails Photography

right before the holidays, but I felt an odd urgency to do so. That weekend, in our backyard under a canvas of trees, a professional pet photographer snapped over one hundred pictures of him. In a couple of the pictures, I joined Chester as he sat with his tongue goofily hanging out the side of his mouth. I gave him a warm, loving hug from behind.

I felt relieved, that now I had pictures of my family and my dog.

CHAPTER 3

THE THOMAS FIRE

The largest wildfire in California history — December 2017

ON DECEMBER 6, 2017, I left the Dallas hotel, jumped into a taxi, and headed for the airport. During this business trip, I was connecting through Phoenix for a quick 90-minute flight home to Santa Barbara. If all worked as planned, I'd be home in time to have dinner with my family. Thrilled that my flight left on time, I sat back in my seat and shut my eyes to rest. As we neared Ventura, the pilot's voice came on the loudspeaker to give an update. He directed, "If you look out the right side of the plane, you will see the Ventura Thomas Fire burning." I looked through my window and out in the distance, there was a huge fire burning in the hills and mountains. *So sad*, I thought. The holidays were approaching and not being able to celebrate the holiday season made the situation worse for the families that were impacted.

A few minutes later, the pilot came on the loudspeaker again. "Well, folks, because of the Thomas Fire, many of the people who work at the Santa Barbara airport control tower have been affected, and could not get into work. In fact, the control tower is down, which means I'll have to land this plane myself. Hang tight, we'll have to wait our turn. I'm guessing we'll be delayed about thirty minutes."

Land the plane himself! I thought uncomfortably as I opened my eyes and adjusted my seat to an upright position.

During the next thirty minutes, I tried to rest, but could not. I was worried about my safety. At 51, I was a mom of two teens and a wife of a loving husband. My family needed me. I tried to relax, and counted the minutes until the plane landed. The difficult flight home felt like a bad omen. The Thomas Fire roaring in Ventura County twenty-four miles from my home was impacting flights into Santa Barbara. Hearing about people affected by the fire, losing their homes, or unable to make it into work, made it ominously real and close.

Once home, I walked in the front door. I could smell the aroma of Bolognese spaghetti sauce and garlic bread that Dave, my husband, was preparing.

"You would not believe my flight home," I said as I walked into the kitchen to give him a quick kiss. I always marveled at Dave, who seemed to be able to do it all. He was a hardworking, self-made man. After his parents' divorce in his first year of college, he was told that there were no more funds for his education. Dave adapted, worked for a year, and then secured a spot at Bryant University. He took a job as an RA in the dorm to offset the cost of tuition. He worked tirelessly, and always with a charismatic smile.

Once married and with a family of his own, Dave embraced fatherhood and was a loyal, loving husband. He became the local Cub Scout leader and Boy Scout Scoutmaster, while juggling an intense work schedule as a busy medical device executive. He'd get a corsage for Lauren and wear a tie matching the color of her dress for the elementary school Daddy-Daughter Dance. We'd also make time for

Dave and Lauren, elementary school Daddy-Daughter Dance

date nights. I knew I was lucky. What I loved most about my husband were his kind heart and his smile that lit up the room. Being an excellent cook was a delightful perk, as was his attentive ear when I needed to talk.

Dave was listening now as he stirred the spaghetti sauce and checked on the garlic bread warming in the oven. He was taking in my angst about my flight and the fire in the hills. A few minutes later, he called the kids for dinner. Jack, 17, strolled out of his room with a warm, "Hey Mom, how was your trip?" 14-year-old Lauren's footsteps came into the kitchen. "Yum, spaghetti!" she exclaimed. She told me about the movie she wanted to see on State Street with some of her friends.

When we purchased our house, I told many of my friends it was our "forever home." It was located down a private lane that was visible through a beautiful columned entrance. A few homes were tucked away down this tranquil lane, and among an amazing canopy of mature coastal live oaks and large sycamores.

When we purchased it, the house needed a lot of work, but we didn't mind. We could barely afford it, but we wanted to be in this community and have the kids attend the well-regarded local school. Although we stretched ourselves financially to buy it, we were eager to set roots and build a life here. Dave was very handy around the house. Over the years, after finishing up his day job, he worked nights and weekends repairing things around the house. As we could afford it, we'd make more improvements. I was amazed to see the improvement Dave's upgraded wood trim baseboards, crown molding, and a fresh coat of paint did for our house.

The location was perfect. I could easily walk to the upper village and to the lower Coast Village Road, a lovely street with boutiques, restaurants, and a quaint Read 'N Post store. The kids' elementary school was just a few streets over. When they were younger, they walked to it on the aptly named Schoolhouse Road.

On Sundays, I'd open our front door and smile upon hearing the church bells ringing at our church a quarter mile up the street. This town was my slice of Mayberry. Every 4th of July, the Montecito Fire Department hosted a pancake breakfast for the community. Dave and Jack would walk with the scout troop in the block-long village parade. Arriving early, Lauren and I would find our spot on the side of the road to take in the short, festive parade. Many of the town's 9,000 inhabitants came out in their sun hats and red, white, and blue outfits to watch. Immediately following the parade, we'd convene at Manning Park, which was set up with snow cone booths, live music, and grills sizzling with hot dogs and hamburgers. Each year, that weekend became an opportunity to reconnect with neighbors. When Jack was 11,

18   WHERE YELLOW FLOWERS BLOOM

Jack waving at us with a gloved hand, left, at the Scouts booth, Montecito Village 4th of July event

he'd delighted in participating in the pie-eating contest. He found it hilarious to have his face submerged in pie, eating with no utensils.

Montecito was a quaint town where I saw people I knew when I went out to dinner, or to the YMCA. We knew the names of the shop owners, and tried to support their businesses.

When we first moved into our home, I noted that a lovely retirement facility was located across the street. I often told Dave, "When I'm old enough, just put me in a wheelchair and push me across the street." Dave, at 49, and I, at 51, assumed that we would have many more years in our home. We looked forward to retirement, when I could garden in the yard, and Dave could enjoy in his woodworking hobby and play more golf.

We appreciated the amazing weather in this California seaside town. Originally from Rhode Island, Dave made a swift adjustment to T-shirt weather vs. snow coats and boots. Most days were sunny

Lauren, enjoying the Montecito 4th of July celebration and cotton candy

Jack, "pie-eating contest" at the 4th of July celebration

and pleasant. Come winter, we'd have some rain, but it was welcomed because it nourished the hillsides and plants. When rain came, we appreciated how it made the hillsides a vibrant green.

A few years ago, when we had our driveway repaved, we had the workers add a berm at the entryway from the lane into our driveway. The berm helped the water flow down the lane to the proper street drainage systems on heavy rain days, and kept it from flowing down our non-absorbent driveway near the house. Dave thought that was overkill since we had a French drain near the house to handle the water, but I preferred this extra level of protection. Each year, we'd do a bit more work on the house to make it just how we wanted it.

Recently, we'd purchased a farm kitchen table with comfortable high back chairs for family dinners, when we'd catch up on each other's days. One evening I asked, "Jack, what was the best part of your day today?" He sighed, as this was a question that he'd heard many times before. He obliged and answered, "My online game is going well, and my teacher gave me his felt Harvard University pennant flag he no longer wanted, so I hung it up in my room." Lauren shared that her dad had taken her to get a peanut butter-flavored smoothie after school. Dave said that his day had been hectic, as he'd had back-to-back sales calls with his global team to help close some year-end deals. Continuing to chat, we dug into our meal.

Lauren had just finished up her 9th grade fall quarter, in which she and her classmates were the leaders of her middle school. Jack, now a high school junior, was immersed in a most grueling academic year; the year that colleges carefully reviewed, come application time. He was taking three AP classes, and fortunately was self-motivated. I kept track of his progress, as many parents told me junior year could be demanding, and that some kids could get overwhelmed and depressed. So far, Jack was handling the pressure fine. He still had time to socialize and play online games.

Jack was enjoying high school. Now having his driver's license, he could stop at the coffee shop anytime he liked, and drive to the beach or to get-togethers with friends. He and his girlfriend broke up over the summer, so he had his first experience of a broken heart. Fortunately, a good friend from school hosted a couple of fun sci-fi Star Wars outdoor movie nights on her parents' deck. After spending time with friends, he came back home happier and grateful for them. When not with friends or studying, he helped to lead community service events with his group, Teens on the Scene, that he co-founded with a couple friends a few years prior. Jack had earned Eagle Scout rank in 9th grade, so as a junior he did not need to attend as many Scout meetings. Instead, he carved out time to enjoy weekend hikes and campouts with the troop. Dave had encouraged Jack to get his Eagle Scout rank before the "fumes" became a distraction. The car "fumes" and the "perfumes" to a 16- and 17-year-old would be an overwhelming distraction from scouting.

Lauren had more skip in her step recently. She was thriving in middle school, and had completed a much-anticipated 9th grade Channel Islands trip. Her class of about 35 students, along with her teachers, lived on a dive boat for five days as they studied oceanography. During the day, they kayaked and snorkeled near the islands, or hiked on an island trail. A highlight was when they kayaked into unique island water caves throughout the protected natural preserve. While deep into the caves, often a teacher would stop the group to read and discuss Plato's *Allegory of the Cave*. The teacher knew this would be a memorable way to learn about this famous work, and to help them think about what was real vs. perception. In the early evenings, they boarded the boat to discuss what they had learned.

When not at school, Lauren loved musical theater, singing, and being active in the National Charity League and Teens on the Scene groups, in which she volunteered around town. Often, we'd hear her walking around the brick patio in the backyard, practicing the song for *Les Misérables*, "I Dreamed a Dream." She was practicing for the role of Fantine, as the play was to open in May at the local Lobero Theatre. Dave and I loved hearing her sing, as did Jack, though in typical brotherly fashion, he'd yell for her to take a break when her singing interrupted his focus on a computer game.

This December, Dave was in his groove, albeit exhausted due to his job as Global VP of Sales. The company had new leadership and was working under an aggressive timeline to meet target revenue and performance goals. Dave worked for a guy we'd both worked with earlier in our careers, and he enjoyed the camaraderie. Dave always worked hard, but he'd never worked this tirelessly. He knew this was an important opportunity in his career because if he helped grow the business, he would be better positioned to lead a medical device start-up, which was his lifelong dream.

His all-time favorite and most invigorating job he'd ever had was in his mid-twenties, when he worked as a marketing intern for a medical device start-up. As an intern, he worked with surgeons who used the high-tech ultrasonic tool in newly developed laparoscopic surgery. The tool was amazing, as it both cut and simultaneously sealed vessels closed while also enabling dissection. Surgeons used this scissor-like device in some cases instead of having to use clips or multiple sutures to close vessels. Surgeons embraced this new technology that streamlined their procedures and was gentle on human tissue. With success of the product and surgeons adopting the new technology, one of the Johnson and Johnson medical device companies swooped in to acquire the start-up, and weaved it into its product offering. Dave demonstrated this innovative technology, called the Harmonic, to over a thousand surgeons, which led to him being dubbed "Mr. Harmonic." During the acquisition, Dave's boss had advised him to get big business experience from J&J, to learn all he could, and after that, to come back and lead his own medical device start-up company. Now, 18 years later, this current job was the culmination of his career and efforts; if he succeeded in this company, he'd be well positioned to achieve his goal and lead a medical device start-up himself.

After working a grueling schedule all summer, consisting of non-stop 14-hour days, by late fall the team had landed new contracts that would increase the company's revenues. The new business would enhance the company's performance. Unexpectedly, the vice president of marketing had recently left the company. With that, Dave was then asked to lead both the marketing and sales teams. By early December 2017, he was days away from another flight to Europe for some key meetings. At the same time, the Thomas Fire continued to burn through nearby Ventura County. Taking a break from packing his luggage, Dave came to speak with me in the dining room. As we both stood there looking out at the mountains through our bay window, Dave said, "Kim, you'll be fine; the likelihood of the fire coming all the way across the mountains and into Montecito is improbable. But if it does, just evacuate to Karen's." My college friend lived in Thousand Oaks, far enough away that we'd be safe from the fire. Although it was a remote possibility, I collected key items and papers, and placed them in a box to take with me in the event of an evacuation.

The fire became the largest wildfire in California history, burning over 280,000 acres. It was all we heard about and saw on the news for days. We were devastated to learn that a Ventura firefighter lost his life defending homes, and tragically left behind a pregnant wife and toddler.

Ever a prepared scout, Dave asked us to sign up to receive emergency alerts that would provide us with up-to-the-minute evacuation warnings. These alerts blasted out from our cell phones in an unsettling manner. As our phones rang with an ear-piercing, shrill blast, like an Amber alert, we'd freeze, stopping what we were doing to read the message. With the Ventura Thomas Fire still burning ferociously, before leaving on his trip, Dave had ordered a full box of N95 masks. He asked us to wear them when going outside. The air thickened with smoke, and soon the kids brought the dog inside so he would not breathe in the dangerous smoke.

Then the following week, when Dave was in Europe, an evacuation signal came through on our phones. We quickly grabbed our essentials and our dog, and headed up to my friend's home 40 miles southeast toward Los Angeles. The kids were calm as we drove to stay with Karen and her daughter for a couple of days, until it was safe for us to return. While there, we constantly watched live updates and videos of fire trucks protectively lining our friends' street on Park Lane, only 1.8 miles from our home. We were acutely aware of how close the fire was to our home. Many of the homes were estates, and we knew that some insurance companies found it more economical to pay to stage fire engines and fire protection teams in front of these large estates if the fire came too near. Our home was smaller and much more modest, and hence our insurance did not pay for a private fire truck or team to guard our lane, although our children's artwork and our family photos were priceless.

After a couple days, when we learned we could head back home, the smoky air was thick as we drove down Coast Village Road. The boutiques and restaurants were covered in ash; an eerie sight. The ominous setting juxtaposed with what was usually a season of holiday cheer was unsettling.

Mid-December, when Dave arrived back from his business trip, he was confronted with a home and yard covered in white ash. With his typical industrious approach, he researched and ordered an ash removal vacuum with a special filter. When it arrived, he put on a backpack-like contraption to vacuum the ash from the house and yard. The box of N95 face masks helped us breathe while we lived in these frightening surroundings.

A few days after Dave returned from Europe, our cell phones startled us again with a loud evacuation message. Winds were picking up in a "sundowner," dry, fast-moving southerly winds that come down off the mountains. They were so dry that our plants wilted. In my teens, I loved the warm, dry Santa Ana winds that blew through Southern California, but I feared these powerful "sundowner" winds that were blowing from the mountain toward our village. I grabbed a mask as I took a step outside onto our driveway, and looked at the orange glow of the fire raging on the mountain. Seeing the flames and smelling the smoke was terrifying.

A few minutes later, when we heard the emergency alert blast through our phones yet again, we loaded up our cars and grabbed our bags, ready to head back to the safety of my friend's home.

"I'll drive my truck; Kim, you take Lauren and the dog in your SUV," Dave directed.

"Jack, you follow Mom in your car. I'll be right behind you," he assured us.

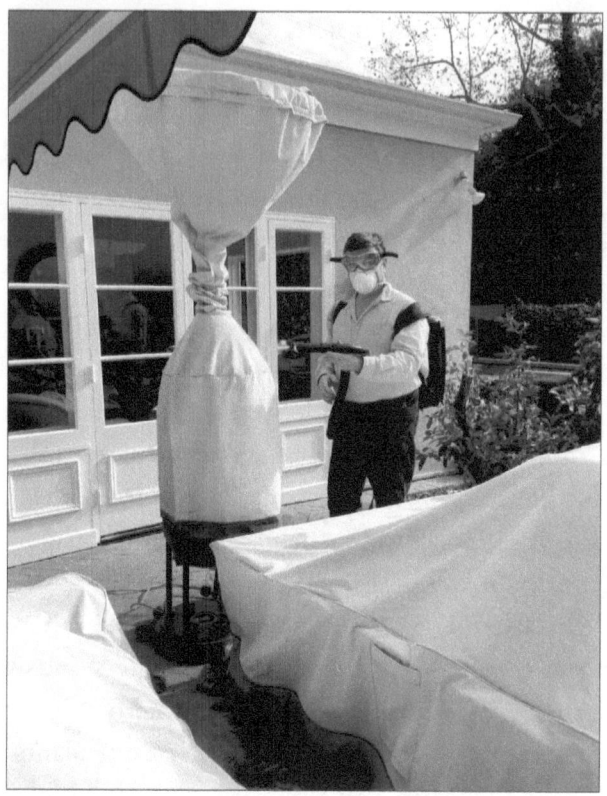

Dave with special ash-cleaning vacuum,
cleaning Thomas Fire ash from the house and patio

At this point, we were nervous, and I felt relieved that Dave was home to lead us out of this crisis. Typically, I was an independent person, but on this day we all needed Dave's direction. We could see the flames on the mountains above Montecito, and the concept that they could race down our way was now a reality. As Lauren, our dog, Chester, and I pulled out into the lane, I rolled down my window to urge Dave and Jack to leave right behind me and not to take more stuff—that we just needed to get out.

They stayed for another few minutes to push three gas heat lamps with propane tanks next to the pool. Dave surmised that if the fire came near the house, the firemen could kick them into the pool and avoid an explosion. The skills he had learned as a scoutmaster came in handy during a crisis.

I felt uneasy and nervous as I drove to Karen's house. The situation was frightening, and I did not like Jack having to drive so far on the freeway as a relatively new driver. I was relieved when we arrived in Thousand Oaks, pulled into Karen's driveway, and we began to unload our cars. Opening the door to the backseat of Dave's truck, I saw our framed wedding picture that had hung in our home's hallway. In addition to the portrait, Dave had saved two queen-sized quilts I had made for him for Christmas the year before. One quilt was aqua blue and teal batik fabric with subtle ocean-themed designs — his favorite colors. On it, I had added a navy silhouette of Dave and Jack on their first scuba dive together. During a summer Scout camp, Jack earned his scuba certification, and someone had snapped a picture of Dave and Jack together, suited up in their dive gear before their first dive.

This picture also symbolized a joyous outcome for Lauren and our family. Dave told me that as he was posing for the photo, he paused to take a call from a middle school headmaster. Lauren had been on the waitlist for a spot in the incoming 7th grade class. She wanted more than anything to attend this school, but she did not want to get her hopes up. We kept in touch with the headmaster over the summer, but we were holding out little hope, as there were few spots available, and many students applied. However, on the day that Dave and Jack had geared up to make their first dive, Dave took a call from the headmaster. He confirmed that Lauren had been accepted, and would start in the fall. Seeing that Dave saved our wedding picture and these quilts made me love him even more.

This time when we landed on Karen's front doorstep, we were much more agitated and frightened. We had no idea how long we'd have to stay, or if our house would be there on our return. My office

Jack's first scuba dive with Dave and when Dave took the headmaster's call

knew of my remote working status, and each of us had our computers. Jack set up a place to work in Karen's daughter's study, where there was a desk and where he could escape; he managed his anxiety with gaming. Dave set up work at a bistro table at the far end of Karen's living room, where he also tried to concentrate. I set up my computer and materials in the game room, and sat on a barstool, using the bar top as my desk. I attempted to focus during the day, but was distracted and worried about the fire and the safety of our home. Lauren sat in the living room, bored, or would shift locations to keep Jack company as she texted her friends. Chester stayed close at my feet.

Trying to infuse our time with some levity and distraction, I took the kids to The Oaks, a big indoor mall nearby. Santa Barbara does not have indoor malls, so Lauren and Jack thought of this visit as an adventure. In addition, it was December, and a good time to do some Christmas shopping. When we arrived at the mall, the kids and I split up. I found the perfect Star Wars sheet set for Jack, and some red flannel Dr. Seuss sheets for Lauren. That night, Dave booked movie tickets for the new Star Wars movie that was showing in a nearby theater. The kids and Dave loved the movie, but I was too worried about the fire to pay much attention to it.

After the movie, when we returned to Karen's, we turned on our computers to listen to the local news in Santa Barbara, hoping to hear something positive. Instead, we learned that strong sundowner winds were predicted that night, which meant that 40- to 50-mph dry, powerful winds would accelerate the fire down the mountains, toward our town and beach. As those powerful winds gusted through the mountains, they would fan the wildfire that had already consumed over 100,000 acres.

I went to bed, terrified that our forever home might be consumed by fire that night. Though this would be a great tragedy, I was grateful that I was with my family in a safe location. However, Dave had had an exhausting work year already, and he felt that to lose our house might be more than we could handle. We tried to focus on the fact that our family was safe, 40 miles away from the treacherous flames. But we hardly slept a wink.

The next morning, we were surprised and relieved to learn that our home was safe. Firefighters had worked tirelessly and strategically to save hundreds of homes, including our own. We were grateful that the first responders' efforts saved our home and the community we loved.

The kids had sensed our fear, and they, too, had been worried about our house burning down. Although our house was saved, December

2017 in Santa Barbara continued to be a frightening time; while others, who had not been affected, were preparing for the holidays.

As we waited to hear when it would be safe to return, we stayed another night with our friends. Dave suggested we see another movie, and we chose to watch *The Greatest Showman*. Now I was able to enjoy the music, the dancing, and the story — all were magnificent. This movie was just what we needed. That night we were more relaxed, knowing our house had survived the sundowner. While in the theater, looking at my family seated on either side of me, I reflected that in our overly busy lives, this time together as a family was priceless. My family was what mattered to me, and I savored the moment.

A day later, when the evacuation orders were lifted, we headed home.

It was a somber drive along the 101 freeway. By now, over 1,000 homes had been destroyed, and, as mentioned earlier, tragically a firefighter was killed. As we drove, we could see the scorched and blackened hillsides; we saw where the fire had jumped the freeway, burning the palm trees on the ocean side of the road. The closer we got to Montecito, the more ash covered our windshield; so much so, that I had to turn on the windshield wipers so I could see.

During the evacuation, the heroic first responder police, law enforcement personnel, and National Guard positioned their trucks to block entry into our town that sat vulnerable and vacant. While the town was evacuated, we worried about home burglary, as ours was a relatively easy street to explore. Once the evacuation order was lifted, the police and National Guard who'd been protecting our neighborhoods left.

Learning of this, we felt an urgency to get home. We worried that some opportunistic and unsavory people who knew that many of the houses were vacant might drive down these streets, and burglarize some of them. We were frazzled. This was a Christmas season like no other; packages and parcels were not delivered during the evacuations, so many were returned to the sender. As we drove into our quiet lane, tape was draped across our little group of mailboxes, indicating there was no mail delivery. It was a visual reminder of the terrifying situation we had just escaped.

We evacuated three times over a 16-day period in December — once while Dave was in Europe, and twice when we were all together.

As we pulled into our driveway that December 22nd, we witnessed a surreal site. Our blacktop driveway was so ash-dusted it looked like it was covered in snow. When we walked to the backyard, it, too, was covered in ash. The pool's water was gray, dark, and ash-laden. Walking through the house, we could smell smoke in everything from our clothes to the carpets, to the inside of our kitchen cabinets. Even our drinking glasses that were in the cabinets were covered in ash and smelled of smoke. Despite all this, we were immensely grateful that our home was still standing, although we were overwhelmed by the amount of cleaning effort that would be required.

Christmas was now days away. The kids knew that some packages would not arrive on time, and they were fine with that. The fire had impacted so many. Businesses were forced to close; restaurants were not allowed to open, and annual holiday parties were cancelled. Despite these changes, we put up a slightly crooked tree in the living room and hung it with treasured ornaments that we had collected over our lifetimes. Each ornament symbolized memories of the time we received it, and from whom. I displayed a four-piece cream-colored porcelain train ornament set that Dave's aunt had gifted us after our daughter's birth. Dave's name was written in gold on the front engine, mine was on the second, Jack's was on the third, and Lauren's was on the fourth. The gift symbolized that our family was complete with all four members. This year, I displayed this special train set on the fireplace mantel, and we enjoyed looking at it as we relaxed together.

Not only was Christmas different this year, but I noticed changes in my son. Typically, each year, Jack would tell us in detail the items he'd like for Christmas. He would provide a computer link to whatever item he wanted. However, this year, Jack surprised me when he said, "I don't really need anything, Mom."

I realized that he was maturing. Without the aid of a wish list, I ordered an outdoor ping-pong table for both kids. In addition, I ordered Jack a new lightsaber. During one of the fire evacuations, when we were at Karen's, her neighbors invited us to play a game of Jenga Giant. We had so much fun playing that game, I wanted it for us to play. Dave and I wanted our house to be a safe, fun place for our kids and their friends to be, before they went off to college.

For New Year's Eve, Dave and I suggested that Jack and Lauren have friends over. Lauren could have her friends swim in the pool and sleep over in the living room, while Jack could have his friends over to play games such as ping-pong, lightsabers, and Jenga Giant. Dave would open the tent camper that sat in our driveway for Jack's friends to sleep in. The kids loved the idea, and made plans for a teenage New Year's Eve.

Christmas was quiet and relaxed this year. We were all so grateful to be in our home, simply enjoying our family time. The only time we dressed up over the holiday was on Christmas Eve, when we headed up the street to our church for the 4:00 p.m. Mass. We saw many neighbors and friends who decided to attend the popular early evening service. We came back to have a traditional seafood dinner. The kids' stockings were out, and we leaned into our family traditions as I turned on the movie, *The Polar Express*. This was our family's favorite movie; we watched it each Christmas Eve. After the movie, I kissed Dave, Jack, and Lauren goodnight as I headed to bed. I knew I had an early rise in the morning to ensure that the gifts were arranged under the tree.

Since the kids were teens, I was less concerned that they would awake before me to check out Santa's loot. In fact, this morning, the kids slept for an hour longer, and I enjoyed my coffee while Dave was in the shower. Santa did come that night, and they were excited for the treasures waiting to be unwrapped.

Soon, we were all seated in the living room and the kids were opening their gifts. Calls from family were coming in, as we shared "Merry Christmas" sentiments with my sister and her family overseas, and our parents on the East Coast. The rest of the day we just hung out, and Lauren dug out a board game for us all to play. She grabbed the board game Clue, and opened the tattered box on the kitchen table. This game had belonged to Dave's late brother; inside were some of the original game scoring papers, still with Michael's handwriting in pencil. Lauren was naturally strategic as she played, and she grimaced and howled when she thought Jack was not-so-secretly helping me. Dave just smiled as he leaned back in his chair, telling us that he expected to win. Dave was happiest when he was with family, playing a fun game together. He was wearing his typical Patagonia puffy vest over his Red Sox jersey. It was a happy, relaxed, and connected day together, with Chester lying on the dog bed next to us.

Later, I prepared dinner as Jack licked his lips in anticipation. Jack adored this quiet family time. He, probably more than the rest of us, loved our family traditions, such as his favorite rib-eye meal on Christmas Day.

Dave and Jack were outside earlier that afternoon, setting up the ping-pong table. Looking out the kitchen window, I heard their laughter as they challenged each other to a match. By early evening, Dave was watching TV in his big comfy chair, with Lauren next to him. It was a relief that we had no big plans with guests on this Christmas. "It's so nice not to have to worry about making the house tidy for guests, or having to entertain this year," I said to Dave. Both of us were tired from our hectic work schedules and the anxiety about the recent fire. We were all home, relaxed, and happy together. The recent weeks had heightened our appreciation for our little home and family time.

During the lazy days between Christmas and New Year's, I pulled out my old sewing machine and set it up at the kitchen table. I loved to quilt, and the rhythmic sound of the machine running was soothing to me. Quilting seemed to help slow my overly busy mind from the intensity of work and running the kids around to their extracurricular activities. I often quilted while the rest of the family were doing something else around house. In a couple days, I already had a good start on a new quilt, and tucked the project away until I felt like crafting again.

A couple nights before New Year's, Dave and I relaxed in front of the TV, enjoying glasses of red wine. Chester snuggled next to me on the couch, as Dave and I chatted. Our nerves were finally calm for the first time since the Thomas Fire. Our conversation moved to the topic of Dave's dad, who'd recently been diagnosed with ALS. The disease was progressing rapidly. During this somber discussion, we moved on to where each of us would want to be buried when we passed. It was an important conversation to have, albeit morbid. Dave mentioned that he'd like to be buried near the ocean. We both thought of the beautiful Santa Barbara Cemetery in Montecito. We appreciated its gorgeous setting that had gently rolling hills and views of the mountains above Montecito to the north. The edge of the cemetery ends right along the cliffs that end at the Pacific Ocean. It was a spectacular location that captured the beauty of our town.

Later that night, Jack strolled out of his room in his navy basketball shorts, T-shirt and bare feet, and laid down on the carpet in front of the TV to join us. Although we'd just had a serious conversation regarding where we wanted to be buried, I was filled with contentment, Chester lying next to me. Dave said, "Jack, it will be a hard day in this household when Chester passes — your mom is going to have a very hard time." For some reason, we had death on our minds. Jack agreed, and said he didn't want to think about losing his dog. He got up to give Chester a kiss on the top of his shaggy head. Dave was right; I would have a difficult time when Chester died.

On December 28th, Dave was invited to stand up at an Eagle Board of Review for twins that he'd mentored through the Cub Scouts and Boy Scouts. Throughout December, Dave had been working so hard. Fatigue from his international trips and having to navigate the evacuations had made him irritable. But in response to the Scout request, he happily agreed. This was his week off, and he looked forward to it. He was glad he could be there for the two young men. So, Dave dressed in his Class A Scoutmaster's uniform and headed off to the Eagle Board of Review. A few hours later, as he walked through our front door, he had a skip in his step. Being invited to support the twins and honor their achievement was extremely meaningful for him. Dave was proud to share in the capstone Eagle Board of Review event. He was thrilled that each twin had earned the highest rank in scouting. Eagle was a rank that only about 4% of Scouts nationwide attain. He had seen the boys learning skills and going through character-building activities that would last them a lifetime. Dave's vacation was off to a good start.

Saturday, as I prepared dinner, he chatted with his mother as he sat in the living room. He tried to connect with both of his parents weekly, to check in with them and share any updates in our lives. As I was cooking, I overheard Dave say to his mother, "Mom, I love you." He emphasized it in an unusual manner. Dave usually ended his calls with his parents by telling them he loved them, but on this night, he sounded different, intense.

I walked to the living room to ask Dave if everything was okay with his mom.

Dave responded casually from his chair, feet on the ottoman. "Sure, she's fine."

CHAPTER 4

A NEW YEAR:
THE FIRST WEEK OF JANUARY 2018

DESPITE THE unusual Christmas and pre-holiday season, New Year's Eve was magical.

During the day, Dave and Jack played a few rounds together on the new outdoor ping-pong table. We had Jack's and Lauren's friends over, and they had a ball. They played the Jenga Giant game on the patio, where they pensively pulled out their target blocks. With each block removed, the players hoped it would not topple the tower and lose the game. Jack still loved all things Star Wars; he ventured into a nighttime lightsaber duel with one of his buddies. Grabbing my phone, I caught the moment as the boys dueled on the patio. Dave joined in the play, picking up a saber. In the darkness, we watched the dueling lightsabers floating and clashing in the night air. We loved that the kids were having fun with their friends. The next morning, Dave helped make a farm breakfast of pancakes, eggs, sausage, and all the fixings. We looked forward to more get-togethers like this for the kids.

We'd made it through a crazy year, and were looking forward to 2018. Dave's company was on an upswing and he was up for a promotion to Global VP of Sales and Marketing. I was in my groove, thoroughly enjoying the company and people I worked with, and the kids were thriving. Jack had a strong group of friends; he was driving, acing school, and dreaming of attending Harvard. Lauren was in her element at middle school, and was busy practicing for *Les Misérables*.

On January 1st, the kids had cleared out, and I was busy tidying up. Dave and I took a moment to appreciate the magical evening and fun morning breakfast with the teenagers, as we considered how much it took to get here. Years of hard work had paid off, and now, having experienced the kids all together, enjoying themselves, safely, we were grateful for the life that we'd built.

In the oven was an herbed roast and mashed potatoes to celebrate New Year's Day. Jack was enjoying a few hours of gaming before he shifted into study mode. At dinner, Dave mentioned that he was asked to go on another trip to Europe, but that he had opted to stay home since there was bad weather in the forecast.

The upcoming week would be busy. As Sr. Director of Strategy and Brand for a medical device company, I had a trip to San Francisco to preview market research results with the leadership team. The kids had school, and Dave planned to work from home. We loved when Dave was home for the week. He had spent so many workdays away over the last five years travelling, we cherished when he could work in the dining room as I plugged away in the home office.

When we bought the house, Dave designed the home office, adding wainscoting, a TV, and chairs that made the front office a quiet retreat. It was a comfortable room to work in. I ended up using the front office. Most of the time, I worked out of the home office rather than the corporate office, which was three hundred miles north. Since Dave often travelled for work or worked in his company's office, he didn't need the home office. So, Dave sat in the dining room that he'd converted into VP of Sales command central, with two large side-by-side computer monitors, computers, and his iPad.

Anticipating Dave working from home more often, we would need two home offices, as we wanted our dining room back. A few months earlier, we'd begun planning an addition. Dave wanted an apartment over the garage so his mother could move in with us in the future, if she needed. The new garage plans had a woodworking area that he would use once he retired.

The first week of January 2018, Dave worked feverishly to understand the company's year-end sales revenue. He enjoyed the work challenge and the team camaraderie. I witnessed that Dave worked harder than ever before with this company. In the evening, when Dave would finally finish for the day, we'd sit down in the living room to chat, turn on the TV, and catch the sitcom we both enjoyed about science nerds.

One night that week, during commercials, I said, "They're saying we may have some heavy rain this weekend; I think I'll take the truck tomorrow to get more sandbags." Dave pointed the remote at the TV to fast-forward through the commercials. "OK, this weekend Jack and I will go out in the backyard to ensure the drainpipe is clear, and that the French drain in the front of the house works."

Every year, we prepped the house for the rainy season. Dave would clean the leaves out of the gutters, have our trees trimmed, and ensure that the French drain in the front hardscape of the house flowed freely, draining water as it should to the back line. Being more nervous than Dave, I liked to place sandbags in front of the garage. Our asphalt driveway couldn't absorb the rain, so it made sense to put extra sandbags to protect the garage, which was detached from the house.

The next day, I drove in Dave's white truck to the Montecito Firehouse to fill the sandbags. A few firefighters helped fill some bags, and thoughtfully loaded them in the back of the truck. Each person was allowed ten bags, as more residents than ever were coming for extra sandbags, in response to the recent Thomas Fire that had left the hills black and barren.

The following day, I boarded a plane to San Francisco to do a market research reveal to the leadership team. The research gave us insights into what levers were driving our business. It was a great meeting, and I knew we had done solid work when the fast-paced CFO thanked the team for the information. I left the meeting, certain that it had been helpful. Later that afternoon when I boarded the plane back home, I was excited to share the news with the sales team at the upcoming national meeting.

It was only the first week of the year, but the pace was moving fast. That weekend, our family was in full swing with activities. On Sunday, to my surprise, Jack strolled out of his room, dressed up in a collared shirt and khaki pants.

"Mom, I'm going to meet some classmates for a school project we're doing on *The Great Gatsby*. We're meeting at Ellie's grandparents'. I'll be home in a couple hours," he said with a smile as he rushed out the front door.

Jack was happy; he had connected with his school's MAD Academy (Multimedia Arts and Design) program, and had met a nice group of friends.

"Okay, sweetie, have fun!" I replied.

Once back home, Jack shared some exciting news. He had been selected by his school to attend a leadership program. Leafing through the program catalogue, he chose the business and entrepreneurship program for high school students at UC Berkeley, B-BAY, which he would attend for two weeks during summer. He went on to tell us that his good friend Ellie also received a similar leadership invitation, but initially she was considering attending Georgetown's International Relations program.

Jack (left, closest to window) simulating a *Great Gatsby* moment for his school assignment

Excitedly Jack continued, "I talked Ellie into switching to the UC Berkeley program! Now we can both go to Berkeley together this summer. It's going to be so fun." He was thrilled that he'd have a friend to join him.

Jack had connected with Ellie and her boyfriend. I wondered whether Jack had a crush on her when I heard him say, "Ellie's one of the best girls in the whole high school — and she's a nice girl." Jack was loyal to his friend, and would not consider anything more than a friendship with Ellie. We were thrilled for him and felt comfortable sending him to Berkeley with a friend for a summer adventure.

Early that morning, Lauren went to her five-hour *Les Misérables* rehearsal, and then joined me at the mother-daughter National Charity League meeting at a local school auditorium. Sundays like these kept us on the run.

I led programs for young women as part of being on the board of the National Charity League, a great organization that fosters mother-daughter volunteerism locally. Lauren saw the impact she could have by helping in the community. Since she was 14, I realized that I wouldn't have this precious quality time with her for long.

During the league meeting, each officer gave a report related to their job. I gave my official VP job-related report, and then moved two feet away from the podium and said, "Now, I want to speak to you all, not as VP — but as Kim, a neighbor in this town." I continued, "As you all know, the Thomas Fire devastated a thousand homes. With the closures and evacuations, hundreds of local businesses lost revenue during the peak season of the year. There is one neighbor in town who lost both."

I explained that a local shop owner lost all her potential holiday revenue due to the fire evacuations, and her home was one of the first locally to be destroyed by the fire. Adding to the loss was that she rented the home, and sadly had no renters' insurance.

I finished by saying, "Please consider patronizing her store to help our neighbor during this difficult time." These generous women appreciated learning how they could help.

After the meeting, Lauren and I returned home, where we could finally settle in after a busy day and relax. Dave and I watched the news and learned that heavy rains were predicted for the next couple days. We planned to monitor the news and check our "aware and prepare" messages. Community members worried about the houses located high on the hills. The mountains' brush and vegetation had burned away in the Thomas Fire, and now massive boulders sat precariously above the beautiful estates set high in the mountainside.

I was unable to fully relax due to the predictions of heavy rain, so Dave humored me by going to buy a sump pump for the French drain. Before he left, he assured me, "Kim, we already have a sump pump in place. But if it will make you feel better, I'll get a second one." He sighed and drove off to the store. We were all traumatized from the repeated fire evacuations and the shrill phone warnings.

Dave, lugging sandbags to place at the entrance
to our driveway, the day before the tragedy

Monday, January 8th, I worked in my office, which had bay windows that looked out to our front yard and driveway. Earlier that day, I asked Dave whether we could get more sandbags. He chuckled, shook his head, and said we had plenty. Even so, he said, "Sure, let's go." We jumped into his truck and headed to the local park with our sandbags to fill. We saw our neighbors and community members working to make more sandbags to shore up areas they felt would be impacted by a heavy rain.

Back at home, we returned to work in our offices. We planned that once Jack was home from school, we'd stack the sandbags at the top entrance of our driveway.

Around 4:00 p.m., Jack drove his car into our lane and slowly turned into the driveway to park next to the camper.

"Hi, Jack," I said as he walked in. "How was your day?"

"Fine." He took off his heavy black backpack and running shoes. In his right hand, he held a half-empty Frappuccino.

"Hey, sweetie, in about thirty minutes, would you mind helping Dad place the sandbags?" I asked.

"Sure," Jack agreed. "It's not even raining yet, Mom — but sure."

Thirty minutes later, Dave and Jack went to stack sandbags along the driveway entrance. I joined them to see how they were doing, and encouraged them to stack them even higher. As the three of us stood at the entrance to our driveway, a neighbor came over to see us.

As he saw us, he greeted us with a cheerful "hello."

He went on to say, "So, you're getting ready for the rain?"

"Yes," I replied, "we're trying to." Dave and Jack paused from stacking their sandbags.

"Well," he assured us, "I've been through these rains many times before, guys. It will be okay!"

We had some small talk, and then he left us, beaming with a big smile.

As we placed the last of the sandbags at the driveway entrance, I asked Dave, "Do you think you should stack one row higher?"

"Kim, we'll be okay! Look, honey, they re-engineered the creek near here after the flood problem over twenty years ago. And look at that house — the large one across the lane. It was built and approved according to the building codes after that flooding. It would have to come down if we were ever to have any problems!" Dave pointed to the main house across the lane.

Looking at our neighbor's house, it was inconceivable it could be destroyed. I felt better about our sandbags. Despite our neighbor's good-naturedly teasing us about our preparations, I called a downtown hotel to book a room for the four of us and our 90-lb. dog. It was worth paying $300 for a room, if we needed to evacuate yet again. I told Dave that I'd booked a hotel. He was okay with that, but said,

"We'll be fine. Let's just keep an eye on the news, and any evacuation texts or emails." As we looked outside, we felt prepared. The rain was drizzling, the sandbags were placed, the two sump pumps were fitted by the drain, and our cars were parked across the lane at our neighbors', to enable us to get out fast, if needed.

Tired from work and the distraction of prepping for rain, we ordered Chinese take-out. While we waited to pick up the order, Jack came out of his room and said, "Hey, Mom, do you mind if I don't do my homework tonight?" This was an unusual question. Jack was a great student, and had never asked to skip his homework.

"Sure, honey. Pass on homework tonight," I said.

I smiled, grateful that he was such a good kid. Even at 17, he had the courtesy to ask my permission, which was sweet. I was one fortunate mom.

Jack went into his room to play an online game, while I ran down to pick up the Chinese food. As I walked up to the cashier counter, I gave them my phone number. Suddenly, the worker looked surprised and told me someone had just mistakenly picked up my order. I waited another fifteen minutes for my order to be re-made, then headed home, walked through the door, and yelled, "Dinner!"

Jack bolted out of his room; he loved Chinese food. We quickly put all the red containers in the center of our long farm table, tossed down a few plates and serving spoons and happily dug in. After dinner, we cleared the table. As Jack was standing in the kitchen, I took the opportunity to say, "Hug?"

"Let's get this over with," he chided, though smiling. After I leaned in and gave him a long hug, I told him, "I love you, honey." He walked back into his room to continue gaming.

About fifteen minutes later, I knocked on his bedroom door.

"Yes, Mom?"

I opened the door. Jack was sitting on his chair. He removed one of his earphones and turned to look at me.

"We should be fine tonight with the rain, but in case it gets heavy, I want you to know that we have a hotel room booked." Jack looked at me and giggled oddly.

"Okay," he said. Jack went on to say to me that Lauren had come into his room nervous about the rain. He'd told her the worst that could happen was that the carpet could get a little wet.

"I doubt that will happen, but we have a plan in case we need to get out. Right now, the officials are not telling us to evacuate. If they do — or if we feel unsafe — we can head out quickly," I reassured him. Jack nodded, adjusted his earphones, and turned back to his monitor.

After dinner, Dave and I retreated to the living room to watch TV. I asked Dave if he would like a glass of wine. "No, I want to be alert in case there's heavy rain tonight."

"Okay, honey," I agreed.

Jack gamed in his room, Lauren chatted with her friends while doing homework, and Dave and I watched TV. Chester lay on the floor in front of the fire. A few minutes later, Jack, in his "Cool Captain Jack" gray T-shirt and bare feet, strolled into the living room. He lay down on the rug to hug Chester, and to catch a bit of TV with us.

"Hey, Jack, do me a favor tonight?" I asked.

"What's that?"

"There's a branch hanging over your bedroom that the arborist needs to cut next week. In case it's windy tonight, would you mind sleeping on the living room couch?"

"Okay." He kissed Chester on the top of his head.

I was relieved that Jack didn't put up any resistance to my request, as he knew I could be overcautious at times.

Around 9:30, feeling tired, I headed to bed. Lauren was in her room getting ready for bed while Dave watched TV a little longer with Jack. Jack had already pulled out his sleeping bag, and put it on the living room couch. I kissed Dave, Jack, and the dog good night, and went into the bedroom. Climbing into bed, I placed my cell phone next to my nightstand in case of any evacuation warnings. Though I was fried from December's repeated text blasts, I wanted to ensure I'd hear if another one came. An hour later, I awoke briefly as I felt Dave crawl into bed.

PART 3
TRAGEDY

"Landslide"
—Fleetwood Mac

CHAPTER 5

THE NIGHT OF THE UNIMAGINABLE

IT WAS 3:15 A.M. when the heavy rain pounding on the flat roof above our bed awoke Dave and me. We bolted out of bed to the living room, where Jack was trying to sit up. He shifted in his sleeping bag when Lauren sat next to him. I flipped on the lights in the kitchen, the living room, and the front hall.

"Hey guys! Get dressed, so we can leave," I called out.

Though our home wasn't located in the mandatory evacuation zone, after Dave checked on the rain, I knew he would want us to leave.

Groggily, Jack stood up, adjusted the warm sleeping bag over his head as if wearing a cape, and walked to his room to change. Lauren headed in the opposite direction toward her room. Dave had already changed, and had walked outside to check on the heavy rainfall.

Minutes later, Dave returned and frantically yelled, "Kim, it's really coming down! Even the large plastic container, the big heavy one by the drain, is floating on water!"

"Oh, my God!" I thought in total disbelief. Two sump pumps couldn't keep up with this deluge.

"Guys! It's raining hard; we need to get out!" I shouted, trying to hide the panic in my voice.

Dave sprinted past me, holding a heavy flashlight. He quickly exited the kitchen door near Jack's room that led to the detached garage.

He yelled from the garage, "Kim, we already have about an inch of water in here!"

Damn it! I thought, as worry and fear filled every cell of my being.

I ran to our bedroom, pulled off my nightgown, and changed into my black turtleneck and leggings. After hastily throwing on my clothes, still barefoot, I was ready to run back toward the living room. Before running out of my room, I stopped when I heard an odd, ominous sound that vibrated throughout the house. I heard a *zing, zing!* As I realized what it was, my heart sank. It was the sound of boulders smashing into other boulders as they bounced down from the mountain to the creek across the lane.

Dave returned from the garage, and I glanced out the bay window to gauge how hard the rain was coming down by the pool. As I looked, the night sky lit up, turning the black night into a light yellow.

I yelled, "Dave, something really wrong is happening!"

Dave headed toward the front door. He adjusted his red rain jacket, rain pants, and heavy work boots. As he paused by the front door to pull his jacket's hood over his head, we heard and felt an explosion. Then all the lights went out. We'd lost all power.

The dark was slightly illuminated by the yellow glow outside that came in through the windows. We could see a faint outline of the room and furniture.

Frantically, Dave yelled, "Guys, out now!"

I raced to the kitchen to grab the dog's leash. Lauren and Jack were in their rooms getting dressed, and would be out any second.

I saw Dave standing inside the front door, again yelling loudly, "Out now!"

He opened the door and was about to step outside, when unexpectedly he slammed it shut.

He screamed, "Back door now!"

I raced toward the back door, dog leash in hand, purse hanging on my forearm, holding my phone.

Chester was at my feet, lying down on the living room floor.

In complete terror, Dave ran past me and bounded out the back door toward the pool.

As he ran, he screamed, "Kim, get out now! Kim, come on, get out, get out!"

Before I grabbed the back door, I frantically yelled for the kids. "Jack, Lauren! Now! Get out!"

Right after I called to the kids, water rushed into the house.

Within seconds, the thick angry flow raced toward me in the back of the living room. I later learned that it was moving at thirty miles per hour.

The dark slime seeped in under our doors. The muddy water came up through the bottom of our front walls and front doors.

I looked down at Chester, lying on the floor near my feet. I told him, "Let's go!" But he tilted his head and looked up at me hauntingly as he lay on the carpet. Chester did not move. He seemed to know there was no escape.

I heard a horrifying, unfamiliar noise that sounded as if I were standing under the walkway of the Niagara Falls. Like the roar of an oncoming train, mere inches away.

The vibration of massive boulders slamming against each other added to my terror as I realized the house was moving. I twisted so I could look at the front of the house, and was shocked to see a wave of mud filling the room. In seconds, muddy water rushed from the front of the house toward me as I stood by the back door. The mud forcefully closed the glass door on my hand, which had been in the door jamb. The force was so strong, I couldn't open the door. The increasing pressure on my hand was excruciating. I watched, horrified, as the mud, now over three feet high, blanketed everything. It completely covered and drowned my dog as I watched, helpless.

As the flow became thigh-high, my panic rose. I tried calling the kids again, but no one answered. When the mud reached my chest, I struggled to keep my footing. A dining room chair from the front of the house floated toward me. I couldn't comprehend what was happening.

"God help us!" I prayed. "Oh, my God, we're going to die tonight!"

The odor of mud filled my nose. My ears rang with horrific, loud sounds.

When I awoke that rainy night, I never imagined that we would be at risk of losing our lives. Now, the unimaginable was happening to my family and me.

As I struggled to keep my footing, my purse fell off my arm. An emergency alert blasted from my phone as it fell into the water. The blast warned to "get to high ground" — tragically too little, too late. The warning came just as the flow immersed me up to my chest.

My body started to spin. I struggled to pull my hand out of the door jamb.

On the other side of the glass door, I could see Dave urgently yelling.

"Kim, come on! Kim, get out!"

"I can't!" I screamed. "My hand is trapped in the door!"

Seconds later, "Dave, I can't stand up! I'm going under!"

The last words I heard Dave say to me before the mud took me under were him trying to save my life. In a horrific instant, he was gone, washed away in a violent river of mud. He had no walls to provide protection.

I was now alone in hell.

I feared for Dave and my kids, whom I could not see. The increasing pressure of the mud pushed heavily against the door, trapping my hand. It felt like it was being crushed in two.

A stronger roaring torrent of water came, pushing me backward into the water. I was entirely submerged. As the house was torn apart, my hand came free.

I knew I needed a miracle to help me survive.

After I lost my footing, I was submerged under the dense, muddy water.

It felt like I had fallen into dangerous white-water rapids with no helmet or protection. The churning mud crushed and tossed my body around as it sped down the terrain's sloping grade. The magnitude of the pain felt like being crushed in a trash compactor from all angles simultaneously. Under the mud, violently, randomly, my body was hit from all directions.

My legs, my back, my arms, my sides, and my head were compressed. Rugged bricks, corners of furniture, large nails from exposed oak floor planks, rocks, and granite pounded my body.

Although terrified, I was alert under the flow.

I thought, *God, if you want me to die now, I will.*

After that thought, my body relaxed like a rag doll in the torrent of mud.

I surrendered and went limp as I thought, *This is how I die.*

While under water, I opened my eyes, straining to see through the dark mud. I thought, *God, show me the light! I'm in so much pain; let me see the light!* I hoped if I saw the light, the unimaginable pain would end, and I would die.

Then I took my last breath. Instead of air, I inhaled mud. As I drew the sludge into my lungs, a stifling, jerking peace came over me.

Then everything went blank.

Minutes earlier, from high up in the barren fire-ravaged mountains, a deluge of heavy water carrying burned trees and car-sized boulders had raced down toward the creek, about 75 feet across the lane from our home. Simultaneously, a torrential rain cell dumped a half-inch of water over a 15-minute period. The water drenched the Thomas Fire burn scar of downed debris, and unleashed massive boulders. In minutes, the creek jammed up with logs and boulders that were stopped at the street underpass. Part of the mountain was falling apart, and was being carried down toward our town by torrents of water. It all roared toward our house in a massive mudslide.

The powerful mudflow did not make the curve in the creek. A huge flow soared up toward the sky. It grew to a 30-foot wave of mud, debris, rocks, and logs that spewed upwards, then crashed down violently as it rolled toward our home. We were at the epicenter of a deadly mudslide.

CHAPTER 6

WE'VE GOT A VICTIM UP HERE

DAZED, I AWOKE in darkness at around 5:00 a.m. *Is this heaven?* I wondered, disoriented.

I felt cold and wet.

As I gained consciousness, I sensed that I was lying on my back. I tried to open my eyes, but it was too painful. My eyes could not open on their own, so, using one hand, I manually opened my tightly closed eyelid. I strained to see through the dirt and grit that filled my vision.

As my eyes tried to focus, I could see the dark sky and two large bent sycamore trees in the distance. I was confused, but, as my head cleared, I knew I was not in heaven. I recognized the tall trees, and thought I was at the back edge of my backyard.

Soon, I could feel my body and how it was positioned.

I was lying on my back, on a pile of mud. My feet were pointing up near the top of the mound, and my head was positioned downward, with my body at a thirty-degree angle. I'd learn that I was lying on the side of a tall pile of debris.

With my free hand, I began to touch my body as much as I could and feel my torso. I felt my black turtleneck top, now shredded with big gaping holes. My hand felt inside one of the holes — I felt my skin and a 6-inch piece of wood. As I felt my turtleneck, I found wood, rocks, and twigs. My bra's underwire was pushed up around my neck under my chin.

I was alone.

As I lay cold and injured, fear filled me. I was terrified for my family.

I reached over to feel my right forearm and found a 6-inch piece of flesh in the shape of a triangle dangling. I could feel the open wound and a half-inch of fatty flesh that dangled, exposed. The serious laceration was covered in muck.

I gently packed the loose triangle of flesh back into position on my forearm. As I did, I unknowingly packed the wound with the dirt and debris.

As I struggled to move other parts of my body, I realized that my left leg and foot were trapped. My head hurt. It was resting on a plank of wood with exposed nails that were digging into my skull. To avoid feeling that pain, I packed my heavy mud-sodden hair into a ball. I used a clump of my hair and mud to cushion my head from the exposed nails driving painfully into my skull. Dazed but now mostly conscious, I felt what seemed like a household spray bottle on my chest. I picked it up and tossed it away.

A spray bottle? I thought, perplexed. I was in a war zone. I was in hell.

To my right, there was a bushy branch of an oak.

Later, I registered a sound nearby.

I heard the forceful torrent of a roaring river. I did not want to fall down this debris pile and drown in that raging water. Above my head and to the right, I saw and heard explosions from dangling, swaying power lines. Nearby, a transformer exploded.

I worried about falling into the river, or getting electrocuted by the dangling power lines that exploded and swung fiercely.

Rain drizzled on my freezing body. I was getting colder by the minute.

I screamed for help, and I yelled for my family. "Dave! Jack! Lauren! Where are you?"

There was no response.

I was alone.

I started to say the Lord's Prayer, beginning with "Our Father." I said the prayer aloud over twenty times. It soothed my frightened soul.

I thought, *I need to rest and conserve energy, because I don't know when I may get help.*

I lay there quietly, shivering, hurt, and terrified.

I moved a little, and adjusted the hair and mud on my head again to alleviate the awful pain from the nails digging into my scalp. Freezing, I used my fingers to move the material of my turtleneck higher on my neck and onto my chin. I felt some slight warmth of body heat as I moved a bit of this fabric onto my chin. That tiny movement gave me some relief.

Later, I saw in the distance white and red lights. They were not spinning like an ambulance, but I registered that someone was there. I gathered all my strength and yelled for help.

It was dark, and I was wearing all black, with only my head, toes, and arms sticking out of the debris. I yelled loudly, "Help!" "Help!" "Help!" "Help!" "Help!" "Help!"

I continued to scream until I heard in the distance a male voice. "Hey, we got a vic up here!" And again, "We got a vic up here!"

I heard footsteps clomping in the dense, uneven debris.

"This is Garet. I'm coming to get you!" he assured me.

I sighed in relief. I could no longer open my eyes. The mud and grit had scratched my corneas so much that they would only open if I opened them with my fingers.

As Garet approached, I pleaded, "Please rub my feet, I'm so cold!"

Garet inquired where I was hurt. I responded, "I don't think I have any spinal injuries, but I have major trauma to my left hip. I think my left hip is broken. My right forearm has a massive laceration, and I can't move."

Again, I pleaded, "Please rub my feet. I need your jacket, I'm freezing!"

God bless him, Garet started warming my ice-cold bare feet with his hands. At one point, he took off his jacket to lay it on me like a blanket, even though I was completely covered in mud.

As Garet continued to yell for help, I heard the footsteps of more firefighters walking up to me. I could not see their faces, as my eyes would not open.

"What was your address?" they asked

"335 Hot Springs Road," I said.

"Who was in the house?" they asked.

I named my family. "My husband, Dave, 49; my son, Jack, 17; my daughter, Lauren, 14. And my dog, Chester, a big Irish Setter."

"Where was your house?" they asked.

I was stunned. *Was?*

This question spoke to the magnitude of the horror I'd just endured and now faced.

It meant my house was gone. Totally destroyed.

More urgently, where was my family?

Is this a horrible nightmare? raced through my mind.

As I lay incapacitated, a firefighter named Ben asked if I could point to where my house used to be. I still thought that the debris pile on which I was lying was somewhere in my backyard. I took my left arm and lifted it over and behind my head. I pointed behind me and said, "My house was over there."

Two of the responders, Ben and Andy, walked toward where I pointed. The other four men stayed to load me onto a rescue flat board.

Where was my family? My children? Dave? I thought, terrified.

"Can you help lift yourself up?" asked a firefighter named Jeff as the rescue board was positioned next to me.

"No," I whispered.

I had no strength, especially since my legs were higher than my head.

"Okay, let's lift on three," one of the responders said.

"One, two, three!"

As they hoisted me onto the immobilizing board, I gave a blood-curdling scream—"My hip is broken!" It was the worst pain I'd felt in my entire life.

The pain was so searing, it overshadowed the pain in my right forearm that was cut down to the bone, and my right knee laceration that cut tendons down through my large quadricep and thigh muscle to the bone.

The four men carried me down the debris pile. As they trod over the sticks, rocks, and uneven terrain toward the ambulance, I wobbled painfully on the board.

Once inside the ambulance, my eyes still shut, I pleaded for pain meds to relieve my hip pain, and for blankets.

I heard someone in the back of the ambulance working fast. I heard a radio call directing them to go to Goleta Valley Hospital. During our 20-minute drive to Goleta, I asked if they could call my parents. "No," someone gruffly replied, "You can't make any calls!" I felt desperate. I needed someone to know about what happened, so they could come help find my family.

Just when the ambulance had driven about ninety percent of the way to Goleta Valley Hospital, the driver got a call to turn the ambulance around and drive back to Montecito for another critical patient. Freezing and in pain, I realized this would delay our arrival to the ER. The ambulance turned around and drove much of the way back to Montecito, when the driver was told to cancel the Montecito call.

I felt dread for that victim, who must have died from their injuries. The ambulance turned around and drove toward Goleta again. At about 8:30 a.m., thickly covered in mud, I was wheeled into the emergency room. Though relieved to be there, I was paralyzed with shock and fear as I worried about my kids and husband.

My clothes were shredded, my feet cold and bare. Surprisingly, my watch, earrings, and wedding rings were still on. As they cut the shredded clothes off my body, I was told the name of the medical tech assigned to me. He sat above my head as I lay on the table. He carefully put pain-numbing jelly, Lidocaine, all over the front of my body to help dull the pain, before he used a sponge to clean off the mud and debris lodged in my wounds.

The front and back of my body were scraped all over, cut in many places, and my left breast had lacerations. The tech tried several times and in different ways to get the mud off me. My hair was such a mess, the team that worked on me used shaving cream to get out the big clumps of mud, twigs, and stones.

A couple of hours went by. Lying in the ER in shock, I felt as if I was not attached to my body. As I lay there, I heard the ER door open, and a woman's voice yelled, "Do you have a daughter named Lauren?"

"Yes!" I anxiously replied.

"She's just been rescued," the nurse yelled as she stood by the door.

A wave of relief filled my mind. My baby girl had been rescued. Thank God! Immediately my thoughts went to Dave and Jack. Where were they? Lying injured and in pain, I hoped I would hear about their rescue soon.

CHAPTER 7

ENTOMBED

WHILE I LAY injured in the hospital, I learned bits and pieces about Lauren's horrific mudslide experience. I had just assumed that she, too, was found on a debris pile. While in the hospital, I had no context about the degree and force of the mudslide that ravaged 30 square miles.

Later in the day, I was able to talk with Lauren by phone. In the hospital, I cried and my heart sank as she told me more about her terrifying experience. I felt so hopeless and a failure as a mother. My baby had been buried alive, totally alone, entombed. My mind wanted to shut out the horror she'd endured. She told me that during the chaos, she felt like the rest of the family had gotten out and left her. That broke my heart. Never in a million years would we have done that, if any of us could have moved from our location to help her. With the slide's power and chaos, none of us had had the ability to help each other. We were separated in our home by the roaring force of the slide that came down the mountain like an avalanche. It flowed like powerful thick wet cement, and rendered each of us helpless.

I was in total anguish, learning of Lauren's ordeal. I feared it would affect her for the rest of her life.

Months later, she wrote about her experience, and my mind allowed me to learn of the terror she had endured. I share it here with her permission. Lauren wrote:

> I had a bad feeling about the impending rainstorm headed toward Santa Barbara. I tried to persuade my family by saying, "I think we should just leave, go to a hotel." But they told me we had a plan, and right now there was no mandatory evacuation order in our location. Out of caution, my mom had made a hotel reservation, so if we were instructed to leave, we'd have a safe place to stay.
>
> In the past, whenever I sensed something bad was going to happen, I'd notice a feeling in the pit of my stomach. I had this feeling the night of the rainstorm. I feared something bad might happen that night.
>
> The night of the rainstorm our family ordered take-out. Mom had run to the nearby Chinese restaurant to pick up dinner. The food was delicious, and one of our favorite choices for take-out family dinner. Mom ordered a whole feast: orange chicken, General Tso's chicken, broccoli beef, fried rice, egg rolls, ribs, chow mein, fortune cookies, and more. It was nice to have us all there for dinner, as my dad usually travelled during the week.
>
> When we went to bed, I overheard my mom ask my brother to sleep in the living room because there was a big tree limb over his room. In case of heavy wind, she wanted him safe. Then in the middle of the night, I was awakened by the heavy rain; it was loud. I went out to the living room and sat next to my brother because I was scared. We talked quietly for a few moments.
>
> My dad got up and started to check on the sandbags and the garage to see how the house was holding up underneath the rain. Soon, Mom, Jack, Chester and I were in the living room, while my dad checked on the house and the rain.

When my dad came back inside, he told us there was water in the garage, and he was really worried because all the bikes and everything we had crammed in there was getting soaked. He then went out the front door to look at the driveway and toward our lane in front of the house.

We heard a deafening explosion.

It was eerie. The sky turned bright orange yellow, as if it were day in the middle of the night. I was terrified, and I knew something was wrong.

My dad came in, slammed the door yelling, "Back door now!"

We all scattered.

My mom to get the dog.

My dad raced from the front door, through the living room and out the back door, past my mom.

Panicked, I darted towards my room to grab my knee-high rain boots, blanket, and phone.

I don't remember where Jack went, but I think he ran to his room to grab his computer.

When I ran outside my room and tried to go down the hallway to the living room, a wave of mud and water came rushing toward me. Without thinking, I turned and raced in the other direction. I ran toward my mom's office as an alternate pathway to the front door.

When I arrived there, water rushed in from the front door which had been knocked open. The furniture was moving and floating. As I dropped the phone, I heard the blast of the 'aware and beware' alert going off.

I was blocked and pinned by a table as I tried to push toward the front door. I was now stuck in my mom's office. The water filled up fast. In an instant, I was treading water, with my head only inches from the ceiling. The printer, office furniture, books, even trees, floated around me.

I screamed for help. I was yelling for anyone to help me. "Come back!! Come back!" as I thought my family had escaped.

I desperately pleaded for them to come back for me. I wanted my dad to swoop in and carry me safely out of this hell occurring in our house. I screamed and screamed in utter terror.

In seconds, the water hit the ceiling, and I was quickly pulled under into a muddy flow. The force felt like a whirlpool. I was spun and thrown around, then something slowed my movement and almost crushed me.

Something pushed my hips together. I felt a horrific pain that was unexplainable. The pain was so intense, I thought I would snap in two like a twig. The pressure suddenly released. Once released from its grip, my body was thrown around again, but now at an even faster speed.

I was drowning.

I couldn't breathe. I tried holding my breath, but I couldn't for long. Against my will, I breathed in mud, twigs, and rocks. I felt the pressure of mud going down my throat. It was scratchy and painful. It was the most disgusting taste and experience I'd ever had. The force of the mud rushed into my mouth. I felt like someone took a hose to my mouth, put it on full power, and filled it with cement. The next instant, my body was suddenly and jarringly thrown against something. After that hit, everything stopped.

My legs felt the rushing flow of thick watery mud for a few more seconds, then even that sensation stopped. I tried to readjust my body, but it was too difficult. I ended up in a sort of squatting position with my knees jutting out painfully. My body folded over, so I was looking down toward my feet.

The "hit" that suddenly stopped me from being washed away was so hard that I barely noticed that I could breathe again. I don't know how long I was drowning, but it felt like at least a few minutes. When my body suddenly jerked to a stop, miraculously, the mudflow drained away from where my head was.

There was stuff everywhere—house pieces, trees, a car, makeup, tree roots. Now, the only part of my body I could move was my fingers. I could slightly wiggle them. My legs and arms were locked in place. I was unable to move, there was mud in every crevice, and nothing would budge. Somehow, by some miracle, there was an air pocket that allowed me to breathe. My face was perfectly aligned with the air pocket.

In my muddy entombment, I pushed with all my strength—a strength I didn't even know I had. I pushed with every ounce of my muscles, but nothing would move. I pushed with all the strength I had, using every limb. My muscles hurt for a very long time after exerting myself.

I wailed and screamed and cried out. I pleaded. I even yelled at God, asking, "Why me, why my family, just why?" I prayed for help and protection.

And I thought I was dead.

My mind couldn't rationalize what was happening. I didn't understand. I thought that maybe I had hit something and died, but instead of going to heaven or hell like I had so often been told about in Sunday School, maybe I would just stay where I died—forever. Maybe I would just stay in whatever position and wherever I was in death. It was a horrifying thought, and I believed it for a long time. To feel that this might be my eternal experience was numbing. I was going numb inside and out.

For six long dark hours, I lay trapped in the mud, thinking I was dead.

I cried, screamed, yelled out, continued to try to push, but nothing moved. I thought about the past few weeks and then my past year. It wasn't like a life review flashing before my eyes, but rather, I was consciously choosing to think about my friends, my family, the places I'd travelled and the experiences that I'd had. I wanted to think about anything I could remember in my life, up until this moment.

I chose to think about the life I had lived because I thought that was what people did when they thought their life was over.

I decided to sing "I Dreamed a Dream," the song I had learned in theater as I prepared for the role of Fantine in *Les Misérables*.

I tried to sing, but my voice was scratchy, and I was sobbing. I don't know why I decided to sing. I think it soothed me. Singing was something I could control, something I loved, and the lyrics of the song resonated with me as I was entombed in the mud.

I screamed and I wailed.

I suffered for six hours.

I felt dead.

My emotions cycled from fear, sadness, terror, and shock.

And I was angry.

I didn't understand how God could do this to me! I didn't understand how everyone who had told me about heaven as a joyful, glorious life after death, had it so wrong. I was angry, confused, and scared. And I was grieving.

I then heard whispers and noises. As I focused, I heard people.

I realized I wasn't dead. I had to get their attention. I had to get them to hear me.

I screamed and cried out as loud as I could. I screamed for a long, long time. Then, terrifyingly, I heard the voices go away. They were gone.

I began to cry and sob. I had missed my chance to be rescued.

More time lapsed, and I heard the voices come back. That time I screamed louder than I ever had before. I screamed and screamed, "Help! Help! Help!" trying to make as much noise as possible. Eventually after I screamed for 30 minutes, I heard a man's voice say, "We hear you!"

I finally could stop screaming. I trusted him. I trusted that he heard me, and would get me out.

CHAPTER 8

HOSPITAL, HAMMOND'S, AND UNEXPECTED NOTORIETY

AT SOME POINT, I was taken from the ER to a hospital room. A nurse told me that both my knee and left forearm were heavily wrapped up and would be until I was wheeled into surgery later that evening. In surgery, they cleaned and repaired the large laceration on my forearm, and repaired my knee laceration, tendon, and quadricep muscle. My left hip was causing me a pain so intense I could barely handle it. I was certain it was broken.

I was dazed, having been given sedatives to ease my pain and quell the shock I felt in response to the trauma I'd experienced. When I was in the ER, Lilli, an administrative assistant at my kids' middle school, and who had been a chaperone on Jack's summer bike trip to Italy, became my advocate at my bedside in the hospital. She was an unexpected angel who helped me in whatever way I needed. "Kim, Lauren is safely at Cottage Hospital downtown, and Anna is with her," Lilli said at my bedside. "Okay," I replied with relief, yet still in shock. No out-of-town family had arrived yet, and I was not sure when they could, with the freeway closed. Torturous as it was to not have Lauren with me, I felt relief that she was in the hospital, and Anna, her youth pastor and former nanny, was with her. I still did not know where my husband and son were.

Lilli became a trusted aide, navigating and supporting all that needed to be arranged. She kept me informed about the chaos that was going on a few miles away in Montecito. That first night, our friends Dave and Lori swooped in to visit me. During their visit, I could not see them because my eyes were mud-scratched. Lying in the hospital bed, my eyes unable to open, Lori held my hand as I told her what happened. I took solace through gently rubbing my thumb on her hand; I heard her sobbing. Her husband Dave was standing behind her, taking in the magnitude of the terror that I and my family had endured. Marco and Kelly, middle school teachers, rushed in to check on me. Then Jack's best friend, Casmali, came in and held my left arm gently. I felt the sorrow in his heart. Casmali tried to comfort his best friend's mother, someone he had known since third grade. We did not know the status of Jack and Dave, but it certainly looked bad.

I called my aunt in Canada; her landline number was still ingrained from my youth. With my cell phone destroyed, I had no cell numbers on hand. My aunt answered, and I whispered that I needed my cousin Marty, ten years my junior, to come right away to help. I learned later that Marty immediately left his work, grabbed his duffel bag and tossed in heavy work boots, and drove to the airport, with a one-way ticket from Toronto to Santa Barbara. My side of the family didn't get to see each other too often, living on different coasts, but I knew we'd be there for each other in times of need, and we loved one another. I had also called Dave's best friend, a cop in Oregon, also named Dave, whom my husband called "DC-2," and asked him to come. At this point, I did not fully understand the magnitude of devastation from the slide; I thought some of my house would be still on the property. I knew that my parents, both in their eighties, would not be able to walk through the mud and debris to see what was left, or if anything needed immediate attention. Dave Clark, "DC-2," immediately boarded a plane. Both Marty and DC-2 were due to arrive the next day.

The second day that Lauren and I were in the hospital, my parents, my cousin, and Dave's best friend all arrived. Lilli coordinated how they could support us. We asked Marty and DC-2 to spend time with Lauren at her hospital and keep her company, playing card games to keep her mind occupied and to calm her nerves. Lauren and I were able to talk on the phone. The first call was brief. I remember such relief at hearing her voice and telling her how much I loved her. We were both in shock, unsure of what the day would bring, but grateful to hear each other's voices.

On this day, the bruising on my body started to appear. *Eggplant purple* was how people described my skin color. My mother told me my skin looked like someone had taken a wire brush to it and rubbed feverishly. I was also cut in areas that were not bandaged like the surgical repairs. My father thought that based on my skin abrasions, I must have travelled in the mudflow on my stomach, which would explain why the front of my body was cut up and scratched more than my backside.

During the early afternoon, the priest and a sister from the church came in to visit me. They wanted to check on me and pray with me, which I found comforting. Even in shock, I felt the mix of emotions — a huge sense of fear and concern, worrying about Dave and Jack, and also profound gratitude that Lauren and I had somehow survived. Those dramatically different feelings were odd to experience together. I also sensed the priest and nun were visiting because they too feared the worst for my husband and son.

Lilli was still with me, and just prior to my guests entering the room, the nurse had given me another dose of sedative to help me relax. I don't know who, but one of them told me that my dog's body was found. Like a bird struggling with a broken wing, hearing these words was like someone slowly trampling on its tiny feet: more hurt. I had seen Chester wash away at my feet. He was helpless, as we all were, when the mud roared through the house. Chester had been an amazing dog, who was such a loving part of our family. I cried as I thought of the pain he must have endured, and as I realized that he was gone forever. He missed out on probably seven more years of living.

"What are they doing with his body?" I asked.

"I've been in touch with the folks helping with the animals. They have his body, and they want to know what you'd like done," Lilli said.

"I'd like him cremated. Please ensure that you get a nice box for his remains, so I can get them back."

Then my mind shifted to thinking about how and when I'd be able to let Lauren know. Solemn, vulnerable, helpless, and awaiting more devastating blows describes how I felt in that moment.

This was the first of the final outcomes I was to hear over the next few days. I learned years later that hearing about Chester's death was a dress rehearsal of sorts. Lilli and others orchestrated who would be in the room and how the news would be delivered, in an attempt to prepare me for imminent news on Dave and Jack. My support team wanted to ensure that I had the right people in the room if, and when, we heard any updates about my husband and son. I believe the nurse even asked me who I wanted in the room, if we got news on the boys.

I slept poorly that night, anxious, sad, and worried about what I'd learn the next morning.

Despite a poor night's rest, I tried eating breakfast that next morning. After about thirty minutes, the nurse took away the food tray and in came my parents, the priest and the nun, and Lilli.

"What's the tube by your nose?" my mom asked.

"A tube for extra oxygen. It's okay, it will help," I quietly replied.

I could see the concern on her face as she saw the extra medical equipment attached to me.

They asked how my night was. I said that I could not get comfortable in any position, and it took all of my strength, along with nursing help, to roll me on one side or another. I could hardly move. By this time, all the bruising was fully exposed, showing how hard my body had been impacted.

After a few more minutes, a uniformed officer who worked for the sheriff walked into my room. He stood at the back of the room, near the door.

"We found Dave," he said.

"Alive?" I asked hopefully.

"No, Kim. Dave is dead. He was found on the surf line at Hammond's Beach."

"Are you sure it is Dave?" I frantically asked, hoping there had been a mistake.

"It's Dave, Kim. I'm so sorry."

I had just heard the words of finality that my husband was gone. I was stunned and in utter disbelief. I felt a depth of sadness I had never felt before. Dave was not even fifty years old, and I adored him. *This can't be happening!* I thought.

Oh God, Lauren. She so loved her dad; she will be devastated, swirled in my brain.

Immediately, the nurse came over to give me a sedative. "I'll have to tell Lauren," I mumbled through the tears. "Let's figure out a way to have her transported to my hospital room, so she can hear it from me, in person, and not some other way. God-forbid she sees it on the news." The media was posting TV pictures of the dead, and I knew it would be even worse if she learned that her dad had died by hearing it on the news.

Later that day, after they transferred Lauren to my hospital, they wheeled her into my hospital room. My parents were with me, along with a few others, including my priest and the sister from the church. We embraced when we saw each other; although seeing me so bruised, she seemed hesitant to put much pressure on my body. As she sat back down in her wheelchair, I continued to hold her hand. From my hospital bed, I took a deep breath and mustered the strength to say, "Lauren, your dad went to heaven. We will miss him terribly, but we will be alright. We will get through this." Lauren's body contorted as if punched in the gut. Her jaw dropped open as she screamed in disbelief, "No! No! No! No!" Wailing, she slumped down in her chair with her mouth open, seeking to get out the pain of what she just heard.

Lauren was a young girl already impacted by the emotional and physical trauma she had endured when buried alive under twenty feet of mud for hours. Now she was hearing devastating news of losing her dad.

This was the saddest conversation we would ever have. After she learned that Dave, her dad, had perished, we wept about him together. And then Lauren asked about Jack. Since Jack was still missing, we worried all the more, now that we had learned about Dave's death.

To get some rest, Lauren returned to her room with two of her dear friends. Now I had to call my husband's parents to share the tragic news that he had died. This news was even more catastrophic because Dave had been my in-laws' last living child; his older brother had died from a congenital disease when he was only eighteen years old. This torturous news was cruel beyond words. Even in their grief, they lovingly showed Lauren and me care and concern. Where they got that strength, I don't know.

This was the darkest time in my life.

The next day, Lauren came to my room and sat by my bed. She looked frightened as she saw the large metal bowl on my nightstand, filled with various prescription bottles. "Do you have to be on all those things forever?" she asked nervously.

"No, honey, these are extra pills right now to help with the pain, and to prevent infection from the mud in my surgical incisions."

HOSPITAL, HAMMOND'S, AND UNEXPECTED NOTORIETY

I sensed her relief. My 14-year-old daughter was looking at her only surviving parent, bruised and battered in a hospital bed. The oxygen tube in my nose and monitors beeping all around were so much for an already traumatized young woman to experience. My heart sank for her. She was scared and frightened about what the future would hold. A little later she asked, "Mom, are we going to have enough money to live?" She had no idea about homeowners' insurance that should provide us temporary housing. "Yes," I reassured her. Injured, traumatized, and now unsure of what her future would look like, Lauren grabbed my hand and softly rubbed it.

Lauren and I had endured horrifyingly painful and traumatic experiences. We continued to suffer as we began to learn more details about where her father's body was found. It was located over a mile from our home, which meant he had been carried down Olive Mill Road, over the freeway, past the train tracks, over more land, and out to Hammond's Beach, where he stopped near the surf line. His body travelled almost a mile and a half. Later we learned that Dave's body was naked from the waist down, which showed the force of the avalanche. A university professor who studied the debris flow later informed us that the force on the victims was akin to a plane crash. My last glimpse of Dave was of him wearing full rain gear and heavy work boots. The deadly force of the mudslide had ripped his securely tied work boots off his body. A few years later, we learned that he had suffered polytrauma all over his body, including fatal trauma to his head. It is possible that every bone in his body had been broken with only his flesh holding him together. We were incredibly sad and horrified to learn these details of how he had suffered.

And my son, Jack, was still missing.

As each day passed, the likelihood of finding him alive became more and more remote. The first responders, nurses, and law enforcement personnel told me Jack was missing. They hoped to find him.

They did not say Jack had perished. I recall a search team member coming to my hospital room to ask me where Jack was when the slide happened. He wondered if he had run outside, or if he was in his bedroom. I recalled Jack running to his room to get dressed to leave. I assumed he had been in his room when the slide hit the house. With this information, I heard that they used excavators to dig out the mud-filled pool area in our backyard to find him. But still no Jack.

After five days, I began to fear what no one wanted to say. My baby boy, Jack, only 17, had perished too. The search teams had not been able to find his body.

If there was hell on earth, in these few days, I felt it. As I lay in my hospital bed, my scratched corneas healing, as well as the lacerations on my body, I was in a living hell. The physical pain no way compared to the pain I was feeling, missing my son, Jack, and grieving my husband, Dave.

Only days before the mudslide, our family had sat at the kitchen table, digging into Chinese take-out food. Eight days prior, the kids and their friends had enjoyed a festive New Year's Eve at our home. We had loved one another and our lives together, and now that life was obliterated.

To get through this nightmare, I asked for a Bible to be placed on my bed tray. I also requested a rosary with a charm of St. Anthony, since this saint is the patron of the lost. I was grateful to God for sparing my life and Lauren's, but we had already lost Dave, and I prayed to St. Anthony to find my son Jack. It was a miracle that Lauren and I had survived the car-sized boulders, massive tree trunks, live wires, broken glass, and everything else that whirled around us. I hoped that somehow Jack had also survived. After five days, I prayed that if my son wasn't found alive, that at the very least, they would find his body.

Little did I know that outside the hospital, our lives were being written about all over the nation.

Lauren's rescue after trapped hours buried alive.
Courtesy Tom Piozet

Our family's 2017 Christmas card was used for a front-page image of the *Los Angeles Times*. The Montecito tragedy went global. My sister in Germany was stunned to see images of her sister and family as central figures in this major natural disaster.

Lauren's rescue was captured on film and published around the world, even becoming a two-page spread in *TIME Magazine*. Media personnel sent my grieving mother-in-law flowers in hopes of getting a newsworthy conversation with her, while others tried to reach my parents in search of a comment, interview, or story.

Once my family was aware of the media activity, we locked down and hid our identity at the hospital. Only those we knew and wanted to visit us were given a special code to gain entry. Unbelievably, a stranger tried to see Lauren in the hospital by falsely saying he was Lauren's cousin. After that incident, Lauren took an alias. My husband's best friend purchased a red baseball cap to put on "Rose" when they went out to get her some basic clothes, once she was healed enough to move about.

In the hospital, I had no access to a phone or social media. Hospital staff had cautioned me not to turn on the TV because it was filled with mudslide coverage. Four days after the slide, however, needing a distraction, I grabbed the remote and clicked on the TV. To my shock, a news update was showing pictures of the mudslide victims. Seeing my husband's picture amid the other victims shattered my heart, and made it even more real. After that screen image of the victims, the news revealed an image of my son Jack and of Lydia, a two-year-old baby girl. Under these two pictures was the word "MISSING."

I turned off the TV, promising myself to never turn it back on while in the hospital. Lilli often slept on the spare couch in my room at night. A couple times when I awoke and looked over, I saw Lilli sitting under a blanket, as if it were a tent.

I learned that Lilli was tracking the news and social media on her phone under the blanket. She wanted to learn whether there was any news about Jack, and to correct any mistruths that were circulating. One evening on a popular social networking site, she read a post falsely claiming that Jack had been found by the beach, alive. Sadly, Lilli had to correct the person posting the falsehood, and she asked that the search and rescue team be the only source of my missing son's status. This went on for days.

In my hospital bed, I felt tremendous pain all over my eggplant-purple bruised body. My left hip pain was excruciating; it was much more than the pain from my two surgery sites. I was sure that my hip was broken, and I requested a higher-level scan to see if they could identify any damage. Desperate to have pain relief since the strong painkillers weren't providing enough reprieve, I asked my surgeon whether my acupuncture practitioner, Kathleen, could come to the hospital to try some pain-reducing acupuncture on my hip. The hospital team agreed, and Kathleen came to my aid. Though I had had a career in medical devices, in which I saw firsthand the wonders of Western medicine, I also believed in the benefits of Eastern medicine.

Kathleen quietly entered my room. She was devastated for me and wanted to help in any way she could. She gently pulled back my hospital gown to expose my hip. While a nurse shifted me to one side, Kathleen began to insert her acupuncture needles. She carefully put in an array of what seemed like twenty acupuncture needles in my hip area, buttocks, and upper thigh. I must have looked like a purple pin cushion. I held on to the hope that I'd soon get some pain relief and healing from her therapy.

No one had given Dave Clark (DC-2), my husband's best friend, a heads-up about what was going on in my hospital room. So, with my pin-cushioned rear end in the air, Dave quickly strolled into my room, ready to update me on his latest assistance efforts. And, voila…

Dave's stunned facial expression made me chuckle; the first time I had been able to laugh since the tragedy. I burst out, "Dave, I think you just got more than you bargained for!"

Dave's eyes seemed to bug out of his head in shock, but he laughed too. He was happy to see a smile on my face during such a dark time in our lives. As any gentleman would do, he raced out of the room to give me privacy.

As each day passed, my hope of finding my kind, humorous son alive dimmed. Jack was strong, but I sensed he was gone. Lauren told me that she too had a feeling, right after the slide, that her brother was not with us anymore.

Multiple times, an officer or detective visited me in my hospital room to ask more questions about Jack. The search team was trying to collect information that might help them find him. An active search was ongoing, with search dogs, search and rescue personnel, firefighters, friends and neighbors, who were all trying to help find Jack. I felt helpless because I could not join the search for my boy.

And I felt even more helpless when I learned that Lauren was ready to be discharged, but I was not. She needed her mom, and I felt I was letting her down by not being able to go with her. As Lilli was no longer spending the nights in my hospital room, she offered to have Lauren stay with her while I was still in the hospital, and I knew Lauren felt safe with her. Lilli had a cute dachshund and a cat. I knew that Lauren would enjoy being around the animals.

"Mom, I'll be okay, I'll be at Lilli's," she said. "You just focus on getting better."

The next day when she came to visit me in the hospital, Lauren told me that some friends had come over to Lilli's house the previous night. They sat around the kitchen table, crafting and making bracelets with beads. As I heard that, I knew she was getting the needed support, yet it continued to pull at me that I was not yet able to care for her. A few days later, Lauren told me that she received a special hair treatment at a salon. Struggling with the smell of mud, despite repeated hair washes, she found a woman who suggested a mineral cleaning treatment. This special treatment helped to get all remaining mud smell out of Lauren's hair. She was relieved. The smell of mud was a horrible trigger to what she endured, and what she lost.

Weeks later, the doctors told me I needed to go to a rehabilitation hospital. "No!" I said. I needed to be home with Lauren. I felt she needed me, instead of being in the care of others. My daughter had been in the hospital a little over a week while still bedridden; I had been there about three weeks. Lauren came to my room one afternoon and stood next to my bed. "Mom, you need to go to the rehabilitation hospital. It's okay, I'm fine at Lilli's." Hearing Lauren say she was okay while I went through the inpatient physical rehabilitation allowed me to accept this, and I agreed to go for a few days. My priest even came to my bedside and urged me to go. I think he thought if I just got to that rehabilitation facility, I would realize how much I needed it.

I was transferred from the hospital by van to an inpatient rehabilitation hospital. As I was being transferred, I noticed a man who sat parked in his car facing me. A pit formed in my stomach as I noticed the camera that he had pointed toward the van, awaiting my transfer.

My life had changed in an enormous and surreal way.

In the rehabilitation hospital one afternoon, the nurse popped in to tell me the sheriff was there to see me. I was terrified that it was to tell me they had found my son. I grabbed the nurse's hand, and asked her to sit with me while the sheriff was in the room. She kindly agreed and pulled up a chair next to my bed, holding my hand with both of hers. An entourage of men in sheriff's uniforms came into my hospital room. I sensed a weird energy about them, as if they felt guilty, seeing me lying in a hospital bed injured, and knowing what they had to tell me. Instead of telling me that they had found Jack, the sheriff proceeded to tell me something to the effect that, "We are still looking for Jack, but not every day now; just weekly." Awkwardly, he tried to grab my hand to give me comfort, but I knew that what he was really telling me was the search was going from a "rescue" to a "recovery effort." I appreciated his visit, but I got a very uncomfortable feeling from his energy. Despite that feeling, I still believed that each week, search teams would be out looking for Jack and toddler Lydia.

Once out of the rehabilitation hospital, people would stop to talk to me at the local convenience store, or in a store's parking lot. Once as I came from Mass at the Mission, a reporter approached me from one of the news-magazine shows to ask for an interview. When I finally logged back into my email, there were many media requests seeking to interview Lauren and me. Each wanted to be the first to get the story of our tragedy. I realized that not only did I have to help Lauren and myself heal, but also, I needed to protect my daughter from the flurry of media attention.

CHAPTER 9

TWO MEMORIALS AND A CHUMASH RITUAL

F ROM MY rehabilitation center bed, I started planning Dave's funeral. I was not ready to include Jack in a joint event, because his remains had not yet been found. Instead, I chose to focus on Dave's memorial, and continued to pray that Jack's body would be recovered.

So many memories swirled in my head. From the day we met, to our engagement, to having our children, to the simple times of pure contentment holding his hand when we walked. A friend had brought in a picture of Dave posing with the Cub Scouts at the scout house. He was dressed up in a ship captain's white outfit, and the scouts were assembled around him with big grins, holding their sailboats they'd each made. The picture drew me back to when we first moved to Santa Barbara from Ohio; Dave had us all go to the local scout house to meet the Cub Scout troop. Immediately we felt welcomed, and sensed the mothers' keen interest in the many scouting experiences we'd had in Ohio. Dave was fully engaged and the moms in attendance noticed it immediately.

The next month was the famed Cub Scout Pinewood Derby event. It was a fun day, when Cub Scouts aged 7–12 would bring the cars they had carved out of pinewood, painted, and prepared in anticipation of racing their cars against the other Cubs' cars. Dave loved this event. He and Jack worked together in the driveway and garage, designing the burgundy-colored car. They added a racing stripe on the side of the car, and a silver-colored design decal, and ensured that the wheels rotated well. They were ready, although Dave wondered if the weight of the back wheels was ideal for maximum speed. Then the day arrived, and the whole family headed up to the scout house for the Pinewood Derby event. Lauren loved to run around and play, often to the scouts' chagrin, while the dads prepped the boys for the races. I enjoyed watching the event and getting to know the other parents. Jack's car won that day and he was beaming with a contagious smile. The parents recognized how Dave had engaged in the event, took a leadership role and made the event fun. He shared his knowledge from participating in the Ohio pinewood derby event and the Montecito parents were thrilled. A mom came up to me and pulled me aside, asking, "Do you think Dave would consider being the troop Cubmaster?"

"Sure, why don't you ask him?" I said.

A few minutes later, I saw three moms scurry toward Dave. They pulled him aside and asked him if he would lead the cub troop as Cubmaster. With a big smile, Dave replied, "I'd be honored." Dave said it would give him more quality time with his son, and he looked forward to the idea of building tool boxes, go-karts, and rain-gutter regatta sailboats with the Cub Scouts and their parents.

A couple months later was the famed rain-gutter regatta. A section of house gutter rested upon a couple of wooden sawhorses that made them about chest-high for the young Cub Scouts. The gutters then were filled with water so that the Cubs could race their sailboats they made with their dads. It was fun to watch them blow with as much air as they could muster, toward the sails of their boats — trying in earnest to win in the race. To make it more festive, I rented Dave a ship captain's uniform. On the day of the regatta, Dave showed up looking dapper in the white captain's suit and hat. The Cub Scouts were excited, and the parents all smiled; they knew they had in Dave a committed leader for the troop. Watching everyone enjoy the event made it a perfect afternoon. For our family, we came home feeling connected to this new community and embraced by the other families. This, and many other memories of Dave and the family flooded my memory as I planned my husband's funeral.

While I organized Dave's service from my hospital bed, my friend Marsha called me.

"This may sound odd, but I got an overwhelming sensation that you need to host a Native American burial ceremony on the beach Sunday morning, the day after Dave's memorial, for Jack."

Sensing the conviction in her voice, I said, "Sure. Let me call Jack's best friend, Casmali, who is Chumash, and learn if something like that is even possible."

When I called Casmali, I told him about Marsha's conviction. He said, "Let me talk to the elders."

Within hours, Casmali called back. "Chumash burial ceremonies are typically only performed for the Chumash community. But," he went on, "my father said that 'we'—all of us who endured the mudslide tragedy—are indeed community, and they would be honored to perform a ceremony for Jack."

And so, I was starting to listen. I was starting to be more open to the nudges I got from others. In this case, acting upon the strong sense of my friend when she told me we needed a Native American ceremony on the beach for Jack.

Because the mudslide was national news and had impacted the entire community, the priest advised me to plan for a large gathering. With our church still closed, Dave's funeral was held at the Santa Barbara Mission. I was using a walker, and a few minutes before the service started, I walked down the center aisle of the church. I took great comfort in how many friends, prior work colleagues, and neighbors showed up to pay their respects to Dave, and to provide support. As I scanned the pews, I saw people representing distinct chapters of Dave's life. Friends from San Diego when the kids were babies, colleagues from our careers, and local friends. Even our friends and neighbors from Ohio had flown out to say their goodbyes to Dave.

The scouts and scout leaders from Dave's troop led the procession into the church, signaling the start of the service. Witnessing a sea of Boy Scouts with pained looks on their teenaged faces, leading their late Scoutmaster's casket into the church to honor him and say their goodbyes, was beyond profound. This sight pulled at every one of my heartstrings. From the faces of everyone in the pews, it moved each of them, too. The boys' wish to honor Dave was a testament to his efforts as a volunteer to make a positive difference in their lives. The look on their faces as they walked up the aisle to their seats spoke volumes about the man they came to honor. To many of these kids, Dave was like a second dad. He was the male mentor that had helped teach them about the backcountry, camping, and even gourmet cast iron cooking. For many years, Dave used some of his vacation time to accompany them at Scout summer camp. Our dear friend and former work colleague, Alan, flew out from Cincinnati, and offered to play "Amazing Grace" on the bagpipes during the processional. Although so sad, it was a beautiful testament to Dave's life.

The sacred beach ceremony was planned quickly, days before Dave's funeral, leaving little time to send out announcements for that event. At Dave's service, I invited some of Jack's friends, family, and teachers to the Chumash beach ceremony for Jack the next morning.

Early Sunday morning, over 100 people gathered at the beach, where Jack's best friend since third grade was leading the ceremony. Witnessing a 17-year-old leading a sacred ceremony for his best friend, dead but still missing, was moving beyond words. During the ceremony, Chumash elders kindly shared the meanings of the songs, so we all could understand the beauty of the ceremony. At one point, they wrapped my shoulders with a special handmade blanket, as a gift of distinction. A blanket draped over the shoulders of a mother who has lost a child is a symbol of honor and acknowledgment. The sunrise ceremony by the Pacific Ocean at Leadbetter Beach, as waves of surf gently crashed onto the sand, was one of the most moving that I had ever witnessed.

Circled up, everyone noticed two large birds that soared above the crowd, as if to watch and be noticed. During the ceremony, I felt more at peace than I had since the tragedy. The message that Marsha had communicated, and that we acted on, transformed into a gift of healing for me, for my daughter, and for the community. Casmali had given a meaningful tribute to Jack, and I hoped that he would also find some peace and healing. I didn't know at the time that his father's home, his aunt's home, and his brothers' homes had also suffered damage from the mudslide. He had kept his losses quiet from us, as he unselfishly focused on helping those injured or killed.

Cracked open, raw, vulnerable, I was listening to people's intuition that I might have dismissed in the past. And this was just the beginning.

The following month, we held Jack's church memorial service at the same beautiful and historic Santa Barbara Mission. We were not allowed to call the event a funeral, as his body had not been found, but I wanted a priest-led church service to honor Jack, and allow the broader community to attend. It seemed as if Jack was now Santa Barbara's son as well, because so many people in the community were affected by the fact that he and the two-year-old baby girl had not been recovered.

Two weeks earlier was Lauren's scheduled Youth Group Winter Camp in the mountains near Los Angeles. I wanted her to attend, as it would be grounding and nurturing for her. The Youth Pastor, Anna, was a mentor to Lauren, and had been her nanny. As I thought about her long weekend getaway, I realized that I did not want Lauren that far away from me so soon. I offered to drive her and her friends up to the mountains, and I booked a room at a nearby hotel. What I did not anticipate was how scary the curvy mountain drive would be for me. I drove cautiously up the mountain, but I could tell that Lauren and her friends in the backseat felt my angst when we drove through the fog. I dropped them off at the three-day camp, where snow beautifully covered the ground. Lauren jumped out of the car, looking excited to attend.

After I checked into my hotel, I headed to a restaurant for dinner. A couple about my age was in front of me at the hostess stand. Wham! It hit me. I was alone. No Dave to enjoy a nice meal and conversation with at a restaurant, ever again. Never again would I enjoy a weekend getaway with Dave. As the couple in front of me walked to their table, I felt overwhelming sadness missing my life's partner. The hostess returned and walked me to my table, set for one.

This sucked. A lot. I ordered a steak dinner, and watched the other couples as I felt the loneliness of missing Dave, and the heightened responsibility I felt for Lauren as her only surviving parent. I thought about how I could support myself the next couple days while Lauren was at camp. After dinner, I went to the front desk and booked a massage in the spa for the next day, knowing it would help my aching body.

Back in my room, I crawled into bed. It was now common for me to wake up in the wee hours of the night, unable to sleep. Often, I would awake at 3:30 a.m.— the time of the mudslide. This night I woke even earlier, at 2:00 a.m. I got up, put on my glasses, and took a seat at the desk. I knew I had to do it; I started to write my son's eulogy for his service that was two weeks away. Tears rolling down my eyes and heartbroken, I wanted to do him justice and to honor him.

My whole body felt off and surreal. Writing his eulogy made it more real that Jack was gone. Missing, yes, but clearly, he had perished. My anguish was all-encompassing, I was unable to speak or breathe normally. As I tried to write the eulogy, my mind darted from one memory of Jack to the next.

One recollection always warms my heart. It was the day I watched Jack at age six take the hand of a special needs boy and walk with him onto the school bus. He sat with the boy to and from school daily. Another day, someone snapped a picture of Jack sitting with the boy in the grass, gently holding his hand. Jack had a natural kindness toward others, and this image in my head was such a strong example of it. I started to write. I wrote about Jack's interest in computers and gaming. He'd built his own computer one summer with his friends, and was delighted to see the finished product. Jack enjoyed it so much that he even designed his own online game on a popular gaming platform. His game had over 5,000 players, and he told me that he was like the CEO of the game. He had players who did marketing for the game, and other players who had other jobs. When he told me this, I was floored. He was leading a large team.

Lauren had told me a funny story about his online game. When Jack was about 16 years old, Lauren decided to log into and join his game as she sat in her bedroom. All of a sudden, Jack came bolting into her room, making a dramatic entrance. "Lauren, what are you doing?" he loudly asked. Sitting on the floor with her computer open, Lauren replied with a smile, "I'm playing in your computer game." She was shocked with Jack's reaction. "You are making us lose points! Wait until tomorrow to play!" he said as he marched back to his room.

What Lauren did not realize at the time, was that Jack went back to his computer and as CEO of his game, he appointed four players with the sole job of protecting Lauren during the game. It assured Jack that she wouldn't inadvertently lose the team points, but it also allowed her to continue to play. When Lauren told me this story,

I smiled. That was Jack. It captured his love of gaming, his ingenuity, and his inclusiveness, love, and protection for his sister.

Lauren told me about another time when Jack came bolting into her room exclaiming, "Never send nude photos on your phone!" Stunned, Lauren could not understand why her brother came in to tell her that. When she asked him about it, Jack told her that he had heard a boy in high school had been circulating a picture that his girlfriend had sent him, showing her bare breasts. Hearing about this, he wanted to caution his sister from ever putting herself in a vulnerable situation. There were so many stories that illustrated who Jack was. As I continued to draft the eulogy, tissue in hand, I wrote down a few of them to share.

My heart was forever broken. I had seen online a picture of a metal sculpture called *Melancholy* by Albert György. It was one of the best depictions of how I felt, as it portrays the void that grief leaves in us. In this sculpture, a human sitting on a bench, head facing down and arms resting on his thighs, has an empty space where his heart and torso would be. It captured the emptiness that I felt in my grief. I knew it would be brutally tough to write a eulogy for my son, but as his mother, I needed to be able to stand up at his memorial service and speak about him and for him. And, in some way, although it was one of the hardest things I had to do, I knew it would result in some healing. Writing about Jack was a way to slightly open the pressure valve of my sadness and anger.

2:00 a.m. rolled into 4:00 a.m., with an eerie quietness in the room as snow gently fell outside the window. I had much of the eulogy written. As the sun rose, I ordered breakfast, and stayed in my pajamas as I sipped my coffee. Later, when I checked in for my massage appointment, the receptionist asked what type of massage I preferred. I described what had happened to me, and said I wanted something relaxing and nurturing. "Well, ma'am, I think you should try Reiki," she responded. I had never heard of it. She told me that Reiki is a Japanese form of energy healing that could help with trauma. Apparently, some top medical centers in the US have used it for cancer patients, or those with PTSD.

In the massage room, I met the therapist. Surprisingly, she told me she had heard of my tragedy from her friend, despite the fact that she lived almost two hundred miles from my home. As coincidence would have it, this massage therapist was good friends with one of Jack's friend's parents. What a small world.

On the table while she did the Reiki treatment, suddenly tears started rolling down my cheeks. "This is good; it is helping to release a bit of the grief and trauma," she said. In an unexpected act of kindness from this stranger, she did not charge me for the massage. It was another situation in which someone compassionately used their talent to help me, and I noticed the impact.

The rest of the day, I thought through more of the details as I planned Jack's church memorial service.

Unlike Dave's service, there would be no casket. Instead, I had poster-sized pictures of Jack framed and on easels by the altar, along with beautiful sprays of flowers in his favorite orange, blue, and purple colors. On St. Patrick's Day, 2018, the ceremony was a somber memorial for my son, who was taken far too soon. I saw a professor of mine from UCLA's business school, who walked up to tell me this was the saddest funeral he'd ever had to attend.

I was filled with anguish, as Jack dying before me defied the natural order of life. I didn't know how I could continue living without my son and husband, yet knew I had to, for Lauren. Lauren could not yet accept that her brother and dad were gone. Her grief would have to be released in layers, in her own time. During this time, she told me that she was numb.

During Jack's procession, a group of his community service "Teens on the Scene" sat together in a few front pews in their blue service club shirts. Jack had co-founded this service group in 7th grade, and continued expanding the volunteer group when he entered high school. The club had over two hundred local teen volunteers in five different high schools. Jack's Montecito Boy Scout Troop 33 also attended, wearing their full Class A scout uniforms to demonstrate their respect for Jack, with a distraught look on their faces. Following them, high school friends, community members, and teachers attended, overflowing the Santa Barbara Mission.

My son meant the world to me, his sister, and my husband. During his memorial, I was able to see just how many lives Jack had touched in his short 17 years. For many of the teens in attendance, this was their first experience of losing a friend so young. Beside myself in grief, I gave a eulogy for my son, after three of his friends and his middle school headmaster gave beautiful tributes.

When Ellie, his good friend from school, spoke, two birds swooped in from the back door of the church and flew up the aisle to the altar, near the lectern. One bird darted to a side window and sat observing the funeral from the thick-walled windowsill. The other bird continued to flutter above the surprised audience. It was so dramatic, that even the Catholic priest paused to comment. He laughed with a touch of awe, saying the bird flitting around the altar must be Jack, in some way letting us know he was with us. I wanted to believe it was Jack flying around, as if to say, "Look at me, I'm here, I'm here!" The other bird must have been Dave, watching intently and quietly from the windowsill. I surmised that Dave was with us, too, but he let Jack steal the show.

During the reception and the receiving line after the service, so many people commented about the birds. Despite how many people had attended the Mission Church over the years, none had ever seen birds fly in.

CHAPTER 10

THE MAGNITUDE OF LOSS AND OUR SURVIVAL

FOR TEN DAYS, the National Guard and other first responders were in Montecito. In a 24-hour period, around 900 people were rescued; 800 on ground and 100 by air. The freeway, a main artery to the north and south, was closed for 10 days. Crews worked 24/7 to clear roads, fix broken gas mains, and reconnect electricity. Once opened, the freeway was full of large trucks hauling away millions of tons of mud and debris. Neighbors whose homes were not impacted were told not to drink the contaminated water for weeks. Many family pets were missing, presumed dead.

Surprisingly, most of the victims and destruction came from an area that was not in the mandatory evacuation zone. I knew that one day, I wanted to learn why the decision was made not to evacuate all of Montecito down to the freeway although I understood that the Fire Chiefs had made that strong recommendation. Tragically, many families were home asleep, unaware of the danger that would soon kill them.

Cantin house, November 2011 (before)

Kim on her lot with car-sized boulders, April 2018

Mere feet and inches determined who lived, and who died.

I had been only a foot away from my husband, who was just on the other side of our door. Dave perished, whereas I did not. Dave's body travelled 1.5 miles, but I travelled two hundred yards. Lauren had travelled one hundred yards.

Twenty-three victims perished that early morning of January 9, 2018. Montecito has approximately 8,700 residents; everyone knew someone who died or who was impacted. Four hundred homes were either damaged or destroyed and over a hundred people were injured. As I understand it, many more might have perished, had it not been

Obliterated lot (after)

for Montecito Fire Chief, Kevin Taylor. Apparently, concerned about the risk of mudslide, Kevin ordered the extra equipment and rescue teams to help in case of an event. Learning what Kevin Taylor did — requesting a quarter of a million dollars in equipment and people resources staged to help the day before the avalanche — indicates that he lives the oath to "protect and serve." If nothing had happened, he would have had to defend his decision. He is one of the true heroes in this tragedy. His decisions helped save many people, and get them to needed care after the devastation. But most don't know this about Kevin because he is a humble, hardworking, kind guy who believes he was just doing his job.

Now the areas hit were unrecognizable.

And many of the victims were unrecognizable. In the days that followed, search teams worked in earnest to find the missing.

Kim next to boulders on her property

CHAPTER 11

STEEP INCLINE

ONCE I WAS discharged out of the physical rehabilitation hospital, Lauren and I went to live at a temporary furnished rental home that our middle school connections helped find. It was located outside of Montecito, which felt safer to both of us. Its one-story layout also helped in my recovery.

My parents discussed the rental home with me as I prepared to be discharged. My dad exclaimed, "Kim, wait until you see the driveway to the furnished rental house, it's a doozy!" His animated tone told me that I would not like it. "It's not too bad," my mom jumped in reassuringly. "Yes, it is steep going up, but at the top there's a large flat area that is big enough so you can park cars and turn around easily." With my nervous system still shot, the description made me fear what I'd soon see.

As my parents drove me home from the hospital, I got to witness this driveway firsthand.

Seeing the steep, long incline, I started to cry. It surprised me that a steep driveway now felt scary. Clearly, my nervous system could not handle any more unknowns. As we started our incline, not being able to see what was at the top activated my fears. I sighed in relief when the car crested the top, revealing the large flat driveway, house, and front yard. Adjusting my walker to get out of the car, I felt sadness and emptiness as I approached the door of our temporary home. It was not my home. My family of four and sweet dog were not in it.

Over the next many weeks, I'd habitually take a deep, slow breath to calm my nerves almost each time I drove the borrowed hunter-green car up the steep driveway to the rental house where we were now staying. A nice family from the middle school had lent me their vehicle. None of the clothes I now wore were familiar. Many were given to me, and often I chose sweatpants and a sweater to be comfortable.

People often described me as an independent person who did not like to ask for help. Instead, I was a helper or fixer of things. Now, in this rental home, I found myself being comforted by others. It was foreign to have so much support, as Lauren and I transitioned into our rental home and new life. The community of Santa Barbara is known to be tightknit, giving, and compassionate, yet it felt odd because I had never had to rely on other people before. Local families signed up to bring us food each evening. A large white cooler sat on the front porch, and it was humbling to find a thoughtful, delicious meal prepared for Lauren and me, for almost two months. What a gift that was. While I was injured, I did not have to struggle to go to the grocery store or spend time cooking. I was being nurtured by this amazing community.

In the rental house, Lauren took the room with twin beds. Immediately, she invited a friend to sleep over each night. It was clear that she feared sleeping alone, and she said that she was fearful of crawling into bed with me, for fear of hurting one of my wounds. In addition to people bringing clothes for us to wear, we experienced a cascade of support, including folks offering to drop off and pick up Lauren from school. A dear friend, Lisa, from my youth, came to stay with me.

She said that I had helped her when her mother passed away in 4th grade, so she wanted to be here for me. She drove 18 hours to help me, and found a place to house her and her elderly dog. I took comfort in friends that I'd known for over 35 years, who helped to ground me with their support. Lisa ran errands and helped advise me on what action items I needed to attend to, regarding the massive amount of insurance and other administrative calls I needed to make. Stacey, my friend since I was 16, when we worked together summers, ran Lauren to and from school, and she and her husband kindly took my parents to a lovely restaurant to help them celebrate their wedding anniversary. Local friends let me have my mail routed to their PO box, until I could get my own. The rental house was lovely, with an amazing view of the Santa Ynez mountain range.

Typically, I would have loved this view, but now I saw evil in the mountains. The mountains now signaled death danger to me. Part of this range had roared down and killed half my family, forever changing our lives. I realized that I much preferred looking toward the ocean, where I found some peace and calm. I knew that someday when we were ready to look for a replacement home, I wanted to ensure that it faced south, toward the Pacific.

During this time, Lauren was clear: she feared going back to the area of Montecito where the slide hit. "Mom, there's no way I'm going back there! I can't even face the smell of mud. The smell of mud was in my hair for weeks. Even a textured smoothie is now gross to me, as it reminds me of the mud and twigs going down my throat." Now, each time she was preparing to head out on an errand, I'd hear, "Mom, please remind my friend's mom who's driving me today to take an alternate route in Montecito!" Understanding her concern, I proactively asked anyone driving Lauren to avoid the mudslide area.

During the day, I used the dining room table as my desk, with a calendar and planner to keep me organized. My sister had come to stay with us. While Lauren was in school one day we went to meet with the staff at the local hospice counseling center that the doctors and nurses had advised me to check out. My sister and I walked into the lobby, and we were quickly greeted by staff, who took us to a meeting room to discuss the types of services they offered. I learned about individual grief therapy sessions that were offered weekly. They told me they'd have a separate counselor for me and for Lauren. They even mentioned that they had a teen group session for teens who'd recently lost a parent. I was amazed to learn about this compassionate service to help people in their time of need.

"Wow, this is making it even more real," my sister said somberly. She realized that Lauren and I would need extensive counseling support to deal with our grief and our trauma.

When Lauren was home from school, I went into her room to chat. "Hey, I went to learn about the hospice center today with Auntie Pam."

Looking up from her iPad, Lauren asked, "Yeah, how was it? And what does hospice do?"

"It was good," I said. "Hospice is the place that so many of the hospital folks kept encouraging us to visit and utilize. I learned they offer a variety of programs and counselors that can help us work through the tragedy and our grief. I was impressed with it. They are dedicated to services to help people who are going through grief and who've experienced sudden loss. They have individual counselors — meaning you'd have your own person, and I'd have my own person. Often you just go one time a week, for one hour. They told me they even have a group session for teens who've lost a parent. How does that sound?"

Lauren perked up a bit, nodding. I also told her about groups being formed by the hospital specifically for folks who'd been impacted by the mudslide. I said that I planned to check those out as well.

"Lauren, we have to take care of our mental health," I said. "We've been through a horrendous tragedy, and we need professional trauma and grief support." We had not had this psychological support in our lives before now, so this was new for us. "Okay, Mom, we can check it out," Lauren agreed. "I feel numb, though, but I'll try it out." I was relieved at her being open to the support.

Soon, we each had sessions on the schedule. While at home during the day, I researched other trauma psychologists in the area, trying to learn who might be ideal for Lauren and her needs as an adolescent and what trauma support I would need. It was a whole new world; learning about different approaches, I read about some well-studied approaches such as EMDR, a treatment known to help with PTSD.

My life of being busy juggling work and family was now a distant memory. My day was now focused on establishing a sense of order for Lauren and me. My focus was scheduling the needed support, driving Lauren to and from school, and handling the massive amount of paperwork needed to try and stabilize my new life. Just at the age when Lauren should be given more freedom and independence as she developed as a teen, I felt I had to work intensely to stabilize her world and surroundings. The trauma she'd experienced made her appreciate and embrace the extra level of motherly attention, but I didn't know how long that would last.

CHAPTER 12

MUSICAL HEALING

SCHOOL WAS A sanctuary and happy place for Lauren. She went to the independent Santa Barbara Middle School, which had a unique outdoor education program, excellent academics, and a strong inclusive community. Dave and I had fallen in love with the school, not only due to the outdoor program in which each year the students and teachers went on three week-long to 10-day mountain bike trips, camping and exploring; but also because of the sense of kind community it fostered at the school. While there, Jack had grown in self-confidence and self-assuredness about who he was and who he wanted to be. Now, I was watching Lauren do the same. In weeks, Lauren would gear up for the winter trip, which this year included a kayak trip up part of the California coast.

One afternoon after school pick-up, Lauren asked, "Mom, can you run me to the harbor this afternoon?"

"Sure, honey, what's happening?"

"Jesse wants some of the students that are going on the kayak trip to practice in the harbor. He told me that he wants to make sure I do okay in the water, after — you know."

"That's thoughtful and smart of him. I'm glad you'll be able to try out the kayak in the harbor, with the teachers with you. I think you'll have fun."

I drove Lauren to the harbor, and sat on a nearby bench to watch. It was the first time she had been near water since the tragedy. Lauren had almost drowned while being washed away and buried by mud. Like others, I did not know how she'd do in the water. My shoulders relaxed as I saw her teacher, Jesse, paddle close in his kayak, while Lauren and her classmate splashed their paddles and learned the nuances of paddling successfully around the harbor's boats. I felt relieved: she could do this. This meant that she could go on the school winter trip, even if she opted not to kayak every day.

Back at home, Lauren and I looked at the calendar. Upcoming were her twice-weekly rehearsals for the May production of *Les Misérables*. To the surprise of the ensemble and theater directors, Lauren had returned to the group to rehearse her role of Fantine. When I saw her at practice, I realized that she was with her tribe. She loved musical theater. In the abrupt transition to our life as a family of two instead of four, engaging in those kinds of events helped her regain a sense of normalcy and stability. I prioritized those events, yet watched with a vigilant eye as to how she was doing.

In addition to the school events and musical theater, we were involved in mudslide community fundraisers and events. Soon after the mudslide, one of Lauren's friends wanted to go help find Jack, but was told by authorities that it was much too dangerous. So instead, the teens came up with the idea to host a teen sing benefit, with the monies they raised to go to a community disaster relief fund. With the preceding Thomas Fire and its multiple evacuations, and now the debris flow closing a main travel artery, it seemed like many local service personnel had lost their jobs. Many shops and restaurants had closed, having lost their ability to sell during the holidays — the busiest and most revenue-generating time of the year, for many shop owners. While Lauren was still in the hospital, her friend had asked her if she wanted to be in the production. "Yes!" she had said from her hospital bed. So, for a busy eight weeks, we also coordinated getting Lauren to these rehearsals. A talented group of local teens was quickly organized, and music icon Kenny Loggins agreed to help co-produce the show. Mr. Loggins provided amazing support, encouraging these kids in what became the Teens Sing for Santa Barbara benefit concert (www.teensingforsb.com).

Lauren and I had never met Mr. Loggins before, but he was known in town for having a generous heart and as someone who used his talents for good. On the way to one of the rehearsals, I said, "Lauren, do you know who this is? Kenny is the music of a generation. He sang and recorded some of the best songs, like 'Danny's Song,' 'Celebrate Me Home,' and 'Return to Pooh Corner,' and his iconic movie hit songs: 'Footloose,' 'Caddyshack,' and 'Danger Zone.'"

"Mom, he's just Kenny to me," Lauren simply replied.

Mr. Loggins was a dad, and he clearly enjoyed mentoring these talented teens for a great cause. I told him how meaningful his "Return to Pooh Corner" song was to me; I had played that song every night for baby Jack to fall asleep to and Jack continued to listen to that CD until age seven. To me, the song meant new motherhood, and the amazement of a new life filling our hearts. Mr. Loggins warmly thanked me, and then he shifted the conversation to how I was doing as I stood there, steadying myself with my cane. He looked just as I'd imagined, with handsome touches of gray in his hair. Soon after, Mr. Loggins gathered the teens together so that the planning and practice for the concert could start.

It warmed my heart to see and hear about the teens' work on the production. One night during show practice that I was unable to attend, Mr. Loggins and the other parents witnessed a heart-warming moment. The next day, Mr. Loggins was eager to tell me all about it.

"In the sound studio," he said, "I was coaching Lauren and another teen on a song they would sing for the show. Behind us, watching through the glass, were several parents. It was getting late, so it was the last take of the song. Suddenly, while Lauren and the other teen sang into their microphones, they started dancing and singing next to one another. Their arms were swaying with the music, their bodies grooving to the beat. Lauren, totally immersed, was smiling. She put her head down as she waved her arms above her head, rocking to the beat. Joy in the moment was palpable." Mr. Loggins exclaimed, "That moment was *the* highlight of the past few weeks! I saw her having fun. A moment of joy. It was incredible to experience, just weeks since the tragedy." That joyful moment was caught on tape by the videographer, and was used in the commercial to promote the benefit show on TV. When I saw the clip, I smiled. It gave me a little hope that she'd get through this, and it reinforced how powerful music and song were to her soul.

On show night, when Lauren took the stage and sang "Defying Gravity" from the Broadway show *Wicked*, we were all riveted. Tears rolled down my face as I witnessed her bravery. Lauren walked on stage six weeks post-tragedy and sang a poignant song that moved everyone in the theater. Sitting there, I knew that Dave would have been so proud of his daughter.

Lauren had told me that when she sang, it was one of the only times when she really felt her feet firmly on the ground. Impressively, this benefit concert raised over seventy thousand dollars that was donated to the local Unity Shoppe relief center and food pantry. With the donations, The Unity Shoppe created a disaster relief section in their center. Now, those in need could get blankets, clothes, towels, or other items that had been washed away or destroyed in the mudslide, or lost in other disasters.

Lauren singing "Defying Gravity" during the
Teens Sing for Santa Barbara benefit concert
Photo credit Steve Kennedy

As I drove home with my daughter, I said, "Lauren, you did amazing! Now that it is over, how did it feel to be part of the show?"

"It was good! I love all the people in the show; they are my people," she responded.

"Oh, I'm glad, sweetie. I'm glad you felt it was good for you. The audience certainly responded to you on stage. I bet it moved each of them to see you singing and dancing after watching your dramatic rescue less than two months ago."

"Sure, maybe," she replied in a tone that made me think she could not believe her impact on others.

"And this concert raised thousands of dollars for the Unity Shoppe! I think it's amazing that all of you worked together to make such an impact that will help others in need," I said, as we pulled into the driveway of the rental home.

"I know, that's great! I feel good about that, but I'm tired," she responded as she walked through the front door toward her room.

I hoped this experience would inspire her and the other teens with the power of giving back to those in need.

A few weeks after the concert, Mr. Loggins had the kids gather at the newly created Unity Shoppe Disaster Relief section, feeling that it was important to show them the direct benefit of their volunteer efforts. This was evidence that even at their young age, the teens could contribute to their community.

I saw the healing benefit when Lauren sang. Yet, the realist in me also recognized that it was a busy distraction to keep us from feeling the loneliness of our family of two, and missing the life we'd had with Dave and Jack. But this was our new life, and I knew we had to keep marching forward.

Other new events came up with short notice. With last year's Christmas card plastered over major newspapers and news outlets, many were interested in Lauren's story as millions watched her miraculous rescue. One afternoon my phone rang. It was a fundraiser called the "Kick Ash Bash" by the ONE805 non-profit. The organization was doing an event to raise money for first responder equipment, and to thank all the first responders and their families for their heroic work on the Thomas Fire and debris flow. It was to take place on a large estate with a field big enough to be a polo field; they'd convert it into a concert and benefit area for the day.

"Lauren, we got a call, and they'd like to have you sing during a major fundraiser for the first responders' families and for some new equipment. Are you interested?"

"Sure, what do they want me to sing?" she asked.

"The National Anthem to open the benefit concert. David Foster will accompany you on keyboard. He's a very famous music producer and composer who's won Grammy awards for his work."

Lauren singing the National Anthem at the Kick Ash Bash Fundraiser for First Responders
Photo courtesy ONE805.org

"Okay, I'm game," she said.

Soon, Lauren was singing the National Anthem with David Foster. The talented lineup included Ellen DeGeneres, Katy Perry, the band Wilson Phillips, Dennis Miller, Alan Parsons, Kenny Loggins, and others. Impressively, this event raised two million dollars for first responder equipment.

My life felt surreal. I took comfort in watching Lauren enjoy singing. Each time she did, people said it moved and inspired them. She has a great voice, along with the inspiration she gave others by showing her courage and resilience, and the results were epic. Lauren, who essentially walked away from being buried alive for hours toward her waiting ambulance, was the epitome of inspiration when she walked onstage to sing. Each note she sang helped to heal a traumatized community.

Barely a month later, Lauren was invited to sing a solo with her friend on guitar at the sold-out Santa Barbara Bowl during the Brad

Paisley/Ellen DeGeneres benefit concert. They performed a hauntingly soulful Ed Sheeran song, "I See Fire."

I was awed to see these celebrities use their talent for good with the local benefit concerts. Before each event, I'd drive to the local department store to find Lauren a stage outfit. Having lost all of our clothes, our salesperson, who by now knew us well, was helpful finding items. During each performance, I was focused on ensuring that no media asked her about her mudslide experience or rescue. Her story would be told on our own time in the way Lauren wanted it told.

Months after the Kick Ash Bash, where we met Ellen, Lauren said that if she was to tell her story, she wanted it to be on Ellen's TV show. Ellen had been a kind neighbor during the tragedy, and was rumored to have ridden her bike around the area, asking if folks were okay. In May, we both were interviewed on her show when Lauren for the first time shared her story more broadly. Following the interview, she sang "Rise Up" by Andra Day and Jennifer Decilveo. The song was perfectly suited for Lauren and the way she was strongly engaging with life, as opposed to recoiling in her trauma.

That year was a year of firsts. As my wedding anniversary arrived, I placed my cane in the passenger's side of the car and drove to the cemetery to spend time at Dave's grave. I had nothing planned, other than taking some flowers to the cemetery plot, where I wanted to sit on the grass in quiet. While there, I recalled that it was a sunny, beautiful day when we married years ago near the coast in Southern California. Today, the weather was also beautiful. From Dave's plot, I could see the cliffs and the Pacific Ocean. Sitting on the grass, I decided that this was a good day to buy a car. Since the tragedy, I'd been driving the owner's car from whom I was renting the house. When I had bought my work car just eighteen months ago, I had chosen out a white SUV. As I drove into our Montecito driveway in the SUV, Dave greeted me in the driveway and exclaimed with light sarcasm and a big warm grin, "Why did you get 'the Montecito mom car'?"

I chuckled, and said, "Because I liked it."

"You should have gotten the midnight blue SUV we saw there!"

I laughed at Dave's comment and replied that the car of his dreams was too expensive for our budget. Today, as I sat on the grass at the cemetery, I replayed so many good memories from over twenty years together. I had married the perfect guy for me, and I missed him terribly. My life was lonelier, and it would be much more so when Lauren headed off to college in a few years. To dismiss that sad thought, I focused on the idea of buying a new car.

From my sitting position, I rolled over to get up. But as I struggled, I realized that I simply could not get up off the ground. Still quite weak and injured, I tried to shift onto my knees and push myself up with my hands, but to no avail. No matter which way I tried, I simply could not get up from the ground to a standing position. Even with my cane at my side, I could not get myself up. What a sight I must have been! A grieving, injured wife and mother, now seemingly stuck, lying on the grass at the cemetery. After I realized my predicament, I saw a woman in the distance visiting a grave. I had to do what no one wants to do in the quiet of a beautiful, serene cemetery: I started to yell for help.

"Would you come help me?" I called out.

With a quizzical glance, the woman tilted her head and looked at me as she placed her flowers. In a minute or so, she started to walk toward me. Although she had no idea why I needed help, she was a kind-hearted person who helped me get to my feet. How embarrassing. In each unexpected instance like this one, I was learning that I needed others' help more than I realized. Once up and after I dusted myself off, I thanked her profusely, and then headed toward my car. After I left the cemetery, I drove toward the car dealer.

In the showroom, I saw a beautiful midnight blue SUV — the exact one Dave would have chosen. I walked in with my cane to steady my gait as I approached the display car. It was a beauty and, in the car's cab, next to the driver's seat, was a handle. It was perfect — that handle made it easier for me to pull myself into the car. "I'll take it!" I said to the salesman. He was generous, and gave me a mudslide discount.

Within an hour, I was headed to the middle school to pick up Lauren after school. Lauren told me her friends were giddy, telling her that her mom was in a new sporty car.

As she jumped in the car, she said with a smile on her face, "What did you do?" She was happy for me, and knew for sure that her dad and brother would have approved.

PART 4
THE SEARCH

"You'll Never Walk Alone"
—Elvis Presley

CHAPTER 13

FACING THE RUBBLE

AFTER ABOUT a month in the temporary living situation, I drove to where my house once stood. I knew I needed to face this head-on if I was to have any hopes of healing. Seeing it would help me know what happened, beyond what I remembered. Kind friends had offered to accompany me, but I wanted to go alone. It was a private experience to see what remained of where our family had once happily lived.

In the hospital, people had told me that everything was gone; our pool, the brick patio, our home's foundation, and the landscaping. All had been destroyed. I knew that I had to see it to believe it.

Sunlight lit the area as I drove toward our once-shaded intersection, which had been graced by a canopy of old, beautiful trees. The sun shone in since many of the mature trees had been washed away. This area used to be lush with graceful coastal live oaks, sycamore and eucalyptus trees, green hedges, and large avocado trees. I was shocked to see that so much had been swept away.

The noise of excavators and trucks filled the air. The road was muddy, and the car was sprayed with dirt and mud as I drove closer toward our home. As I turned left on our street and then into the lane that just weeks ago was framed by a columned entrance, only a dirt path remained. No columned entrance. No paved lane. No trees. Nothing.

Sitting in my car, I looked onto our property, which was riddled with massive boulders and dirt. A few of our trees still stood on the side of the property that once held over fifty trees.

I sobbed.

Seeing the property made our home's absence more real, yet still utterly unbelievable. The absolute fierceness of our losses hit me. Seeing the ravaged land allowed me to understand that I would never again have my family back. Everything was lost: my husband and son were gone. All of our family photos, my children's baby books, my wedding album — our home that held our memories — gone. Not a piece of foundation, not a remnant of brick patio, not even the metal rebar framing our pool, was left.

Just a month before, we had been a happy, vibrant family of four. Now Lauren had lost her dad and brother, and I had lost my husband and son. Life as we knew it would never exist for us again.

Looking at the few remaining trees, I noticed how high the mud line was on them. By where Jack's room was, the mud line on the oaks looked fifteen feet high. Jack hadn't had a chance of surviving such an onslaught. I was grateful that Lauren and I had somehow survived.

A few of the boulders on the lot were the size of a car. Hundreds of rocks and massive boulders were scattered on our property. As I walked, I saw a twenty-foot piece of three-inch-wide metal that was twisted and bent. Nature's incredible power had contorted this once straight piece of metal into the shape of a curved pretzel.

Standing where our home once was, I pictured where I had been when the mud roared in. It looked to be 200 yards to the intersection where I had been found on a debris pile, trapped and wrapped in electrical wires. I was clearer than ever that it was through sheer luck, or the grace of God, that I survived the impossible. I imagined that many angels must have rallied that early morning. Based on what I saw standing there, I knew that I must have had help.

Two miracles had occurred that morning. Lauren's survival and rescue was clearly one of them. It was a miracle that somehow, buried alive under twenty feet of mud, a car, a refrigerator, an electrical transformer, and a heavy truck toolbox, there was miraculously a pocket of air by her face, and a tiny straw-sized hole that allowed air from the outside to flow into her muddy entombment. That tiny hole enabled her to breathe, and she survived six terrifying hours before her two-hour rescue. When Lauren's two rescuers came to visit me in the hospital, Fire Captain Ben told me that it was a miracle that the direction I had pointed them to from my debris pile led them straight to Lauren. Now, seeing the area where Lauren and I were found, I believed him.

As I looked at the boulders, downed trees, twisted metal, and electrical wires scattered all over, it seemed impossible that we had not been crushed to death, drowned, or electrocuted. I could not imagine what would have happened if Lauren or I were left without one another, totally alone, since Dave and Jack had died.

As I started the car's engine and quietly drove away from our destroyed home, the nightmare of losing my husband and son was even more real. I kept thinking that it was a miracle Lauren and I had survived. As I drove away, I was shaken. I determined that I would work to show my thankfulness for having survived. I wanted to show my gratitude for being spared.

Back at the rental home, I walked into the kitchen and started to prepare salmon with asparagus, one of Lauren's favorite meals. She strolled out of her bedroom. "Hey, Mom, how's it going?" she asked as I trimmed the ends off the asparagus.

"Hi, sweetie. How was your day?" I responded.

"Pretty good. We picked our new electives at school, and we're starting to practice our Shakespeare play in Jesse's class. I'm Juliet, and I get to do my lines on the balcony toward Romeo. I'm cool with that," she said. "What did you do today?"

"Do you really want to know?" I asked her, raising an eyebrow.

"Yes."

"I decided to drive by Montecito and our damaged lot. When I saw the area, I pulled my car over on our little lane, parked, and had a good cry."

"Why'd ya do that?" she queried in a tone of disgust and angst.

"I wanted to be able to see it, and to be able to drive by it again. Work will need to be done, like clearing the lot and getting a fence up."

Drawing in a breath, I continued. "Quite frankly, I also needed to see it for myself. To face my fear, and see firsthand the area where we'd been rescued. I got to see the five trees clumped together that saved your life; those trees slowed down the debris you were in and helped the pile form, so you didn't get whisked away."

"I never want to go back," she said firmly.

"That's okay, Lauren. You never have to. Yet one day, you might change your mind. Take it a day at a time, sweetie.

"Would you mind setting the table?" I asked, and we continued chatting about school until dinner was ready.

After dinner, I had to leave for an hour to get to my "How We Heal" group that had formed after the mudslide. I knew I really needed that session tonight. Hosted by the local hospital, the sessions were offered to people who were impacted by the mudslide. By now, I was going to three different counseling appointments a week, and this was group versus individual counseling. I found the group sessions the most helpful, being with people who "got" what I'd gone through. When I tried a widow's group, I felt like I just didn't fit in. I loved the women in the group, and we became good friends, but I'd feel even more sad when they'd talk about being able to sit in their late husband's favorite chair, or take comfort seeing a favorite sweater or memento the two had collected while married. I had none of those things. Mine, I was told, was a complicated grief: losing my husband, and my son, our dog, our house, and truly my daughter and myself as we had been. Lauren and I were now different people, working to navigate our new reality.

While in my chair at the group session, I kept my eye on the large round clock on the wall. As the hands of the clock advanced to 7:00 p.m., I quickly excused myself. As with most appointments or errands, I'd dash to get home because, understandably, Lauren did not like being home alone.

CHAPTER 14

THE CROOKED HOUSE

MY HIP HAD been badly contused or bruised and had a labral tear. I spent my days attending physical therapy sessions, making administrative calls, and replacing some of the things we had lost in the mudslide. I attained our passports, submitted death certificates, grieved, and cared for Lauren. Early on, I cried in my grief, which was helpful in the process. Yet often Lauren said that she just felt numb. I was sad for her. She told me that sometimes, when she headed out of her room toward the kitchen and saw me crying, she'd quietly head back into her room again. Although I told her it was healthy to cry to let the grief out, it must also have been scary and unsettling for her to see her only surviving parent cry. I tried to reiterate that it was good for me to get the grief out, and I hoped she would be able to, as well. Through the various experts I'd spoken with, I learned that adolescents grieve on their own time, not mine. I focused on trying to be supportive through it all, though my emotional tanks were nearly empty.

One day, about 65 days after the debris flow, sitting at a paper-cluttered dining room table at the rental house, I called the sheriff's department to get an update on the search they were doing for Jack, and to get more specifics about where Dave was found. I was given the contact information of a search and rescue individual who had found Dave. I dialed the number. When she answered, I told her, "I'm Dave's widow, and I'd like to learn more about where Dave was found." She breathed deeply, paused, and kindly, in a soft voice, she shared that she had been one of the people that found my husband's body on the surf line at Hammond's Beach, a beautiful, serene part of the beach near a Chumash sacred burial ground. I was stunned to learn how far Dave's body had travelled from our home. Though painful to hear, I needed to know the details of his death, as knowing about my husband's last minutes might provide clues or information we could use in our search for Jack and Lydia's remains. As she continued to share the details of Dave's death, I told her I was grateful that they were still out there searching for Jack and Lydia, the other family's baby daughter.

There was a deafening pause on the other end of the phone.

Then, softly, she she replied something to the effect of, "Kim, we stopped searching on Super Bowl Sunday."

Astounded, my voice rose a few octaves. "The sheriff told me personally that you weren't searching every day, but that you were searching every week!"

"No, Kim," she responded definitively and gently. "We stopped searching on Super Bowl Sunday."

Drained, I thanked her for her candor, and hung up. I was furious.

Super Bowl Sunday was only a few weeks after the day when the sheriff came to my hospital room, saying that they would be searching weekly for Jack, just not daily.

My mind raced. That Sunday was the weekend of Dave's memorial, and I was never told anything about the active search for Jack being halted. I'd been waiting each day for a call from Search and Rescue telling me, "We've found Jack." I had even called a couple times to the funeral home, to ensure they'd kept a matching casket to Dave's in stock, so that when Jack's body was found, we would be ready. Now, it had been over a month since Jack's memorial when I learned this shocking news on the phone.

I was angry, stunned, and overwhelmingly sad.

After learning that the search team had effectively stopped actively searching after the biggest football game of the year, I made a decision. Nothing is more powerful, no matter how hurt and injured one is, than a mother in search of her child. Especially if their child is dead and missing.

It was not okay to think of my beautiful son's body left in debris. I needed his remains found for our closure, for the respect and dignity of his body, and to lay him to rest next to my husband at the cemetery. Not just for me, but for the entire community that wanted Jack and baby Lydia found. Through the tragedy, these two kids became the community's children, with the local parents and community members praying they'd be found and properly laid to rest.

I was now a mom on a mission.

Various folks told me that so many of the search and rescue personnel got PTSD from what they saw post-mudslide, and they needed a break. I certainly tried to understand, but I also had PTSD. I had survived being washed away by the mudslide, and I had lost half of my family — my husband and my first and only son, who was still missing. I felt my fury in my gut, knowing that I didn't get to take a break. I didn't have the luxury of a time-out. I knew that time was of the essence. I had to put on a smile and friendly demeanor to get continued help, when some had given up. Each day that passed meant more body decomposition, and the risk of the many hired earth mover teams inadvertently hauling him away as they cleared the lots and streets. I knew that this was very possible. In my search efforts, I'd learned details regarding the condition of the bodies of some other victims that made me even more concerned about debris being cleared and hauled away without proper oversight.

It was a dark time. A lot of labor and energy was being expended. I knew there were many heroic efforts, and that some errors were made, in the rush to clear the streets. I just hoped that the errors made throughout the entire mudslide event would be acknowledged honestly, and the experience learned from, so history would never repeat itself.

One thing I was clear on was that I was not okay with hearing that the active search had essentially stopped. Picking up my phone, I called the man in charge of the search. Hearing his voicemail, I left an urgent message for him to call me back.

Later that day, I ran an errand on Coast Village Road in Montecito to distract myself as I waited for his call. This street was a favorite of mine, where I refueled my car and strolled the various locally owned stores, curbside restaurants, and the Friday Farmers Market. Being on this road was a warm reminder of an area I considered home.

As I walked by my favorite store, my phone rang. It was the search team guy returning my call. Still reeling from my call with the woman from Search and Rescue, I told him who I was, and that I wanted a meeting to understand the status of the search.

The poor guy on the other end of the phone did his best to try to calm this ferocious mama-bear. Toward the end of the call, he insisted that he leave me his cell phone number and name, so I could call him directly any time for updates. However, I didn't have a pen or piece of paper on me.

I darted into the store and asked the owner if I could borrow a pen and paper. She stopped what she was doing and handed me both; I proceeded to scribble down the contact information. After the call ended, I felt obliged to fill her in on why I had dashed into her store so swiftly. I shared that I was on a call with a search person about the effort to find my missing son from the mudslide. At that point she asked me something that I'd soon learn was important. She said, "Kim, do you know Catherine Weissenberg?"

"Nope, never heard of her," I said.

"Oh, I think you need to know her. She has special intuitive abilities. She worked the back channel after the slide with some first responders, and her clues helped find two of the victims."

My mind raced. "I'm in. Tell me more."

She proceeded, "You'd really like her. She's local, very private, and kind of off-the-grid regarding her unique communication abilities. She's Catholic, too. She is low-key about it all, and she's a mom, like you."

Hmm, I thought.

I wrote down Catherine's number.

I knew I needed all the help I could get.

I was suddenly open to the idea, sensing that help could come in various forms.

In every fiber of my being, I did not think that Jack's body made it out into the Pacific Ocean, as some had suggested. I had a feeling that my son's body was buried in the mud and debris, somewhere in the mile-long path toward the ocean that was over half a mile wide. The large mudflow path impacted a 38-acre natural preserve. This area also had a trail, and an open space that was graced with coastal live oak, sycamore, and olive trees. The private property lots were now damaged and many of the elegant homes that once stood in the village were destroyed. We had to check those large piles, too. Another area to search was the thick debris-caked sidewalls of the creek that had overflowed and changed the topography as the landslide travelled down the mountain toward the sea.

Once I returned to my rental home, I called Catherine to introduce myself. I explained that her friend at the store had given me her contact info. I wanted to let her know that it was safe to speak with me, and that I was aware of her unique communication skills, which she strived to keep private. She knew who I was, due to the extensive media coverage.

Catherine told me she'd be willing to do whatever she could to help in the search for Jack. She shared that she did hear from many of the souls that were lost that night, and had received clues that helped find two of the victims. Because she was a person of deep faith, she prayed daily and continued to seek information about Jack and two-year-old Lydia. She sounded pragmatic, and I liked her right away.

By the end of the call, we had scheduled a time when she would do a "writing" for me. Before hanging up the phone, Catherine offered to walk the land with me anytime. She said that she did not know how it all worked, but thought if she walked the area, she might sense something and get information about specific places to search.

A few days later, we agreed to meet in Montecito. As we walked the flow area, we discussed how since the slide, she had walked some of the areas in Montecito to see if she got any energy, or clues in terms of finding the missing kids. Having a daughter and husband of her own, she could only imagine the enormity of my loss, and the grief I was feeling. She understood the importance of finding my son and toddler Lydia.

Catherine shared that when she walked by railroad tracks near Butterfly Beach, on Super Bowl Sunday, early February 2018, she felt knocked over and almost fell down near the corner of a property near the train tracks. She also sensed more strong energies and presences in a garage area on that same property, as well as from a huge debris pile that was on the nearby tennis courts. In fact, she went on to tell me that she felt so strongly about this feeling, that she resisted her natural inclination to stay quiet and under the radar. She called the sheriff's office involved in the search to plead for them to send dogs right away to search that particular pile.

Making that call, she knew she risked being considered a "whacka-doodle" by those who did not believe in people with intuitive abilities.

During the call, the person on the phone told Catherine that they did not have anyone available to search that area. As she told me this story, I couldn't help but think back to the call with my husband's first responder, who unbeknownst to her, had told me that the search had ended by Super Bowl Sunday. Despite Catherine's plea and follow-up calls, she got no support to search the two piles she felt so strongly about.

Piecing these clues together, I knew I had to learn more details about the search.

Soon I became aware of a house that had formerly stood on a large lot in the debris flow path from my property.

This farmhouse-style home had been badly damaged by the debris flow, with mud throughout the first level and crawl space under the home. Two of its brick chimneys stood precariously crooked and heavily damaged, cuing any observer that this home was unstable. The house was one of the few homes in the area with a basement-like area. That sub-area had not been searched, as it was too dangerous for dogs to enter while the house stood. Sometime in May, about five months after the slide, the house was finally scheduled to be demolished. Knowing this, I encouraged the search and rescue team to be on-site with cadaver dogs. It would enable them to search areas that they'd had no safe access to earlier. The search and rescue (recovery) team was happy to oblige, and for that I was immensely grateful.

The day the house was to be demolished was a big day.

As I drove up to the property, personnel from multiple agencies were at the site. It looked eerily like a crime scene investigation, rather than a house demolition. Vehicles lined the corner street lot with "Search & Rescue" in large letters. There was a team of three handlers and cadaver dogs. Leading the group was Fred (not his real name), a handsome, powerful-looking man in an orange vest. The entire scene was somber. Nerves were rolling in my belly.

Catherine had written down some of the clues she had received following the slide. She thought some of them referred to places where we'd find baby Lydia and Jack. We shared some of these clues with a local general contractor who'd been clearing many of the destroyed lots, and who had been trying in earnest to help in the search. When he heard the clues, he thought they sounded like this very lot and this general area. The contractor surmised that the eddies that formed and boomeranged in this area also made it a high-probability area.

Today was clearly not a typical house demolition. On this day, everyone knew there was the real possibility of finding the human remains of two treasured children.

Everyone on the scene felt it. And now the mother of one of the missing children was with them on the lot.

Prior to the demolition day, I called Catherine. I asked her to come join me as the house was coming down, to walk the area and see if she sensed anything there. Catherine was still a new person in my life and, to be honest, I was a bit cautious. Now a single woman who had the sole responsibility for my daughter, I had to take more care to ensure I could make my daughter's life safe and stable. A little bit of "stranger danger" surfaced when I met any new person.

Catherine and her husband drove up in her soccer-mom-style black mini-van. They strolled up to me. Catherine was wearing a big cross necklace, and gave me a warm smile that immediately helped ease my discomfort. Seeing them, they looked like a middle-aged, normal couple. Catherine came here out of kindness. She came to help, asking nothing in return.

Catherine brought three beach chairs that we positioned on the far corner easement close to the street. That way, we could watch the demolition and the cadaver dog and handler, without being a distraction. As her husband went to get sandwiches for us for later, we watched the work begin. I sat in the middle chair, flanked on one side by Catherine and on the other by Grant, a dad in the Boy Scout troop and a friend.

What I learned in my new role as mama-bear engaged in the search, is that no dog handler wants you anywhere around his or her dog when they are working. Before they began, the handlers made it sternly clear to not touch, talk to, or to distract the working dogs. Search dogs need to focus when working an area alongside their handlers. Also, these dogs are super smart, and like most dogs, they want to please. If others are around to distract the dog, it might result in a false positive alert. These dogs are so smart, that many understand lots of human words, which can bias their efforts.

Initially, some of the handlers came off as not the "warm and fuzzy" type. These folks were there to do a job and not to engage in niceties with me, the grieving mother. I'd heard that the Santa Barbara team was traumatized from the heroic efforts they had performed after the massive landslide. They saw things people should never have to see — ever. Seeing me was a sad reminder that they had not yet found the two missing children. Later I heard from many that it affected them deeply.

The long day began.

With each scoop the excavator dug, fear rose in the pit of my stomach. Abe, a devoted volunteer who was working the excavator, took a deep breath when he entered the earthmover machine cab, nervous about what he might uncover. Along the backside of the property was a hill embankment. As Abe used the machine to gingerly scrape a layer of soil, he exposed a Wolf oven range.

"Does it have red knobs?" I asked.

"Yes!" he hollered.

"Okay, I think that was our oven," I replied.

Our kitchen range was so heavy, one oven tune-up guy I had hired two years earlier gave up, saying, "It's too heavy for my equipment-raising machine to lift it off the floor."

Now, this massive, old steel range was wedged into the hillside, having travelled three hundred or so yards before landing there. The significance was clear: this range came from my kitchen, which was the room closest to Jack's bedroom.

Then, a stunning thing happened; something I will never forget.

Catherine, my friend Grant, and I sat in our low-to-the-ground beach chairs on the far corner near the road. I was seated in the middle chair when one of the search dogs broke routine, left her search effort, and ran toward the three of us. This dog made a beeline directly for our group, in front of the retirement community with the acres of beautiful open trails. A few feet from us, this search dog swiftly darted behind the backs of our chairs. Then, she stopped behind my chair and gently licked me on the back of the neck. Seconds later, she ran in full sprint back to continue her search effort.

The three of us looked at each other, stunned.

The dog handlers were surprised, too.

This search dog was known as a "bitch," not because she was a female dog, but because she had a tougher attitude. Her handler would say, she is "a working dog and not to be petted—she is not friendly." This particular dog, we gathered, was not the type of dog to give strangers kisses. And it was atypical for a search dog to break their search protocol — especially in this way.

Catherine looked at me and said, "Wow! That must be Jack knowing you're here. He's trying to give you comfort."

It was such a soft, gentle kiss on the back of my neck. I felt it as a loving gesture. Later, I wondered if the dog was somehow trying to point me in another direction in which to search.

I didn't know if communication really worked from those who had passed, but after this stunning occurrence, what Catherine said did not sound too off-base. Somehow, some way, this kiss could have been a loving sign inspired by my late son.

As we watched more of the property demolition, I overheard one search dog handler say, "I'm glad we're searching this today. We never got to search this pile before — it was too soggy and wet. It would have been like quicksand, and too dangerous for the dogs."

Many debris piles were too wet and dangerous to be searched. Inground pools on the damaged lots were filled with soupy mud. During the search effort, if mud was too wet, it masked the smell of human remains for which they were searching. The various discussions I heard between the dog handlers revealed that there were multiple areas that had never been searched.

We were at the house demolition for two full days, observing sadly a once-treasured home get demolished and torn down. A couple times during the demolition the search dogs gave the alert of human remains. Once a dog alerted, the handler would exit that dog from the area and bring in another dog to see if the second search dog also alerted in the same location. This was protocol to validate dog alerts. Typically, if three dogs alert in the same area, it means there is 90% accuracy of human remains detection. Unfortunately, in the mudslide flow area, if a victim had left a trail of blood from injury, or if the sewage system that was destroyed caused fecal matter to mix into the debris, a dog might correctly identify the human blood or matter and therefore give an alert, even though there was no body present. This search was extremely complicated.

After lunch on the second day of the house demolition, the head of the search team, Fred, in his big orange Search and Rescue vest, called me over to sit and talk with him. We quickly found a log at the base of the hillside to sit and chat.

He kindly began by expressing how disappointed he was that our efforts at this site did not help us locate the missing children. Fred then pulled a large paper map out of his vest pocket. It was a map of the debris flow area, almost completely marked up with tiny scribbles.

"Kim, all of these tiny, wiggly lines represent all areas searched by the dogs. Each dog was wearing a GPS tracker on their collar." Crisscrossing lines made the map look like an angry toddler with a red pen had made designs all over the paper map. It was evident there certainly had been extensive searching. It was impressive, and I was grateful.

He went on to tell me that he felt the dogs and search team handlers had searched thoroughly every square inch of the debris flow area. He continued, "Kim, I think you better get it in your head that Jack's body probably made it out to the ocean."

I was heartbroken. And I was mad. Every part of me felt that was just not true.

Every fiber in my body did not believe that Jack made it to the ocean. I don't know why or how but that did not feel possible to me. Logic even convinced me it was not so.

"Let's look at this logically," I began. "Jack, Lauren, the dog, and I were inside the house as the slide hit. We know that Lauren and our dog Chester were found 100 yards south, one football field distance from our home. I was found 200 yards south from where I had started, which was 100 yards from Lauren. Jack, who was also in the house, would probably be within 400 yards of our former home. Dave's body travelled over a mile to the surf line at Hammond's Beach, but Dave had been outside the house in the backyard when the slide hit. There was no part of the house around Dave to slow his movement or to protect his body, or to help his body get caught up in large clumps of trees or big parts of the home like Lauren, the dog, and I experienced."

Fred nodded his head politely, but proceeded to tell me, "Well, there was a mudslide in 2005 about 15 miles south of here in Ventura County, in a tiny village called La Conchita. We still have not found some of the victims from the La Conchita slide."

This just pissed me off. Unbeknownst to him, he had poked this mama-bear.

I thought, *Last I checked, your orange vest says "Search and Rescue" and that is what you are supposed to do! So, keep going! The job is not done — not in La Conchita or here in Montecito.*

My head was ready to explode, but I managed to stay calm, and I held my tongue. After taking a deep breath, I thanked him and his team for all their help and efforts at the crooked house.

I knew this crew had worked extensively through very tough circumstances with a job most would never have signed up for. And they were volunteers. They were driven to help in a significant way. I was grateful for their efforts, but despite the GPS map, I remarked, "I do think there is more to search!" I was even more convinced of this after hearing members of his search team talk about debris piles that were too wet and dangerous to be properly searched.

During our conversation, Fred informed me about search protocol. He explained that because it was now May 2018, it was more challenging for his team. "Why?" I asked.

He patiently explained, "During a period of search and rescue, when victims might still be found alive, search teams are allowed to go anywhere to search without search warrants. In urgent situations, the search team has full rights to enter private properties to search. Once the search transitions into a search and recovery effort, things change. Now, my team needs the private property owner's permission to enter and search the property. As you can imagine, that requirement makes it cumbersome and challenging; even more so in this community where homeowners with severely damaged homes are now living elsewhere temporarily, which makes it difficult to track them down."

I thought about the type of people who chose to live in Montecito; many chose this seaside town for both its beauty and privacy. Many homes were built with tall hedges or protective entrance gates affixed with camera security. Needing permission to search private property made our mission more complex.

As I struggled to get up from the log, I thanked him and the entire team.

I walked away with the conviction that if we were to find my son and baby Lydia, I needed to lead the charge.

CHAPTER 15

THE SACRED SEARCH TEAM

FIVE MONTHS after the tragedy, and after watching the crooked house come down, I knew I had to fully engage to help lead the search efforts. Catherine was committed to helping in the search. She never asked for a dime, but told me she felt compelled to use her intuitive skills to help find Jack and baby Lydia. Some of the clues she had written down on January 12, 2018, three days after the mudslide, included:

Fractured femur
Pieces of me
Appendage traces
Olive Mill too swift
Femoral artery
23 paces from the left bank
Hand Tied

I believed that she was moved to continue helping in the search, as it would help her potentially piece together a puzzle that would lead us to the children's remains.

A few weeks later, she came to my home to give me a reading to see if she got any messages from Dave and/or Jack.

This was completely new to me. Raised Episcopalian and converting to Catholicism when I married Dave, I was not aligned with "mediums" or "channeling." I had been a Sunday school teacher for the middle school kids at my Catholic church and there certainly was no curriculum chapter covering mediums. Thus, I felt a bit strange getting a reading. But, knowing that Catherine was a Catholic, and because I was open to any information that might help in the search, I was all in.

During the reading, Catherine took out a pad of paper and pen. As she started, I watched as her hand wrote vigorously and quickly in cursive. Catherine then started writing what Jack was telling her. Jack was saying, "Don't worry about finding my body" and that "It was just a shell" and "I'm okay! I'm okay!"

Although it was healing to hear Jack say he was "okay," I certainly was not okay with his body being somewhere in mud-ridden debris. It made me ill to think that his remains could be in a pile mixed with twisted chain link fence, housing material, broken glass, or items from someone's garage. Toward the end of the reading, I asked Catherine if I could ask a question, to which she pleasantly replied, "Sure!"

My question was an obvious one.

"Jack, do you know where your body is buried?"

I was desperate for some clue — any clue — something to help us in the search.

To this question, Catherine wrote what she heard:

"I don't know where the shell is, Mom, but I know I will be found!"

Then, I asked, "When will you be found?"

To that Jack said, "I do not know."

Catherine said she heard Jack's *I will be found* in a very distinctive, matter-of-fact, and definitive way. She described it like someone just placing a staff into the ground firmly, stating a fact. "I will be found."

As you can imagine, it was very emotional to get a reading with my late husband and son. I so desperately wanted them back in person; not just in an invisible spirit, talking through someone I had only recently met. Yet, it gave me hope that Jack was so certain that his remains would be found. I found it maddening, however, that he could not offer a clue as to the location.

At different times, Catherine would call me randomly on the phone with a new clue she received. Early in the search, she got the clues *archipelago, purple umbrella, teacup,* and *red falcon.* Unfamiliar with the term "archipelago," I looked it up: "scattering of like things." Maybe that was a clue referring to the boulders scattered around? Or perhaps, Jack's bones? I had no idea.

I wanted a clue with the exact GPS coordinates. Instead, I got these cryptic clues that at the time made no sense. Yet each time Catherine called, I noted them so I could recall them when we were in an area searching.

Another day in 2018, while we were walking around a lot near the creek, she got a message that said, "foot bone and careful, it could be mistaken as a rock." Not a GPS coordinate, but a more specific clue.

By now, many months post-mudslide, hundreds of property owners were hiring different companies to help clear lots and/or repair damaged lots. This made me nervous. I felt compelled to inform the workers when I saw them. As I experienced it at the time, I knew of no coordinated effort by the city officials to ensure that property owners knew to advise their workers to be conscientious while clearing debris piles. I was sickened, knowing most of these property owners were now living temporarily elsewhere, and had hired crews from out of the area who were unfamiliar with the fact that two children were missing and likely somewhere in the debris that was being moved.

I was terrified, thinking my son could be found and inadvertently hauled away like a muddy log. I also recognized that it would be horribly startling if these unsuspecting workers stumbled across human remains without any mental preparation.

After many attempts to share the information with debris clearing crews, I learned that some of the crews spoke Spanish and very little English. Understanding this, and concerned about getting the needed information out, I went home one day and drafted a one-page flyer. On the flyer, I placed pictures of the two missing children, and I inserted an image of a skeleton in the dirt so the visual would help explain the cautionary notification. Not knowing how to speak or write Spanish, I wrote out in English a few sentences about the mudslide. The request on the flyer was simple: be conscientious and aware while digging and moving dirt and debris, and if any suspected remains were spotted or unearthed, to please stop and call the fire department immediately. I knew the fire department would know best how to proceed.

Once I had a draft, I called Jack's former Spanish teacher and asked if she would translate a version into Spanish. She quickly obliged, and the next day, I had a stack of both English and Spanish flyers in my car. Whenever I was in the village and happened to see earth-moving teams, I'd often pull over and hand them a flyer. Each person I interacted with seemed grateful for the notification, and each left me with the impression that they'd be aware and follow the protocol if needed.

One day, while driving down my old street after picking up my mail at my PO box, I noticed a big earth-moving machine on the damaged lot two lots down from mine. That property was right in the path of where my house and all the contents would have travelled, and it was near the crooked house that had recently come down. I quickly pulled over and parked next to the chain-link fence hastily erected to keep looky-loos out of the damaged property. Seeing the gate ajar, I slipped through it and started walking with my wobbly gait, toward the person working the machine. The machine operator immediately stopped the engine of the excavator and hopped out of the cab to come talk with me. To my surprise, a pretty, blond-haired woman walked toward me. She had been operating this big piece of earth-moving equipment.

"Hi, I'm Ann," I heard her say in a warm, friendly voice.

"Hi, my name is Kim. I stopped by because I'm the mom of the missing teen killed in the mudslide. I wanted to make sure you were aware that two kids are still missing in the mud somewhere. I just wanted you to be aware, so you can be very careful and observant."

"Nice to meet you, and I'm so sorry for your loss. I have two teens myself, and I'm heartbroken for you," Ann responded. She continued, "Yes, for sure! I'm being very careful, and will continue to do so. Do you mind if I give you a hug?" she asked.

Wow, I thought, *how kind.*

I smiled in assent.

So on an empty, mud-ridden, damaged lot near a busy intersection, Ann leaned over to hug a stranger in an act of pure human kindness. Leaving the lot, I felt more relieved, sensing her compassion, and that she'd be conscientious and aware as she cleared the lot.

What I did not realize at the time was that Ann would soon become part of my small sacred search team, and a dear friend, as we searched together over the next three years. When she wasn't doing her work as a general contractor, Ann volunteered for a neighborhood second responder team called the Santa Barbara Bucket Brigade. This volunteer group formed one day as a group of neighbors came together to help dig out other neighbors who were struggling with their mud-filled homes. In a matter of days, this group grew to over 3,000 volunteers who literally moved millions of tons of mud and debris for neighbors, for free and out of the goodness of their hearts. Their efforts defined what community resilience means. Ann, who could run big excavation equipment, was a pivotal volunteer within this group.

Soon Ann would be the one who'd meet and walk with me throughout the creek flow area, assessing large piles of debris. We'd make plans as to when she, and typically another neighbor, Sherri, and I would go try to tackle it, once I secured the property owners' permission. Ann would drive the excavator, while Sherri, Grant, my friend from Scouts, and I would typically lend our eyes to spot what was scooped up. We'd separate any debris or personal items from the mud. Ann became known as "Angel Ann" to me and my core search team, with her tireless volunteer efforts.

Sherri was a friend of a friend; prior to the slide, I had never met her. She was a pretty, blond-haired woman who had a lovely, quiet presence. Sherri had hired Ann to clear her lot and demolish her damaged home. To help her and her boys feel more empowered, Ann even let them in the excavator cab with her, to take hold of the levers with her as they took down part of their damaged home. Most often, Sherri was a spotter for the excavator operator. Her keen eyes would help her pull out of the pile or excavator bin a once-treasured household item. Sherri's eyes found family pictures, articles of clothing, kitchen pots, or a child's toy in the rubble. Thoughtfully, and quietly, she'd take them home, clean them as best she could, and put them in a baggie with a note of where the item was found. Often, she'd put the item on the new social media page for missing and recovered slide items, so the items could find their way back to the owners. She was a "mud angel" like so many of the volunteers in the Bucket Brigade. Soon she would come to help me in the search for Jack.

She, too, had lost her home in the slide. Apparently, Sherri heard the roar of the mountain at 3:30 in the morning. As she looked out her back window, she saw trees snapping like toothpicks and the roaring mudflow racing toward her house. Immediately, she ran to her young boys, fortunately sleeping nearby in the same queen bed. She jumped between them, doing her best to secure one on each side, and yelled, "Hold on as tight as you can!" The three of them rode the mattress out on the angry mudflow as their home washed away. Holding on tightly, they rode the mattress all the way to the roof of a neighboring house. It was truly by the grace of God that they survived.

Sherri would tell me quietly that using her free time to help in the search was helping her heal. She did not lose her life or either of her sons that horrifying night. Helping to search for the two children was in some way cathartic, and a way to thank the universe for sparing her and her family. Sherri soon became a trusted friend; one who'd say, "Kim, we're only done searching when you tell us we're done." She became known as "Sweet Sherri" on our core search team.

As the team went out often, one of the Search and Rescue handlers, Rick, and his ginger-haired Australian Shepherd dog, MacGyver, came to check an area of recently moved dirt. Rick had a quiet, soft strength about him. He had been in great physical shape his entire life. Even in his seventies, he went extreme skiing, ski patrolling, or traversing an area like an athlete decades younger. Soon, he became the lead search dog handler helping us. I had his cell number and email to keep him abreast of all our debris clearing and search efforts.

One day while out in the open trail spaces, searching as we walked together, Rick told me that he had lost his son to a car accident when the young man was in his twenties. I sensed that Rick's compassion for me as a parent who'd also lost a child was the reason he continued to show up to search, when other handlers believed that their job was complete. The more I got to know Rick, I realized that he was absolutely the person I needed to help in the search. One day, while we were walking in an area with Ann and Sherri, I overheard Rick say, "I'm the luckiest guy in the world!"

Stopping in my tracks, I was stunned.

How could Rick, a father who'd lost his son, say such a thing?

Rick's simple phrase was an important tonic to my soul. It gave me some hope that in the future, I might find joy in my life again. Rick was the right guy to be part of my sacred search team.

Rick and his search dog MacGyver
Photo credit JC Corliss

The core group of folks who would engage to search, to excavate, to spot for me, and to provide moral support were people I had not known before the tragedy, except for Grant. I came to learn that they were the people ideally suited for the job.

Grant was the dad of an Eagle Scout from Dave's Boy Scout troop, who lived a few streets over from us. A quiet man, Grant was the guy who walked up toward the mud-covered road and was one of the first to see our damaged lot, after the first responders. Grant was heartbroken for our family. Unbeknownst to me, for weeks Grant collected all the "Cantin" debris flow items. He took them to his home, and he and the scouts carefully cleaned them and stored them in plastic containers he had purchased. Months later, I was stunned to learn that he had stored the six big containers in his family's living room until I was ready and able to receive them. He had grown up in Montecito, and knew so much of the town's history, neighbors, and the community ins and outs; it was great to have him on my team. Often, on days we searched, he'd show up and pick up the team's lunches and waters that he'd bring over in a cooler. I sensed that Grant felt compelled to be there for me in honor of my late husband, and in the event that Jack's remains surfaced. A few other neighbors were regulars on the search, including the gracious and kind neighbors Allison, Jacques, and Noelle.

When back at home with Lauren, I often asked her if she wanted the update regarding the search. She always did, but she never wanted to see anything we'd found while it still had mud on it. She got used to seeing the trunk of my new SUV filled with boots, a shovel, a hard hat, a soil probe, landscape flags, and gloves. Not the typical items in what Dave would have viewed in his dream car.

One day, Ann and I worked to clear an open space on the trail area near the creek. We carefully scraped away the mudslide layer, hopeful that we'd find more items that would serve as clues leading us to Jack. Toward the end of the afternoon, feeling frustrated and sad as we had found nothing, I slowly started to walk away from the excavator. I happened to glance down. Looking up at me was the muddy face of a buried teddy bear. "Hey Ann, I found what looks like a teddy bear," I called over.

Carefully I dug around the toy bear and pulled the mud-laden stuffed animal out of the dirt, with plans to take it home to wash it. Once home, and four cycles in the washing machine later, it was all clean. When Lauren got home from school and settled, I asked, "Hey, can I show you something we found today?"

"Sure, as long as it doesn't have mud on it," she said.

As I held the bear in my outstretched hands, I said, "I think it was Jack's, and I'm looking for a picture to ensure it was his. Do you remember it?"

Jack's bear, with its face peeking out of the muddy path, offered an energetic push during the search.

"Yes, I recognize it, it was Jack's. I recognize the green shirt too. That was the bear he built at my birthday party in Ohio."

I strongly sensed that it was Jack's, and started to look at any pictures that had been sent to me by friends and family. There was the picture. Jack, holding his newly made Build-A-Bear, was looking adoringly at his little sister, which warmed my heart, maybe even more now than back then. Jack had made the bear at one of Lauren's birthday parties years ago, and it had been in his closet ever since. It was the jolt in the arm we needed to keep going.

CHAPTER 16

NEW TRADITIONS

WHILE SOME weeks included time spent searching in the debris flow area, I knew that my main job was caring for Lauren and working to create a stable environment. School was in full swing, and during the upcoming spring break I wanted to create new memories for us. A dear friend invited us to go skiing in Mammoth with their family. Skiing was not possible for me due to my injuries, but I told Lauren about the opportunity. Though I grew up skiing, our family had never gone skiing together, nor had the kids ever been on skis. We gladly accepted our friend's invitation, and I scheduled ski lessons for Lauren. I knew I'd feel safer with someone expert skiing with her. It was an enjoyable week, and it felt healthy to get out of town and to the snow. While Lauren skied, I would often get a much-needed pain relief massage. One afternoon, as I made my way to the ski lodge, I noticed some people sitting outside and enjoying a beverage. As I sat at a small table, a woman came up to me and asked if my name was Kim. Surprised,

I said, "Yes." She told me that she was one of Lauren's nurses in the hospital. I was amazed that by chance, Santa Barbara folks who helped in the tragedy were at the ski lodge.

A week later, as Easter approached, Lauren said that she was still uncomfortable driving through Montecito to get to our church. So we adapted, and joined the family of one of Jack's dear friends for Mass at the Santa Barbara Mission. We continued a tradition of going to brunch with friends, but this year we chose a different restaurant. Lauren loved Easter brunch with her friend Katie, but it would have been too much emotionally to go to the same place we'd enjoyed as a family. For Easter dinner, I had found an artistic iron candle holder that held three candles, for our holiday table. My grief counselor had suggested I have something to honor my loved ones. The candle seemed perfect. We would light a candle for Dave, Jack, and Chester, in their memory. I was starting to lean into some rituals that would help me honor my family, especially on special occasions.

During this holiday, my thoughts went to one of our last ones together, as a family. I recalled a fun Easter egg hunt that Jack, Lauren, and her friend Katie enjoyed. After brunch, we were invited to my friend's yard for an Easter egg hunt. Despite the kids being in their teens, my friend still thought it would be fun for them, especially her daughter and Lauren. Marsha hid the plastic eggs in her garden and yard, and gave each a basket. Before they started, Marsha told the kids there were two "golden eggs" hidden along with the plastic eggs. Jack, always game for fun, eagerly joined his sister and Katie for the hunt. Marsha, Dave, and I watched the kids running around the front yard and garden. In typical form, Jack chased Lauren around the yard, making her feel like he'd get all the eggs, and we heard Lauren scream with a hint of glee and delight. Moments later, I saw Jack walking quickly toward Marsha as the girls continued their hunt. In his hand was one of the coveted golden eggs.

In a soft voice, Jack said to Marsha, "My dad didn't want me to take it. Here you go, you can re-hide it."

"Oh, bless your heart, Jack; thank you, honey," Marsha replied.

Marsha's daughter caught a glimpse of the golden egg Jack was handing off to her mother and immediately exclaimed, in a panicked voice, "Mom! That was a golden egg!"

"Yes, honey, Jack found it and gave it back," Marsha told her daughter in a quiet voice as Lauren was still running around the yard searching in earnest.

Both Marsha and I were capturing this moment on video, and we each smiled behind our cameras. The moment caught Jack's kindness, his sense of humor and brotherly instigation as he teased and chased his little sister. As I remembered this memory, I shared it with Marsha. Marsha smiled, remembering it fondly too. Then she started tapping on her phone, looking through videos. Moments later, she found the video of this precious last Easter Egg hunt with my family, and shared it with me. What a treasure that video is, to see and hear the kids' glee that day.

Around this time, I started to think about summer vacation. Lauren would be off school for about two and a half months, and I wanted her to have some new experiences. I called my sister, who lived in Europe, and we discussed the idea that she and her daughter would meet us in London for a few days. I met with a travel agent, and asked her to help us plan a fun two-week trip. It was something to look forward to, and I thought it would be good for both of us. We'd do that trip following a memorial service that some of my former work colleagues at Johnson & Johnson wanted to host for me in Cincinnati. As the Cincinnati memorial service was being planned, Bob, a dear high school friend of Dave's, arranged for Lauren to sing "God Bless America" at the Great American Ballpark in Cincinnati. As Lauren would sing, the billboard in the stadium would dedicate the song to Dave and Jack.

As the days progressed, we kept focused on stabilizing our lives with school, physical therapy, grief counseling appointments, and appreciating all the support from friends and family. In the interstitial spaces of our new daily routines, I'd feel the waves of grief. Often when I was driving, the loss would hit me, and tears would stream down my face. Other times, it was seeing something we'd once had in our now-destroyed home that triggered a memory of happier times. These items were a mirror for me, showing that my life had changed forever.

CHAPTER 17

STAIRS AND A VIEW

STANDING IN a store's shoe department, I ran into a friend and her daughter. "Hey, Kim, how's it going?" my friend asked. "Okay," I responded as we gave each other a brief hug. As we chatted, I mentioned I was looking for a furnished rental, as the owners were due back to the place Lauren and I were currently renting. It was a daunting time to try to find a rental. With over 400 homes damaged or destroyed in the Thomas Fire and debris flow, so many families were displaced and now renting. The outlook was bleak.

"I just heard about this great home that is available, and it's furnished," she told me. I quickly looked up the ad and immediately called the agent.

"You can come see it at noon tomorrow, but I have another client coming at one o'clock," he said. Leaving the store, I was so grateful to have bumped into my friend and to learn about this rental. We ended up renting this furnished home, which Lauren liked more than I did. "I like the more modern feel to it, Mom. No offense, but your cottagey, traditional vibe is not what I like as much," she told me. I chuckled, noting her style preference.

We secured the rental, and moved in the following month. I knew upon moving in that I'd want the locks re-keyed. I called a local locksmith I'd never used before. He came right over and diligently re-keyed all the house entrances so Lauren and I would feel more secure. When I went to pay him, he shook his head. "No, no, I will not charge you; it's the least I can do for all you have lost." I was so moved that a stranger did the unexpected, using his skills to help another going through a difficult time. Those gestures were so helpful, as Lauren and I tried to heal.

As I settled into our new rental, I wanted to make Lauren's room areas especially nice. I turned one of the adjoining bedrooms into a TV-teen room, with a couch and table to play games. I knew she'd have friends over, and this room would be ideal for them to hang out. A kind mother of one of Jack's friends, an interior designer by profession, asked me if she could help decorate Lauren's room as a gift to her. She found the perfect comforter, pillows, and wall art that turned a basic room into a welcoming space ideal for my teenage daughter.

This house was fine, but I felt it was too high up in the hills and too remote. The houses were spaced out in this hilly area in such a way that you often did not run into neighbors, or feel connected as a local community. Lauren was delighted when a mama deer and her fawn strolled into the backyard. They would lie down outside her bedroom window, and each deer would gaze in, looking at her. She named the two deer with some of her friends one night, and was thrilled each time they'd return.

One warm July night, we heard again the shrill "aware and beware" blasts ringing out from our phones. Apparently, a fire was burning about 20 miles away, in a neighboring city. We were not in the evacuation zone, but when our power went out, I went to Lauren's room.

"Lauren, grab a bag. Let's go to a hotel where we'll have electricity and can feel safer," I said, with every effort to sound firm but calm. "Okay," she said, and quickly got ready to leave. I felt a heightened responsibility at being her only parent. I alone had to prepare her to leave and make her feel safe.

We drove to a local hotel but there was no vacancy. We drove to a few others in town and got the same message. Around 4:00 a.m. we started driving south toward Ventura. It was anxiety-provoking that each hotel we stopped at was full. Finally, we drove to my good friend's home in Thousand Oaks, 40 miles away. It was still dark, and I did not have my friend's cell in my new phone. I knew her daughter's bedroom window faced the front of the house. At 4:30 a.m., I pulled into my friend's driveway, stood outside her daughter's window, and said in a loud voice trying to wake her, "It's Kim and Lauren. It's okay. Can you please let us in?" I worried if I just rang the doorbell, it would scare my friend and her daughter. Fortunately, they heard it was us and opened the front door with the same open arms and warmth they had during the Thomas Fire evacuations. I was spent emotionally. The fears and triggers surged back.

We crawled into the guest beds and tried to get some rest, but I quickly came to the realization that the rental house we were in was just too high up and remote for Lauren and me. The next day, I called my realtor and told him to find us a house to buy. I wanted something closer to town and other people.

The next week, my realtor showed me a few different homes. My preference was a one-story home. I liked the elegance of the layout and with my hip and knee injuries, I preferred a home where I could easily get around. We narrowed it down to a few homes and I was ready to show them to Lauren. I wanted her to be part of the final selection.

One home was just a few lots down from the school she had attended, where she felt connected to the staff and students. I liked the location, in that it felt more like my neighborhood; it was not Montecito, but it was the route I took for five years, while driving the kids back and forth to school. The house had a nice view of the ocean, and from the deck I could even see the cemetery where Dave was. Everything seemed good to me, except the stairs. Built on a hill, the home had steep stairs to the master bedroom, and more steep stairs down to the family room. When I showed the house to Lauren I heard in her voice her excitement about it, compared to the others we looked at. As she pointed to the pool area, she said enthusiastically, "I can have friends over to swim in the pool!" She was envisioning herself in the house, having fun.

"But, Lauren, all these stairs," I replied pensively.

"Mom!" she said in her most persuasive tone. "Get over it. The exercise will do you good! And, Mom, if I need anything and you're not here, I can run to the school to get help from the teachers."

I was sold.

If she was going to feel safe in this house, it was worth every step I had to climb. And I agreed; climbing the stairs would be good for me. As we drove home, my friend Marsha was also in the car. We pulled into the driveway of the rental home and suddenly stopped. In the driveway were the two deer, the baby deer suckling from its mother. We turned off the car, and quietly watched this beautiful nurturing scene. I sensed symbolism in the moment.

Later that day, my agent and I wrote up an offer on a house that would soon be ours.

It felt good to think about the prospect of nesting, and in so doing, perhaps stabilizing a bit.

As we thought about moving in, it was clear that we didn't have a stick of furniture or anything else for a home. No couch, no mattress, no hammer, no toilet bowl plunger. Nothing. Our prior neighbor from across the lane was an interior designer. Mark graciously came to my new house and suggested some furniture that would work perfectly. He even met me at a store to help me pick out what would work well. While there, I realized that I viewed furnishing the house as more of a functional effort than a sentimental one. I'd lost it all, and now a couch was simply a thing to sit on. I did get furniture that looked nice, but my attachment to it was significantly less than in our old home.

I also realized that I did not want the same style I'd had in our other home. In fact, while shopping in a store, I'd had a visceral negative reaction to seeing the dish pattern I'd had before. I took that in, and then told myself it was okay to find something else. Simple white dishes it would be. Clean, simple, easy.

I surprised myself even more—instead of more traditional décor, I went with a coastal contemporary look that felt right for Lauren and me now. I wanted new visual cues. I found freedom in that; freedom, or an escape from memories I did not want to face daily.

Amazingly, one of the items found in the debris area, by my friend Grant, was an art folio of Dave's from high school. Miraculously, the zippered leather art folio protected the artwork inside. I had never seen this work before, as it had been stored in our attic. As I opened the folio, to my delight I found some beautiful black and parchment chalk drawings that Dave had drawn and signed in 1986. I took three of these pieces to be framed, and added them on the walls of our new home. They worked perfectly.

Thoughtfully and deliberately, adding some items to remind me of Dave and Jack helped me feel more grounded as we created our new home. Since Jack liked the color orange, I used that as an accent for a few items. Dave's love of blue and yellow made it easy to select the perfect tile mosaic bistro table for the deck.

Next door lived one of Jack's friends and his mom. Bram would come over to go for strolls with Lauren, or he'd take her in his car for a

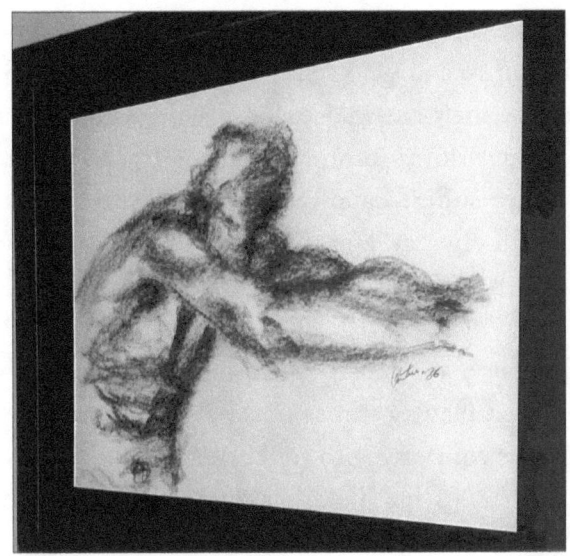

Dave's artwork from 1986 that survived
in an enclosed zippered art folio

burger. Having her brother's buddy next door comforted her. As Jack's friends headed off to college, I sent them each off with a Stitch plush doll to remember their friend. Cool, college-aged kids each packed a plush doll for their dorm in remembrance of Jack; this warmed my heart. I knew they suffered a lot when their friend never returned to his desk at school one day, and they were told that he was "missing." I appreciated each and every time that they'd drive by and say hello or text me.

Soon the house was mostly furnished, and Lauren had friends over. They enjoyed playing games in the family room and swimming in the pool. It was comforting to see her happy in this new place. The over-protective part of me liked her at the house with her friends; I knew they were safe and having fun.

Now that we were getting settled into our new home, I started to look for a puppy. Lauren said that she did not want another Irish Setter, as that would be too hard for her. She was interested in a doodle-type dog. As I sat on the couch thinking about looking for a doodle puppy, I felt overwhelmed. The thought of all the energy needed to train a 10-week-old puppy seemed just too much for me now. *I wonder if they have trained doodle puppies?* I thought. I typed in a search for trained goldendoodle puppies. Up came a site, www.doodlecreek.com, which had 5-month-old trained doodles. And there was a picture of a cute black-and-white Old English Goldendoodle, a mix of Old English Sheepdog, Poodle, and Golden Retriever, that they had appropriately named "Oreo."

I showed Lauren the picture of this cute pup and she thought he would be terrific. I called the breeder in Canada, and he was so gracious helping us make Oreo our own new puppy and part of our family. When I brought him home, it warmed my heart to see Lauren sitting on the ground, playing with her new adorable puppy. Oreo filled our home with a positive, loving energy that we both needed. But soon I realized that Oreo also wanted dog companionship. He'd been professionally trained with other dogs, and I felt he missed them. So, three months later, I called the breeder and asked him, "Which other trained puppy do you have, who would get along well with Oreo?" "Lucy, a Goldendoodle," he said. Looking at the profile, she seemed perfect. A few weeks later, we added Lucy to our family. These two pups immediately brought joy and comfort into our home. Barking at strange noises or when people came to the door was an added security feature.

CHAPTER 18

PAINT-COVERED HANDS

AS A WAY to honor Dave and Jack, I engaged with the Scouts, volunteering to help during the district's Eagle Board of Review (EBOR). About once a month, I'd be asked to join a meeting with other Scout adult volunteers to host the EBOR. This is the meeting when an Eagle Scout Candidate goes before a board that reviews their Eagle project and verifies that they have met all the requirements to earn the highest rank of Eagle. Only about four percent of Scouts ever achieve the rank of Eagle. These board reviews were meaningful because I'd hear from each Scout what he or she learned through giving back with their project, how each learned about their leadership style, and what knowledge they'd take with them to college and beyond.

One evening, as I drove to a board of review for a Scout, my mind drifted as I remembered Easter weekend 2015. The week before, Jack was on a weeklong middle school hiking and camping trip in the back country of Santa Barbara. As the winter trips approached, the students got to choose which of four adventures they wanted to join. One was backpacking on Catalina Island; another was a rigorous mountaineering expedition in the snow; another was a Santa Barbara backcountry backpacking trip that included mules carrying much of the food. Jack took no time choosing the backpack and mules trip. He was familiar with the backcountry from his many Scout weekend trips. He told me, "Mom, this trip has the best food. We get steak dinners, and the mules carry all the food." I chuckled, recalling his rationale. He liked adventure and good food. The weeklong trip included a day-long hike to the next campsite, meals, and the day's wrap-up with songs around the campfire. Jack felt confident in this setting. When I picked him up and all the parents circled up to greet the kids, I recognized that most of these tired teens would go home and sleep in the next day and throughout the week during spring break. Jack would not be so fortunate. His Eagle project would start at 8:00 a.m. the next morning, and last throughout the long weekend.

The elementary school where Jack chose to do his Eagle project is a Title 1 school in which some kids who attend live under the poverty level. The school building and grounds looked run-down. We passed by this school twice daily as I drove to and from his middle school. We talked about it during a car ride one day. "Mom, why is this school so run-down looking?" he asked. "Jack, I don't think they have as many resources as your school had."

"That doesn't seem fair," Jack said, in a tone that made me realize he felt the inequity of it.

When Jack was looking for a service opportunity with his Teens on the Scene community service group, he went to this school one day with his team to repair the soccer nets. While there, he noticed that the recess area had eight very dilapidated basketball hoops and nets. The backboards were faded white, with rust covering them. A few months later, when Jack was looking for a meaningful Eagle Scout project, a project designed to benefit the community in some way, he approached the principal to repair the basketball area. Jack chose an ambitious and extensive Eagle Scout project. Some projects take up to 100 hours of effort, but this one would take more like 250 hours. Jack led a Scout team and their parents over Easter weekend as they painted and repaired the basketball recess area. Learning that the school mascot was a dolphin, Jack designed the dolphin on his computer, and had the image made into a large stencil he could use on each backboard. Each backboard was painted a vibrant cobalt blue with a large white stenciled dolphin as the target to aim the basketball at. The basketball posts were painted a bright school bus yellow, and each hoop was repaired with a new net. He even had the trash can lids on the playground painted cobalt blue. Once repainted and repaired, the playground came alive.

On the last day, Jack's hands were white with paint, and he was tired. A young boy who came to the school to play over the weekend walked up to Jack. "Thank you for making my school beautiful again," the child said, with a big grin on his face. That was so meaningful to Jack because it was why he did it. During his eulogy, his friend Bram told a little story about it. Bram had asked Jack about the recess area refurbishment that had been highlighted in the local papers and on the news. "I don't know what the big deal is," Jack had replied. "They had something that needed fixing, and I just fixed it, no big deal."

After the project was complete, the school was so impressed with the refurbished basketball area, every 5th-grader colored an individual thank-you note for Jack. Many had images of the new dolphin backboards.

Rusted backboard before Jack's Eagle Project refurbishment

Jack, tired but pleased with the refurbished basketball hoops and backboards at a local elementary school

One card said:

Dear Jack,
We are so grateful for you spending a long time on our basketball courts. Thank you for painting the trash cans. It has brought joy to our school and brings us pride in our playground when we play other schools. Thanks for making this a better school.
                                                  Sincerely,
                                                  Jason

The 5th-grade teachers invited Jack to the school so the students could thank him personally. I recall picking him up early from middle school as he quickly changed into his Scout uniform, along with his sash filled with the merit badges he had earned. In the classroom, the kids sat at their desks, and others sat on the floor, asking Jack questions. They wanted to know what was his favorite merit badge to earn. "Scuba diving," Jack replied. He liked that he now could scuba dive with his dad, and he looked forward to those adventures. I could tell that for many of the students, this was the first time they learned about Scouting. Seeing a young teen in uniform, with a series of merit badges that displayed areas he'd learned about, was intriguing for the kids. At the end of the visit, the teachers asked to take a picture with Jack with the kids. I smiled as Jack sat on the floor cross-legged with the children. His smile said it all. He felt gratitude in the moment. He had used his efforts to help others and he realized that it made him feel good.

I was in awe to observe Jack, at 15, with genuine interest and ease speaking with the 5th-graders. Leaving the classroom, I could tell that he felt a sense of pride because he had worked hard on a project that positively impacted these students. As we got in the car, he said, "Mom, that was really nice. I'm glad they like the playground." Jack knew that if he was blessed with resources in life, what he did with those resources made a difference. My heart overflowed, seeing the genuine love and kindness Jack had in his heart for people. It was a moment where I as a parent, was learning from my child.

On the way to the EBOR meeting, I took the car on a brief detour to visit that elementary school where Jack had done his Eagle project. I drove up to the school and pulled into the parking lot. I walked over to look at the playground. The playground still looked great, with the cobalt blue backboards and white dolphin image on each still looking new. On this early evening, a group of kids were in the area playing basketball, with their parents chatting to one another as they looked on. I took a moment to take that in. I was filled with a mix of appreciation and love for what Jack's heart led him to do, along with a wave of grief because he was not here with us. After a few minutes, I got back in my car and drove over to the Scouts' board of review.

CHAPTER 19

A TEACUP, A FALCON, AND A SUPERHERO

BETWEEN APRIL and December 2018, almost every other week, we cleared an area to search or I walked an area to investigate. My brother-in-law, Ronny, flew in from Europe to help me as I moved into my new house. One day he asked if he could help in the search for his nephew. "Of course!" I replied. We went to an area by the creek, where we were carefully removing a massive debris pile filled with downed trees that were jammed up next to a neighbor's large tree, which had miraculously stayed standing. That day, Ann, Sherri, Grant, and Rick were helping. Piece by piece, we pulled big downed branches off the pile. At times, we found personal items, from kitchen pots and pans to pieces of china. This day, the pile gave us quite a revelation. During the effort, we found a chipped teacup, an umbrella, and a six-inch action figure covered in mud. I recognized it immediately as Jack's childhood figurine. Earlier, Catherine had reminded us that she'd received clues about a teacup, an umbrella, and a red falcon. Maybe we were getting closer to finding Jack.

Jack's superhero figurine found

As we walked onto another area, across from where we were clearing the debris pile, we noticed a rather large 3x4-foot statue sitting on the ground near a destroyed backyard next to the open space preserve.

Stunned, we stopped immediately. It was a statue of a red falcon.

At the end of the day, I took the items home and logged them on a poster-sized map of the debris flow. I used blue circle sticker dots to denote where clues were located on the map, and red dot stickers to areas where anything "Cantin" was found. Out of the entire debris flow area from my home to the ocean, the blue dots and the red "Cantin items" dots seemed to cluster together in a relatively small area. As the team saw this, it helped prioritize debris piles to focus on clearing.

We were in awe that some of the clues Catherine had received started to surface in one general area near the creek. If nothing else, finding these treasures seemed to give our group the emotional boost to keep going.

Someone suggested I call an intuitive renowned in California. Apparently, this intuitive had helped police find the remains of buried murder victims. Hearing about this woman, Marisa, and her talent to help find victims was enough to make me grab my phone and start dialing.

When Marisa picked up the phone, I heard a voice that sounded kind and willing to help any way she could. During the call, she told me she would not take a dime to help in this sacred effort. With quiet, human kindness, she said she simply wanted to deploy her talents to help us. Her assertions made me feel better about working with her, as she wanted nothing from it at all, other than to help. It was out of a place of human compassion and love, and for that, I trusted her.

As we wrapped up our call, she told me she felt compelled to take the long drive to spend time "in the field" with me and my tiny team.

The next day I picked Marisa up at a local hotel and drove her to our first stop, a condominium complex. There we met Rick from Search and Rescue, Grant, and Catherine. While walking this property, we strolled over to the general area that Catherine had walked by on Super Bowl Sunday, in February 2018, where she had experienced those strong presences and called authorities to ask them to send a team to search the debris-filled garage and nearby pile.

On this morning, over six months later, six of us spoke to the folks who had been on-site when the condo property was cleared. The property managers shared with us that they had cleared the mud-filled garage areas carefully, and where everything went. Rick from Search and Rescue had sensed that this area, where the underground garages were filled with mud and debris, was a high probability area. But when we arrived there, most of the mud and debris had been cleared and hauled away. We were staring at cleaned-out, empty condo garages. We also learned that the property clearing had occurred without search dogs and their handlers nearby. The pit in my stomach grew. I was frustrated that it appeared there was no central oversight, no central coordination to help guide property owners considering the two missing children. *Who is providing oversight and careful direction?* I wondered. *Clearly, no one is*, I thought to myself.

Learning this, I realized the chances had increased that my son's remains and those of a two-year-old baby girl could have been hauled away without anyone realizing. My horror and anger fueled my search efforts. Abe Powell and his team of Santa Barbara Bucket Brigade volunteers helped by trying to contact owners of properties where large visible piles of debris and mud remained. These amazing volunteers offered their muscle, sweat, and tears as a free service to help clean the piles, and they too helped search for the missing children.

One day as I drove by, I saw big earth movers clearing out the debris in the catch basin near our damaged property. I saw no one was spotting what was being moved and hauled away. I quickly called Abe and soon I saw a regular volunteer, Denise, standing in the midst of the mud-ridden catch basin, spotting for what could be a very sobering find. I was so thankful for her kindness helping me at the spur of the moment.

Prior strangers were now friends volunteering in the search. Back in January 2018, while I was in the hospital, unbeknownst to me, a friend contacted renowned evidentiary medium and author Suzanne Giesemann. Soon she too would be a helpful, compassionate intuitive trying to help solve the mystery of Jack's location. Prior to her mediumship career, she had been a Navy commander who served as the aide to the Chairman of the Joint Chiefs of Staff during the Bush Administration. What an amazing shift in careers, from high-ranking Navy officer supporting the President's chief military advisor, to a sought-after author, speaker, and medium. I nicknamed her "Navy Suzanne." Adding the descriptive adjectives was my way to keep the different intuitives straight in my mind. Catherine was "Catherine the Catholic" and Marisa was "Magnanimous Marisa." I was immensely grateful that each woman, out of the kindness of her heart, was using her unique talent to help find the remains of these precious children.

On this day, Marisa and I walked toward the corner of the property, toward the train tracks. One of the site workers yelled to me, "Hey, Kim, they found a victim just up here." He pointed to the exact area where Catherine had gotten weird vibes on Super Bowl Sunday. Hearing this, I paused and turned back to watch Catherine walking about ten paces behind me.

I said, "Hey, Catherine, this man just told me that a victim was found up there." I pointed.

Suddenly, out of nowhere, Catherine fell and was lying on the ground.

She was stunned; she could not believe it, as she had no idea why she fell. There had been no uneven ground or stick in her path. As she worked to get up, she realized she had hurt her hand, and in fact, she had heard a "crack" as she hit the ground. Our group rallied around her, and Grant helped her up. After some discussion, Catherine went to get her hand checked out at Urgent Care, where she learned that she had broken it and would need surgery and pins to fix it. We all felt horrible, and could not imagine how she had fallen.

With Catherine getting her hand checked out, it was now just Marisa, Rick and his dog MacGyver, Ann, Grant, my friend Stacey, and me. As we walked the flow areas with our guest Marisa, she sensed that Jack did not make it that far south over the freeway, but that his remains were higher north. I certainly had no clue how she was doing what she did, but soon we were all back to the big open area and the creek. We ended up back near where many damaged homes had been, and coincidentally, where many of my family items had been recovered. And also where miraculously some of the specific clues had been found — like the teacup, the umbrella, the action figure, and the red falcon.

As we walked near a bridge, Marisa paused a moment. "I sense that a victim was recovered near here," she stopped to tell me.

Her intuition was accurate, as Rick had told me that months ago a victim was found at this particular location. I was fascinated that Marisa picked up on that fact, which was not publicly known. As she walked by a huge boulder, Marisa said, "I think there might have been two victims here, and I'm hearing the music on a piano of 'Für Elise.' Did any of the victims play piano?" she asked.

Quickly, I texted the next of kin of the victim recovered from the bridge area, to ask if her family members had played piano. She immediately texted back, "No, none of the family played piano." I passed along the information to Marisa. Then I paused; although Marisa was probably referring to the piano piece "Für Elise," I had clearly heard it as "fleur de lis." I remembered that a fleur de lis is the symbol the Scouts use. Jack was an Eagle Scout.

I had no idea how Marisa's intuitive talents worked. I'd spent a life in Western medicine and the corporate world, often working with surgeons and scientists. This new spiritual arena was foreign to me, but I was open to what I was experiencing, and both desperate and intrigued by the clues she was sensing. I had shown Marisa the recent items we had found. Marisa looked at the superhero action figure and said that somehow it was a significant clue. "That's important," she said. "Don't know how, or why, but it will be important to finding Jack."

The dry, hot summer weather had evaporated all the creek's water, and we could safely climb down to walk the creek bed. Marisa and I were walking about 30 paces behind Rick and his search dog. Rick was particularly interested in walking the dry creek bed.

As we walked, Rick said loudly, "Kim, you know, I found some of Jack's homework down the creek there." He pointed ahead of us.

"Really?" I said.

During our search efforts, I was always learning new pieces of information. I wanted to log it all down as a way to piece together the puzzle of where we should focus our efforts. *If Jack's homework made it down to this area, maybe Jack did too,* I thought.

In the distance about 25 feet was a wooden footbridge that gracefully curved over the creek. Rick had walked up ahead to have MacGyver sniff. Soon he headed back toward us. Once in hearing range, he said disappointedly, "Kim, there's nothing down there. Mac isn't getting any scent, and the mud is only a foot deep at the bottom of the creek anyway." Rick and MacGyyver continued walking upstream together while Marisa and I stayed back.

Although disappointed, I felt compelled to continue walking forward along the creek bed. In a minute, I was right above the pedestrian bridge, wanting to see the area myself. At that moment, a neighbor walked out onto the bridge. He looked straight at Marisa and me, sternly and quizzically. Weeks earlier, a nearby home was broken into by burglars. Due to all the mudslide news coverage, crooks felt like it was open season to attack this neighborhood of vacant or heavily damaged homes. Seeing two adults walking the creek behind his home was enough to get this man's attention, and he strolled out onto the bridge.

I quickly introduced myself. "Hi there, I'm the mom of the missing boy lost in the mudslide. We're just walking the creek with a Search and Rescue search dog."

Hearing this, he relaxed his shoulders, and we chatted for a few moments.

"Hey, is this a foot deep of mud?" I asked, referring to the creek floor below, and just south of his bridge.

"No! Not at all . . . this is 12 feet x 40 feet-ish, a big swim hole. In fact, my kids when they were young, they would drag in a tall

10-foot-long ladder along the side here to climb in and out. They'd play in the water like a pool. Now, it is just filled with mud and debris. In fact, I've been calling for months, asking to have it cleared, so if another heavy rain came, we wouldn't have flooding. So far, they've told me they have no plans to clear all the mud that's filling it now," he said.

I could hear the frustration in his voice. Learning that this was an unchecked basin filled with mud and debris that was over 11 feet deep and 40 feet wide, I replied, "I'll call today, and this basin will be checked out by tomorrow!" Then, I turned to face upstream and yelled for Rick and his dog to come back.

As we waited for Rick, the man went on to say that he travelled extensively for work, and it was very unusual that he was home today. Marisa turned to me and said, "Kim, this was no coincidence that the neighbor walked out on that bridge right when we were near it, and for him to tell us about the deep mud-filled basin."

Once back, Rick used his auger pole to penetrate the soil to check depth and to help aerate the area, to allow underground bacteria smells to rise. These aerated holes aided search dogs so they could smell deeper and more effectively.

Down, down, down, we watched as Rick's auger pole easily glided down and sank, all five feet of its length. This was astonishing, as in most other places mud was caked like cement, making probing very challenging. Air pockets were making the pole glide easily. Rick's strained, pensive expression indicated that we'd stumbled on a very important location to search. After multiple probes, he stepped away and gave the command to MacGyver to sniff-search the area.

Within seconds, MacGyver alerted.

Watching this, Rick said somberly, "We're going to have to check this area out."

My heart raced. The rest of the group joined us and quickly the discussion began about Rick calling flood control to schedule a time in a few weeks when they might be able to help clear the debris and mud-filled basin out.

"A few weeks!" I said, "No, this is being checked out tomorrow!"

Ann, a general contractor by trade, offered to clear her workday, to help search the creek basin the next morning. Hearing this, Marisa offered to stay another day, as she felt strongly about this area. Rick said he'd bring Mac.

Early that next morning, as the small team assembled, Ann quickly suggested we all huddle up together to say a prayer. "Pray that we will be guided to find the missing kids," she said.

Then I said, "He's here." I surprised myself a bit as I said it. I'd never been compelled to say that before on any of the other days we had searched. I felt so strongly about this area that for the first time, I called my pastor. I asked him to come and say a prayer before we started searching through the mud and debris. It was a sight to see a middle-aged priest in his black pants and shirt with white collar climbing down into the dry creek bed, weaving between boulders as he walked toward us to say a prayer.

Marisa had received other clues that she thought related to Jack's remains, and had shared them with us prior to the basin-searching day — "he's near" was one of her clues. She also sensed that his remains were near a tree that had something significant about it. She did not know what that was, but something about the tree would be unique. She also felt that a horse property was near where he was. Near this basin was a property that once had housed a horse corral and horses; an interesting coincidence.

Near the catch basin was a huge tree with roots growing out of the side of the creek, which made it unique. Marisa looked up at the tree's branches and noticed that one branch had unique burl markings.

"Kim, come look at this branch," she said. As I looked at it, the burled knuckle of the branch looked like a face of a monkey or giraffe, some animal's face. We thought maybe this was the unique tree we were supposed to find.

For two days, we dug, sifted through debris, and visually searched that basin. We found part of a bicycle and other items from homes. As we did, Marisa said she heard Jack say to her, "I'm here, I'm here, go broader, go broader!"

What the hell does 'broader' mean! I thought, frustrated.

Did "broader" mean out the creek toward the land on the private lots? Or did it mean north or south from where we were?

In my new surreal life, I was quickly learning was that clues were not always literal. I was assured that once we found Jack, then the clues would make sense. "Purple umbrella" could mean literally a purple rain umbrella, or a patio sun umbrella, or it could mean a Lily of the Valley purple flower that looked like a purple umbrella. Or it could mean two distinct things — something purple, and something else umbrella-like in shape. This clue world was certainly not easy for my rational mind to wrap itself around, or to surrender to the process. As a Type A personality, who desperately wanted results and fast, I struggled to remain open and patient with the clues.

The basin was carefully searched, but unfortunately, we did not find anything that resembled human remains. However, this catch basin experience was a pivotal moment for our search team, and specifically for Rick. Finding this area that was assumed to be only one foot deep of mud, and that turned out to be a debris-filled, unsearched, 12 x 40 catch basin, made it clear for us that there were areas still unsearched that we needed to find. And we only found this catch basin through the synchronistic timing of the neighbor who was usually out of town for work, but who happened to be on his bridge as we were walking the creek bed.

Marisa told us to remember the clues, and keep looking. She was sad that she did not get a sense of where Jack was exactly, but she felt we were in the right general area, and that Jack did not make it as far as the freeway. "We missed him somehow," she said, shaking her head in disappointment. As she hopped in her car for the long drive home, she bade us well, and promised that she'd keep trying for any clues that might help us. Before she drove away, she rolled down the window and said, "I stand by this . . . he is near a horse property, and his superhero is a clue that is important." She left with the conviction he was in this general area, somewhere buried deep. From that day on, Marisa used the picture I sent her of Jack as her phone screensaver. She wanted to keep him front of mind, to help with any clues. It was a gift to me to experience her kindness and efforts in the search. She had been a stranger. I appreciated her gift of compassion to a person in need.

Once back at home, I cleaned up from being out in the muddy, dusty area and then I checked my phone messages. To my surprise, one was from Navy Suzanne. She had done a reading for me early on after the tragedy and kindly kept in touch trying to help with clues if she got them. She is a renowned evidentiary medium and as such is asked to speak across the country at various meetings. She called to tell me that she and her husband would be driving through Santa Barbara from one speaking engagement to another in Northern California. I was thrilled she was going to be nearby as I knew she lived on the East Coast. She'd heard about my search team and she wanted to know if I'd like her to walk the area with me. "Of course!" I responded. I quickly added, "Please come to dinner so you can meet some of my sacred search team." She and her husband happily accepted my dinner invite.

On the day Suzanne and her husband met me in Montecito to walk the slide area I made a conscious effort not to inform them in advance about locations, dog alerts, items found, or clues we'd received.

That afternoon, we just walked the area together. Interestingly, Suzanne stopped near the side of the creek by a log that lay on the ground under a canopy of trees.

She sensed Jack could be near the side of the creek in this location. I was awestruck again. Like Marisa and others, I was being drawn back to the same general area to search for Jack.

CHAPTER 20

SEARCH DOGS, CREEK WALLS, AND TREASURES RETURNED

AFTER THE debris-filled catch basin and a few other revelations, Rick changed his mindset from *I think we may have exhausted the search area; I just don't know where else to look*, to *There's more work to do*.

I was relieved to hear Rick verbalize this, as I valued his help, and we really needed it. I was becoming more open to listening to my intuition, and not letting others diminish my hope that the missing children would be found. This catch basin was one example.

As it happened, I found more areas that had never been searched. This included an area closer to my damaged lot, where the owners had hauled away 15 truckloads of mud and debris without anyone running search dogs through the area, or having anyone spot each bucket of mud as it was transferred into the truck.

Astonishingly, I learned that my husband's bag had been recovered in the creek near this property. I returned to the area and spoke with a nearby property owner. When I told her about some of the clues to see if any resonated, I mentioned Marisa's conviction that "a horse property is near where he is." The kind neighbor stopped in her tracks, looked at me, and said, "Kim, turn around!" As I did, standing behind me was a living, breathing horse, looking me right in the eye. With that, I rallied the team, and we had dogs run the area that same week.

A few weeks later, walking with a retired firefighter, we wound up near properties where I learned over 30 truckloads had been hauled away. Another large lump formed in my throat, to think that this area had not been searched prior to anyone hauling away the debris and mud. With this new knowledge, more dog searching ensued. I was grateful to all the property owners who showed me compassion and allowed dogs to search their lots.

At another location while searching, one of the property owners came out to speak with the team. In casual conversation, she told us that she had lived at a house that was destroyed by the mudslide, in the very area we had been searching near the creek. As she described the home, we realized it was the same area where earlier our team had found the superhero figurine and the chipped teacup. Sherri leaned over to me after the owner shared that information. "Kim, I find it so curious that we seem to be drawn back to the same area where we've seen the clues show up."

"Exactly!" I said.

In late summer of 2018, I had to put the search on hold to help my daughter get ready for 10th grade and make back-to-school preparations. Her middle school went through grade 9, so in 10th grade Lauren would start at the public high school. She had her new books and class schedule. I hoped that she would be able to cope, considering the losses she had experienced. Her school offered parent sessions hosted by the administration to help parents learn more about the school, and to share the school goals for the year. One Thursday night in September, I drove to her high school, walked through the front doors, and took a seat in the theater, where the parents' session was scheduled to start at 7:00 p.m.

Sitting there, I felt sadness. I should have been sitting here with Dave. I sensed that to others who knew me, I must have been a sad sight, sitting alone, doing this parent thing, as a single parent. Filling out the school paperwork days earlier, I felt similarly when I had to check the box about being a single parent; I felt this any time I had to fill out paperwork listing me as Lauren's only parent. I took a few deep breaths to calm myself as I saw many familiar faces entering the room. Wanting a distraction from my feelings, I tried to focus on the movement in the room, and think about what I needed to learn tonight for Lauren to start in the new school.

Attending these events was a chance to reconnect with friends and neighbors I had not seen in a while. Entering the theater to my right was beautiful Allison and her handsome silver-haired husband, Jacques, who lived close to the area we had been searching. They too had lost their home. I knew Allison from the Charity League group that we and our daughters were members of. I admired Allison. She was gracious, sweet, and involved in the community along with her four daughters. She and Jacques also were members of the search team. Jacques walked areas looking for underground wells that might be places to search. He pulled historical images of the creek so we could compare sidewall grades and depths. Jacques was a quiet ray of light who supported us all.

Minutes before the school program started, Jacques nudged Allison and whispered, "You have to tell Kim! You have to tell her of your experience the other day!" Allison pulled me aside after the meeting. I could see that she was nervous; her hands twisted the program as she recounted an experience she'd had in late summer.

"While our new house was being built, we took our family to Europe to get away and get some joy back into our lives after the mudslide. We were all fatigued by the contractors working on our house. Before the trip, I parked my car in the neighbor's driveway down the lane, mainly to keep the car protected and provide more parking for the contractors. When we returned, it was evening. I walked over to get my car, feeling jet-lagged. But the oddest thing happened as I drove across the bridge over the creek. Over my right shoulder I saw an image of a teenaged boy in the air, looking like Jack and wearing a white T-shirt. Then I heard, 'I'm here! I'm here!'

"Kim, I've never, ever had an experience like this before in my life. I was shaken up and stunned. Actually, I was more than stunned; I was freaked out. I pulled my car into my driveway, jumped out, and raced into the house to tell Jacques about it. I thought you should know, in case that is some sort of a clue to find Jack. Both Jacques and I feel the side and top elevation of that part of the creek looks a lot different than before the mudslide."

As I listened to Allison's story, I realized that the message of "I'm here, I'm here" came at the part of the creek where we'd found the superhero — and close to where Marisa had heard in her mind what I call the *fleur de lis* song on a piano, when she said, "I think there might have been two victims here." We all felt that this message was another call to us to return and search that part of the creek again.

Before the mudslide, I would have taken a story like this with a grain of salt; maybe even concluded it was jet lag that made my neighbor have this unusual experience. Now, after all the inexplicable experiences I'd had, I was more open to accepting her experience as real. Somehow this was part of the journey leading us to find our missing children. I was so grateful for my sweet neighbor's courage to share her story with me.

Back at home, I filled Lauren in on the back-to-school night. We chatted a bit, and then I retired to my bedroom for much-needed rest. I would update the team and the map with my neighbor's experience, which might prioritize searching the debris buildup on that part of the creek again. I was starting to take the messages and act on them, without an expectation about the outcome. I was more open to how things were progressing and manifesting. More keenly aware that I could not control the outcome. I may be able to influence things with the search effort and methods, but I could not control things. I was vulnerable to what would happen next, and I was learning to be more okay with that. I hoped that somehow, all these unexplainable parts of this journey would one day, in God's time, lead me to Jack and Lydia's remains.

When Jack's would-be 18th birthday arrived, I invited all his friends, the scouts, and prior teachers to an evening BBQ and games. Jack's friends commented that they liked knowing where Lauren and I now lived. Some said that they liked seeing the pictures of Jack that were hung in the house. The night felt healing. "That was so fun, Mom," Lauren said, as the party wrapped up. "I miss seeing Jack's friends."

A mother of one of Jack's friends said it really helped the kids when they heard me talk about Jack in conversation. She said it let them know it was okay to do so. For many of these kids, it was their first experience with death. They, too, had been traumatized. Appreciating the value in the get-together, I made a mental note to get the kids together in the future.

CHAPTER 21

PHOTOS AND BABY BOOTIES

AS I WALKED back into the house after collecting my mail, a hand-addressed envelope, thicker than normal, was in the stack. I sensed it had pictures tucked inside. As I opened the note from a longtime friend, I saw five pictures included with it. They were duplicates I must have sent my friend years ago. She wrote that she wanted to send me these pictures because she knew that all mine washed away. Whenever friends did this, I was moved. Each time, they seemed to arrive right when I needed them. I treasured getting back some images of my life before the slide. This set of pictures included an old Christmas letter we had sent when Dave and I got engaged. Dave wrote about our engagement; he took me to a nice location in West Virginia, and had a horse-drawn carriage drive us throughout beautiful grounds one afternoon. Dave had the carriage driver stop by a weeping willow tree near a pond. Blanket spread out on the grass, a picnic basket with chocolate-covered strawberries and champagne laid out. A moment later, down on one knee, Dave proposed to me, and I gave him an enthusiastic "Yes!" I remember the day vividly;

all the red tulips were in bloom that April day. Dave was a perfect match for me. I knew I was lucky.

When I first met Dave at work, I was not only taken by his charismatic smile, but I was also impressed by his can-do attitude and work ethic. I came to learn that, like me, he had started working at a young age. Dave's first job was delivering newspapers in Portsmouth, Rhode Island on his bicycle. Come winter, his dad would drive Dave and his brother around in the car, stopping at every other house so that Dave could run out and place the newspaper near each customer's front door. One customer, Dave told me, wanted his paper placed on his kitchen table, and Dave would quietly enter and oblige the request. My first job was at age 12, cleaning a house for an elderly couple a few streets over from my parents' home. Both of us seemed to have always worked since a young age, and each of us felt we'd have to work until a late retirement.

Also in the envelope was picture of the two of us when I was pregnant with Jack. It made me recall that time, and when I found out I was pregnant.

Married almost a year, Dave and I were looking forward to having kids. We both had careers, and Dave was also taking MBA evening classes, yet having a family was important to us. Each month, I'd take a couple of pregnancy tests, hoping to see the double line of "you're pregnant" appear. With my impatience, who knows how many tests I took, but it was impacting our budget. One evening while Dave was away at class, I took yet another test. This time, there it was! A double line. To be sure, I ripped open another to see if this second test would signal the same. It did and I was overjoyed. I immediately thought about how I could best tell Dave the happy news. I got in my car and made a run down to the local Target store. I went to the baby section and bought two pair of baby booties: one pair in pink, and another pair in blue. Once home, I put each bootie on the floor as if in a path, so Dave would see them when he came home. As I sat in the family room and heard Dave come in the side door, I sensed his pause when he noticed the baby booties. Then his footsteps sped up. "Kim, are you pregnant?" he asked with a huge grin. "Yep!" I exclaimed.

We were overjoyed at the prospect of having a child. Dave looked at the calendar, and said he would be finished with his MBA before the baby was born. That was great news, knowing he would have more dad time when our baby arrived.

Come November, I had a planned C-section. I invited my father into the delivery room along with Dave, as he expressed regret that when my sister and I were born they did not allow fathers in the room. I wanted to give him the unique experience of seeing his grandchild take his first breath. Having experience in operating rooms with my career, both Dave and I were calm and happy as I was wheeled in. As Jack entered the world, the doctor exclaimed, "He looks really good," in a tone that indicated behind her surgical mask was a smile. When I heard Jack's first cries, I teared up in joy. The nurses wrapped him up in a white blanket, and handed him to Dave. As I was flat on the operating room table with no ability to sit up, Dave walked toward me and put Jack near my face so I could see him, for the first time. He was just perfect. I was overwhelmed with relief that he was safe and healthy; it blended with my excitement as I looked forward to holding him once I would be moved to the recovery room. "Dave, stay with the baby," I said, so he would not feel compelled to stay with me as the medical team closed me up. I think it was about thirty minutes to an hour before Jack was brought to me in the recovery room.

The moment that I got to hold my son for the first time was a highlight of my life. I looked down at this little soul who was just starting out his life. He was born to a mom and dad who were eager to love and support him. As I looked at his face and eyes, he looked like an old soul. Even the doctor said the same as she looked at him. Dave and I, a couple, now had become a family. My dad was moved by watching his grandson take his first breath; he seemed animated about the experience for hours. It was a blessed day, and I felt more complete than ever.

The last picture in the envelope was of Jack's first Christmas, when he was about six weeks old. The tree was all decorated, and Dave's mom and my grandfather were in town, as were my parents. I remember feeling that I didn't need or want anything under the tree. I had all I needed. I had my husband and my baby, and I felt the most complete I'd ever felt. It was a sense of complete gratitude for the people in my life that no "thing" or "gift" could impart. I knew that future Christmases would be more active, with a toddler in the house.

I carefully tucked the pictures away in a special place on a bookshelf in my office, and texted my friend to thank her for sending them. It had been a draining time with the search for Jack's remains and trying to rebuild a life. That gesture meant a lot then, as it does years later.

CHAPTER 22

A MESSAGE OF HOPE

SOON IT WAS early December 2018. The searchers and I were losing steam, but we still wanted to dig out a muddy chain link fence area just north of the pedestrian bridge. We'd focused south of it, in the catch basin, and now we decided to hand-dig mud trapped between the chain link fence and the sidewall of the creek, a four-foot width that was filled with cement-hard mud.

A few of us from the search team and some amazing Bucket Brigade volunteers dug the mud out by hand, with pickaxes and shovels. Among the volunteers was Carol, a petite, 70-plus woman, who I'd heard had had knee and hip replacements. I was in awe of her as she slung a pickaxe and heaved her scoops of heavy mud away to help a grieving mother.

By now, we'd been searching for almost a year. We had cleared all the obvious areas that seemed visible with piles that could entomb my son's and baby Lydia's remains. We were getting tired, and I sensed that many of the volunteers were losing hope after such an extensive period of searching.

As we dug one day, I heard Ann yell from the corner of the chain link fence. She was wedged about five feet down in the crevice between the fence and the creek.

"I found a quilt!" she yelled.

"A quilt?" I made quilts! I had hoped so much that one day we'd find one of the quilts I had made.

"What color is it?" I asked.

Ann was digging out a fifty-pound clump of hard mud that enveloped the quilt. As she worked to free it, Ann could see a fabric color emerge.

"It's black-and-white checked on a border," she shouted.

"That's Cantin!" I called out.

Minutes later, Ann single-handedly lifted out a huge clump of heavy mud that held a queen-sized quilt as she stood precariously deep in the mud hole. She tossed it on the ground by my feet.

The quilt Kim made for Dave, with the silhouette of Dave and Jack on their first scuba dive together

338 days after the disaster, the mud-laden quilt was unearthed during a search. It was wedged by a chain link fence.

As I laid it out, I realized that it was not just any quilt I'd made. It was the very quilt I had made for Dave that had the silhouette of him and our son on it. It was the quilt that Dave had grabbed to take with him during the Thomas Fire evacuations. Dave had grabbed it as one of his personal treasures that he could never replace, if the house was destroyed by the fire.

This Dave-and-Jack quilt discovery was clearly a jolt in the arm of hope for us all, and especially for me.

Out of all the things that we could have unearthed, Ann had found a treasure that was stitched with love for my late husband, that included an image of my husband and son. It was not a random umbrella, or a hammer from our garage. It was something uniquely special. Found buried six feet under a bridge, and wedged by a chain link fence in the creek.

This was a clear message to me, not to give up hope.

"Keep looking!" was the take-away message, 338 days after the tragedy. Three hundred thirty-eight days since I'd last seen my son. It gave the team the much-needed inspiration to keep searching. And, keep searching we did.

The team was so inspired, in fact, that Rick soon called to tell me that a few more dog handlers and search dogs were coming to town for a training event. He asked for them to check out a couple areas near the side of the creek, and we scheduled it for the following weekend.

During that search, multiple search dogs alerted in an overgrown grassy area on the side of the creek. Knowing that mud was unexpectedly deep at the catch basin, Rick worked to secure County Flood Control to clear, the following week, this upper portion of the creek next to where the dogs signaled.

While the dogs and handlers were in town, aside from the grassy area of the side of the creek, they also walked the dogs around other nearby debris flow areas we'd been targeting. As we were wrapping up, I heard my phone ring. I saw on the caller ID it was Catherine.

"Hey Catherine, what's up?" I asked.

"I just got a message from Jack," she exclaimed. "He said, 'You just walked over me.'" Then Catherine asked me, "Where are you now, Kim?"

"Catherine, we are out with the dogs searching, just finishing up!" I said, feeling a pensive hope rise in me.

"Gosh Kim, I got this message about fifteen minutes ago, and thought it was really weird. I'm glad I called you now with it. Where were you all walking fifteen minutes ago?" she asked.

The dog handlers were getting ready to leave in their cars, but with this news, I asked them to wait. I told them about Catherine's call, and asked them where they had walked. They walked the dogs again over key areas, but we got no definitive alerts and, frustratingly, we did not know where that certain location was fifteen minutes prior, aligning to the timing of Jack's message.

Although disappointed, I logged it as very interesting that somewhere in this general area we'd been scouring might very well be where we'd find his remains.

The next week, Rick was back out working with the County Flood Control excavator team, clearing the area of the creek where the dogs had alerted.

I stayed away during most of this effort, as someone said to me, "Maybe Jack does not want you to be around when his remains are found." So, trying this out, I stayed away for most of that week's clearing. Toward the end of the week, I swung by and saw Rick standing in the dry creek bed, while an excavator operator cleared the layers of mud in a section of the creek. Rick's sweet wife Ellen was on-site to spot the mud and debris pulled up. That day, I saw in Rick's face fatigue and sadness. This effort at times seemed to haunt our souls when we came up with nothing, yet we wanted so desperately for these children to be recovered. Clearly, Rick felt that sadness. I managed to keep my wits around me, even when we came up with nothing. But, that day, as I walked in front of Rick heading to my car, tears started flowing down my cheeks. *Why? Why could we not find Jack, my baby boy?* I thought.

This was beyond torture; we'd been looking so hard.

As I neared my car, I turned to wave goodbye to Rick. He must have seen the grief on my face; he said in such a kind voice, "Hey, Kim, if you ever want to talk about it, I'm always here." He was not only the most ideally suited search and rescue dog handler, but also, Rick was my friend.

CHAPTER 23

A COMMUNITY SEARCH

SOON IT WAS 2019. I noticed feeling more agitated toward the holidays. It was not just another New Year; the anniversary of the mudslide was soon approaching. For the first-year anniversary, the village hosted a beautiful vigil, and thousands from the town gathered. Lauren was asked to sing "God Bless America." Seeing the girl whose miraculous rescue had been aired on television taking the stage to sing for them moved many to tears. As my daughter sang, I saw the impact that she had on those assembled. Many had tears in their eyes. I knew that her dad and brother would have been so proud of her. I know I was. I was in awe that she sang with such strength and grace.

2019 became a very active year in terms of the search. Some weeks, a search was set in motion based on new information or clues. Other times, we went out to search piles and catchment areas that we knew had to be cleared. We diligently marked up our master map, trying to be methodical and thorough. Some weeks, the search went quiet. During those times, I'd typically be at home working on paperwork trying to replace key documents that had washed away.

My mind prefers to think and work on the big picture, rather than tasks that involve small details. I found the level of administrative detail difficult, but necessary in order to reestablish my life with Lauren's and my social security cards, birth certificates, passports, and the like. I realized that chipping away at it a little at a time was the best approach for me. One early afternoon, I took a break from my computer, and called Ann.

"Hi Ann, how's it going?" I said.

"Good, Kim — how about you?" she cheerfully replied.

"I'm okay, just doing some paperwork. Hey, I have a question. I was driving down this one street closer to the train tracks. I noticed some debris piles there. Maybe you can run out with me to look at it and if you think it worthwhile, I can work on getting the owner's permission to search it."

"Sure, I'm happy to walk that area with you. When do you want to go?"

"Whenever you're free," I said.

"I can go at 3:00 today, if you want to meet me there."

"Perfect," I said.

I shared the location with her, and set my phone timer to head out at 2:30. That would give me enough time to get the car filled with gas and meet her at the location.

When we walked the area, Ann agreed that we probably should search a couple of piles we saw there. As we assessed the location, I noted the nearby address. I wanted to reach out to the property owner to learn about the history of the slide and clean-up efforts in that specific area. Also, to find out if I needed to secure any permissions.

Once back at home, I started dialing the number that I had found for the property owner. I introduced myself, and requested access to search the two debris piles. The lovely lady who answered the phone seemed very receptive and said that she'd get back with me the next day to confirm we could search the area.

The next morning my phone rang, and it was the woman I had spoken to the night before. I was hoping for a quick call where she'd just approve us searching the pile. But instead, she first told me a story that she felt important to share with me.

"Kim, I need to tell you something that happened the other month, as it may help you with the search," she said.

"What's that?" I asked.

"This may sound odd, but I have to tell you about a get-together some local ladies had one night, a few months ago."

"Sure, please do."

"My friend invited some girlfriends to her house, and she also invited a known intuitive from Southern California. The lady hosting had lost her child years back, and found relief hearing from her loved one. She thought the rest of us in attendance might also find this experience with a medium interesting. Well, as we all sat around with the medium, Jack came through in the reading. I think we should invite you over to hear the recording we did that night. We were trying to ask him where he was."

Wow, I need to learn more about this, I thought.

"Sure, I'd be happy to come. And I'm so glad you shared this with me. I'm taking any and all clues that might help in the search," I said.

"I'll call you back with a time we can meet with my friend, and you can hear the recording of the session," she replied.

The next day, the kind lady called me back with a time to meet at a home to hear the recording. They were gracious people who lived in the community. Before she played the recording, one of ladies gave me a preface and overview of the event. She told me that the women were all in her living room, and as the medium started, one of the women asked if she could show a picture she'd brought in her pocket. The medium said that she did not need to see the picture, but that someone was coming through.

In the recording, I heard the intuitive describe the person coming through. She said to the women in the group, "Do you know of this person but not personally?" The group said "Yes." The lady with the picture in her pocket said, "I wish he'd just tell us where to look for him."

The medium went on to ask if this person was swept away in a mudslide or rushing river of mud. She then asked the group, "Are you convinced that he is in one place?" Apparently, she sensed that his remains were in different locations, and there could have been cars around him, and a ravine perhaps. She then said, using her hands to gesture directionally, "He went this way — and then that." Later she said that there could be bones found at some point, and maybe part of him may be found.

I was taking it all in.

It was hard to think of Jack's remains being dispersed. But I had hope, hearing some part of him might be found. I was most keenly interested in the directions the medium was indicating when she said, "He went this way, and then that." In my mind, that was sending us back to the location near the creek, which we'd been drawn to numerous times.

I thanked the women. I knew that they were keenly interested in helping me, and they showed their vulnerability and concern in sharing with me these details from their evening together.

Leaving their house, I was immensely grateful. I was not alone. It was not just me and my core team searching for the missing children. Neighbors that I did not even know were also doing what they could to try to help us find Jack and Lydia. Months after the slide, I had heard about some of the dads in Montecito and some of Jack's friends who went out to search an area by the creek where Jack's backpack had been recovered. I even heard about the school headmaster, Brian, who went out to scour the area and search for his former student. A local general contractor and builder, I learned, walked the area on his weekends, searching and trying to discern how the flow moved, and where unsearched pockets could be. Fire department personnel would also drive into the village on their days off, to walk and search. Hearing all this, I was humbled. I realized that this was not only a community tragedy, but also in many aspects a community search. This was one amazing town, filled with many compassionate people who were doing whatever they could do to help.

CHAPTER 24

VALENTINE'S DAY, 2019

HIGH SCHOOL was in full swing for Lauren. I felt fortunate each time friends reached out to see how I was doing. When friends from far away happened to be flying into Southern California, often they'd call so we could connect. I appreciated every single gesture, and vowed to do the same for others during their time of grief or need.

The first year after our tragedy was our year of firsts. Experiencing the first birthdays, my wedding anniversary, and the holidays without our loved ones — the newness of feeling so different, lonely, and empty, as if a big part of me was gone. The second year was even harder. After the year of firsts, the shock subsided. The second year was one of realizing the permanence of our loss. The reality that this was not a bad dream, but that Dave and Jack's absence in our lives was permanent. The second year, as Valentine's Day approached, my heart ached. During this time, out of the blue, one of our friends, John, called to say that he'd be in Los Angeles for work and would love to connect with Lauren and me. It was Valentine's weekend, and we were planning to be in Los Angeles, so it was perfect for us to meet John at a hotel restaurant next to LAX. John had been Dave's boss early in his career, and had been a groomsman in our wedding.

Just after we arrived in Los Angeles, I received an urgent message from another mudslide survivor. She shared that an ultrasound image with my name on it had been found and posted on the Montecito Disaster Lost & Found webpage. She urged me to check the website posting. *Ultrasound?* I wondered. What could this be?

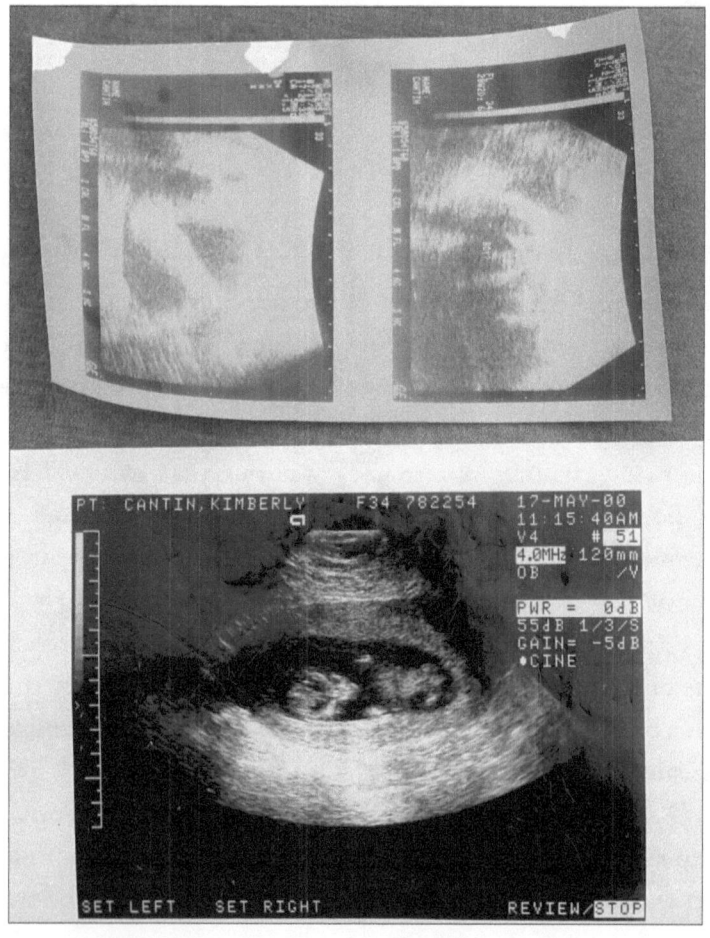

Prenatal ultrasound image of Jack, found at the beach

As I clicked onto the internet to scroll the lost and found page, there it was. I was in utter disbelief. It was now 409 days after the mudslide, and someone today — Valentine's Day — had found the sonogram image of baby Jack. I was stunned.

A few days later, I met the person who'd found the ultrasound. This fragile ultrasound, inside a simple plastic sleeve that could be used in a 3-ring binder, had been wedged between two rocks by the ocean at the base of the bluffs at Butterfly Beach — for 409 days. 409 days in the elements at the base of an ocean-front cliff. This delicate memory had travelled over a mile and a half from our home, and it survived in perfect condition.

These were the ultrasound images I had carefully tucked away in our master bedroom hope chest, and carefully inserted inside Jack's

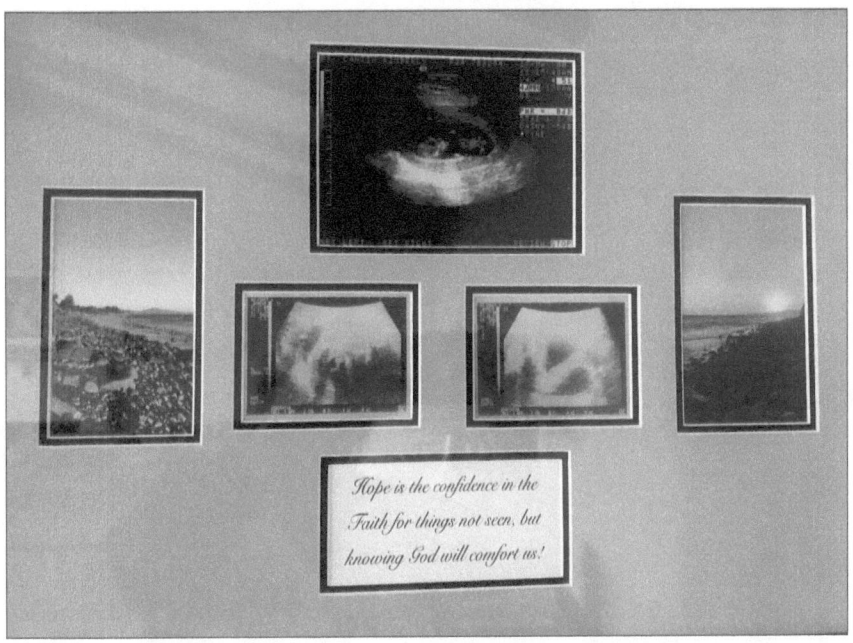

Ultrasound images of Jack in utero, found over 400 days post slide, in the elements, by the beach, wedged by rocks. Found in perfect condition, on Valentine's Day, 2019.

baby book. On the upper left of the ultrasound, clear as day, was my name and the date of May 17, 2000. This sonogram was taken on the happy day that Dave and I learned we were having a son.

It did not get past me that it arrived on Valentine's Day.

Jack's remains had not yet been found, but the ultrasound was clearly a message to never lose hope.

CHAPTER 25

"LOOK AT ME"

CONSISTENTLY, each time we had heavy rain, new items revealed themselves. A kind neighbor, who knew we were searching near her house by the creek, called me one day to tell me, "Kim, I think you should come walk the area. I think there is more debris and there may be more household items after our last rainstorm."

After I thanked her, I called Sherri and we met by the creek's ledge to walk the area. The neighbor was right. As we walked near the creek, we noticed a clump of cloth. It was Lauren's burgundy-colored Christmas dress from the year before, mud-soaked yet visible, clumped at the base of the tree that stood next to the bridge. We'd scoured this area many times over the last eighteen months, but until now, we hadn't seen the dress. Today, after the heavy rains, it was revealed. We also found a baby toy in the shape of a mouse. I thought it might be Lydia's. When we found it, I texted the woman helping Lydia's mom. Lydia's mom did not speak much English, so this social worker was my conduit to pass along information related to the search. I texted the social worker the image of the stuffed toy mouse we found sticking out of the ground, to ask if it was Lydia's. I also asked if her mom remembered what Lydia was wearing to bed that night. She sent me a little video of her daughter in pajamas, in hopes that it would help the team. We heard back that she could not tell for certain if the toy mouse was Lydia's. Regardless, it was clear to Sherri and me that after each rain, we needed to walk the area. Rain revealed what was hidden.

After another rain, a few of us went to walk near the side of the creek. We always went near the same area that we were drawn to. Not long after we'd gotten out of our cars, we noticed a piece of red fabric sticking out of the mud on the side wall of the creek, about thirty feet from a bridge, as if to say, *Look at me! Look at me!*

Jack's costume that was revealed after a rainstorm

Jack in the superhero costume as a toddler

Since we'd started our search efforts in 2018, we'd spent many days inspecting this creekside wall. But this was the first time the fabric had revealed itself. Upon closer inspection, we determined that the red cloth was the leg of a child's Halloween costume. We gently worked to free the costume from the tight tomb of cement-like, hard-packed soil; finally, we got it free. There it was — a child's superhero costume. I knew in my heart it was Jack's.

CHAPTER 26

BOOMERANG

FINDING JACK'S superhero costume from when he was a toddler was just the fuel the team needed to keep going. It was now August 2019; nineteen months since the debris flow. Superhero was a clue that Marisa had said would be important in locating Jack's remains. Now we'd found two items matching the clue — one figurine, and one Halloween costume. Both were Jack's, and both were found in the same general area by the creek and the open walking space we'd consistently returned to. Finding Jack's Halloween costume was significant; even the local news ran a story on the find, as the community was interested and hopeful the missing children would someday be located. People realized that if items were still being revealed, then there was a real possibility that one day, our missing children would be recovered.

Finding the costume inspired our team to go back to the area, to see if there was more built-up debris flow to search. Again we searched it, and again we came up with nothing. We thought for sure, we could cross this area off as "searched" on our map filled with clues and items found.

Back at home, I was settling more into a routine. In fall, much of my time was spent shuttling Lauren to and from school, and to her activities or appointments. When she was in school, I'd find time to continue the search. Soon, I knew, I'd have to think about driver training for my daughter. This frightened me. A lot. Dave had taught Jack to drive, as he had a calm demeanor and plenty of patience. I knew that I'd be more tense about it. Even Lauren worried about the prospect of me teaching her. Fortunately, Jesse, one of Lauren's middle school teachers, offered her six driving lessons as her 9th-grade graduation gift; clearly, this was a gift to us both. I was relieved knowing she had someone to teach her. We took Jesse up on his offer, and I also planned to add additional professional driving training sessions to her experience before I ever got behind the wheel with her. The plan was shaping up in a way that made me much more at ease.

CHAPTER 27

BURLED TREE, DRAINS, AND REUBEN

AS NEW CLUES or target areas surfaced, we continued to search. It seemed like the team would go out a couple times a month. We always walked the area after a rain to see what revealed itself. One Friday, I swung by the local gas station in Montecito to fill up my tank. A woman walked toward my car, as if she wanted to tell me something. Cautiously, I rolled down the window to see what she wanted.

"Are you Kim?" the woman asked.

"Yes, I am. How can I help you?" I responded with reservation in my voice.

She went on to explain, "I was one of Lauren's teacher's aides in her elementary school, many years ago. I've been trying to find a way to connect with you, to tell you something."

"Oh, okay, hi. Please tell me," I said politely.

"Well, I just felt you needed to know an experience I had. I preface this by saying, I've never had anything like this happen before.

When I was walking one day in the open trails area by the creek, there was a tree with a unique, big, burled trunk. It is distinctive. Just as I walked by that tree and the area on the path, I got this overwhelming sense, thinking about your son, Jack. As if I was feeling his remains might be in that area. I don't know what any of it means, but I felt you should know, as I know you are still trying to find his remains."

"Wow, thank you for telling me." I went on to say, "And, please, don't feel the least bit silly for having that experience. I'm learning to be much more open to any clues or messages that help us in the search. I don't know where this tree is, so maybe you can show me."

She agreed, and after my tank was filled, I followed her a few streets over. She walked me to a tree with huge, burled wood at the base of its trunk. This tree was a different one than the unusually shaped tree by the catch basin that we had cleared out months earlier. This tree had a base that was distinctively large and burled, almost like the shape of a plump pear at the base of the trunk, then thinning as the trunk grew taller.

This tree was across the creek from where his superhero costume had been recovered. It had happened again — I had just received another message that brought us back to the same general area again. We kept being drawn back to a section representing only 2% of the mudslide area. Again, I thanked the kind woman for sharing her story. As she walked away, I phoned Rick to see if he could bring MacGyver to sniff that area, yet again.

Rick did better than just bring MacGyver; he told me that over the next weekend a few other handlers with their dogs would be in town again and they'd offered to come work in the area. I was so appreciative.

So, over the weekend, search dogs were deployed to search the ground near the burled tree in the open space, just off the walking path. As I watched the dogs work, they quickly blew past the tree

Out on a search with Ann (on the excavator), Rick, handler Shirley, and search dogs

and darted toward another area about twenty-five feet north of it. All three dogs independently alerted on this particular area. With that response, Rick asked that we all come back the next day with Ann and the excavator, to search that area.

The next morning, Ann, the dog search teams, Sherri, Grant, and I were all in place to excavate. As Rick walked into the search area, this time he carried a 4-inch square metal mesh sifter device. I was startled. I knew by now that we were more likely looking for parts of dismembered human bone, instead of what we had expected soon after the slide: a five-foot-eleven, 170-pound young man. And I had also learned that a couple of the other victims had incurred such polytrauma during the slide. Seeing the sifting device, however, made it a more somber event, and more real and terrifying. This was my baby boy—and now I was seeing a metal dirt sifter. It felt brutal.

Scoop by scoop, we cleared and dug, until Ann was certain she had cleared down to the original grade of the soil that was not mudslide debris. All of us were losing hope, and we were so perplexed that after three dog alerts, we were finding nothing. We all felt it. Sadness and disappointment descended on us as we worked together. As Ann's scooping bin cascaded the collected dirt into another area, Sherri yelled, "Stop!" Ann immediately stopped the excavator, and we paused while Sherri went in to grab what she had seen.

It was not bone, or anything human. Though it *was* something amazing that had survived without even a scratch, after traveling over four hundred yards in the debris flow among boulders, bricks, cars, and trees.

Out of the cement-like dirt, Sherri pulled out a very dirty ivory-colored porcelain Christmas tree ornament. She carefully brushed off some of the caked mud, and the item became readily recognizable. "That's Cantin!" I exclaimed.

I recognized our Christmas ornament; part of the four-piece train set sent to us as a gift from Dave's aunt after Lauren's birth. On this search day, the ornament found was the engine car, which still had *David* written on it in faded gold lettering. The Christmas before the mudslide, I had placed the four-car train set on our fireplace mantel: the *David* engine, then the *Kim*, *Jack*, and *Lauren* cars.

Standing in the big dirt field, we were amazed. *How on earth could this fragile porcelain ornament survive the force of the mudslide for over 400 yards?* We did not know, but we all recognized the symbolism in the moment. This special item was part of a set that represented the connectedness of the Cantin family. To us, it meant that we should keep looking. As we were gearing up to leave, Sherri overheard Rick say, "I think we need an anthropology team." It was the first time I'd

Porcelain Christmas ornament with the name *David*, found without a scratch after traveling 400 yards and buried in mud

heard that suggestion. It not only signaled that so much time had passed, but also that we needed higher-level expertise in finding small pieces of bone. I wanted to dismiss what I was hearing.

A month later, after thinking we'd exhausted searching this area, we moved on to check some of the sewage and storm drain areas that were filled with debris and mud, and that needed inspection. The day before our search team was going to meet the drainage-clearing crew, an intuitive called me randomly with a clue. She was interested in the possibility of one of the children being caught in a large drainage pipe. She mentioned three names that would be present when we searched.

BURLED TREE, DRAINS, AND REUBEN

She said that "Jeff, Mike, and Reuben" would be part of the drainage system clearing as we searched for our children. My focus was on Jack and Lydia, so I paid little attention to her comments, other than to write down the names.

The next day, Rick, Grant, Ann, and I waited on the corner of Hot Springs and Olive Mill Roads, at the triangle median area, for the drainage guys and their truck outfitted with a camera system to scope the drainage lines deep below the roads. Rick often chuckled quietly whenever I gave the team any update on the clues the intuitive folks sent me. Rick was rational-minded, and didn't particularly (if at all) give any credence to intuitive clues. To humor me, he'd smile, and nod his head as if taking in the clue, but it just wasn't his thing. As the two workers jumped out of their truck, I walked toward them and introduced myself.

"Hi, Kim, my name is Jeff, and this is my partner today, Mike," the truck driver informed me.

"Wow, thanks for coming to help us today," I said. I called Rick, Ann, and Grant over to greet them as well.

"Hey guys, this is Jeff and Mike; all we need is a Reuben and we've got the names of the people the intuitive mentioned." I said this in a tongue-in-cheek tone, knowing full well we did not have a Reuben in our midst.

But then, startled, Rick said, "My Hebrew name is Reuben." I chuckled in disbelief. The coincidence was amazing. I imagine Rick would say that it was at that moment he went from a disbeliever to someone with a cautious wonder about things we simply couldn't explain.

During this search, I witnessed some of the best of human kindness. My core team faithfully came out to search. Ann excavated, the Bucket Brigade volunteers helped, County Flood Control cleared a catch basin, and neighbors graciously let us run search dogs on their private property. Their kindness and gift of access was one of the most meaningful gestures of compassion we received during this time.

Life marched on and in my spare time I read some books to help me. Since the loss of Jack and Dave, I had read books on grief and other books suggested by friends. One afternoon, I searched online for an interesting book. I was drawn to a book called *Rare Bird — A Memoir of Loss and Love* by Anna Whiston-Donaldson.

I paid for it to be shipped in two days.

When the book arrived, I looked forward to reading it while Lauren was studying. A warm cup of herbal tea in hand, I headed to my bedroom to sit in my chair with my feet up and delve into my new book. I had not read the synopsis, only the book's title. I knew it would be about a woman's journey through grief and loss, but I had no idea how uniquely so, until I started reading.

While reading a chapter, I yelped. The author described that her adolescent son, named Jack, was washed away and killed in an overflowing creek. *Oh my God!* I thought. Of all books to read, I picked the one about a young boy with the same name as my son, and whose death was from falling into an overflowing creek. Horrifically, this mom ran to find her son; he had drowned, and his body was recovered in the waters.

My Jack was killed by an overflowing creek caused by the mudslide. I called a friend to tell her about the coincidence. As we talked, we discussed how this might be a gentle nudge for us to stay at the creek in our search.

The superhero costume and figurine had been found there.

Three cadaver search dogs had alerted there.

A neighbor had had an experience driving over the creek bridge there.

Marisa had walked the area and sensed "two victims," not one.

Catherine's clues of "teacup, red falcon, and umbrella" were found near there.

Suzanne, who walked the creek area with me and her husband, sensed something in this area.

Now, a book I selected from thousands of choices was about a sweet boy named Jack, killed and his body recovered in an overflowing creek.

We needed to return to the creek to search.

Core sacred search team who helped Kim for three years.
Standing (from left): Rick, Ann, Jacques, Grant, and Sherri.
Sitting: Catherine and Kim (not in picture: Allison).

CHAPTER 28

GIFTS RETURNED AND KINTSUGI

WHEN I WASN'T engaged in search efforts, I was working to establish a new life for me and my daughter while we were both trying to heal. Even while trying to move forward, I was often pulled back into grief over the enormity of our losses. Most significant of course, was the loss of my husband and son. We also had to deal with the loss of all our personal items that literally washed away — all over town — in the early morning of January 9, 2018. The debris field encompassed an area a mile and a half long and half a mile wide, and included property lots where homes once stood. Other homes still stood, but were heavily damaged. Besides residential lots, this debris field also encompassed the sides of the 101 freeway, the sides of the creek, along the walking trails in a protected open space, and all the way down to the beach — where dozens of people, if not more, strolled daily. Our search area was about 110 acres in size. This fact alone was highly daunting.

As mentioned earlier, a kind-hearted local resident created the Montecito Disaster Lost & Found website, where anything found from the mudslide could be posted. The goal was to make it a forum to help folks who had lost so much get back some of the muddy treasures that people found.

I routinely checked that page, looking items from our house.

One day, while looking at this website, I did a double take. I saw what looked like my handwriting in a little book, and it was posted online.

As my eyes struggled to focus, I realized that, unbelievably, someone had posted pages from my personal diary!

Could it get any worse? I thought in disbelief.

I recognized my own handwriting from my diary, now posted on the internet for the entire world to see.

Luckily, I realized that the diary was from my youth, so the worst I wrote about was perhaps a boy crush. But this very real example gave a sense of the lack of privacy that followed the mudslide. Not only did we lose cherished loved ones and our home, but also all privacy as we knew it.

On a positive note, however, it seemed like at times when I felt particularly low and sad, treasured items would find their way back to me. One item was unique because it became a beautiful symbol that a friend shared with me after the mudslide.

A couple of years before the slide, I had purchased a whimsical, inexpensive lime green wooden pig as décor for Lauren's bathroom. One night after a long day of physical therapy and counseling appointments, I decided to scan the lost and found page, and I recognized the little green pig. A volunteer helping to clear an area had found it and then carefully dug it out of the mud, and had posted the damaged, muddy wooden pig on the site. I messaged the site that I was its owner. Although he was badly damaged, anything that was once in my home suddenly became a cherished treasure. These finds were important to me, as they were proof of my life prior to the mudslide. They reminded me of my life that had existed, and helped me maintain my hope that one day we would find Jack.

As a gift to me the volunteers arranged for a local artist to lovingly repair the pig. The artist used the ancient Japanese art form called Kintsugi: the art of gold lacquer repairing something broken, like a porcelain vase. Also known as the "the art of precious scars," Kintsugi expresses a belief that the break and the repair are both important parts of an object. It is better to show the repaired break, rather than trying to hide it. The break, once repaired, shows the valuable and authentic history of the item. Often, once repaired with the gold lacquer, the item seems perhaps even more beautiful.

This was the same art form that a colleague and friend had told me about, months ago when we talked on the phone soon after the mudslide. During that phone call, Kristin had used Kintsugi metaphorically; she said that if I fell apart emotionally from the magnitude of my loss, I, too, could reassemble. As I healed, perhaps I would be more beautiful, like a Kintsugi piece at the soul level.

Whereas before I would have considered this just a fluke, now I was more attuned to noting the synchronicity of such events.

The pig was more beautiful after it was repaired with gold paint. It is now on display in our new home. It reminds me of the human kindness and love I experienced from strangers after the tragedy, and it works as a metaphor for our lives. From what I've read, this art form relates to aspects of the human experience. It can symbolize non-attachment, the acceptance of change, and fate. It is also about repair; and through the repair there is perhaps a rebirth or evolution. Based on my experience, I could not think of anything more appropriate as a metaphor and a gift.

I marvel at how this metaphor was first presented to me by my friend, and then manifested by an artist who beautifully repaired our pig. It reminds me to accept my life's changes, and to work to thrive and move forward. I know for sure that this is what my husband and son would want for us. And, maybe, just maybe, they helped this coincidence to happen.

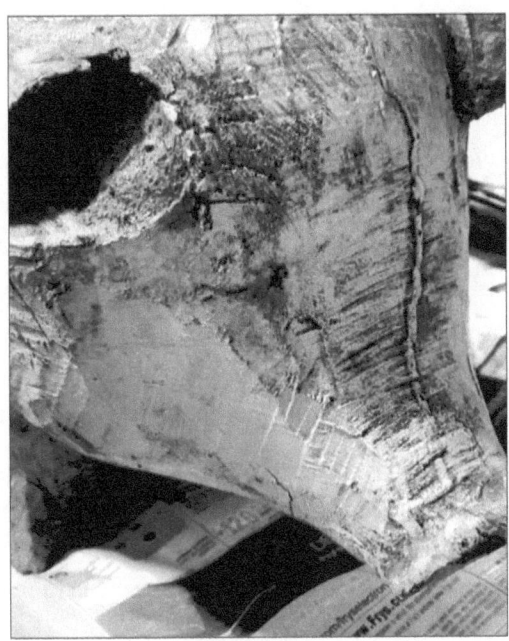

Wooden pig figurine; hooves, ears, and tail all damaged in the slide
Photo courtesy of Amanda Hockman

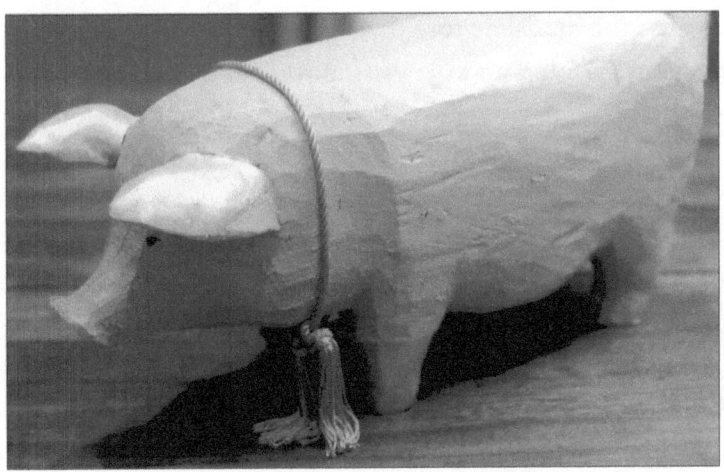

Pig repaired by an artist, Kintsugi style, with ears, hooves, and tail now painted gold

As our search continued, I tried to get more "science" into the process. Marisa texted me one day with the idea of trying to locate a GPS ground-penetrating radar machine. These machines are used to find buried murder victims. As it rolls over the ground, the device detects soil disturbances and locates a body beneath the surface. Willing to try anything that might yield results, I started calling places locally. It seemed that no place had one of the devices, so finally, I called a manufacturer in Ontario, Canada, which offered to rent a unit to me. I gave them the credit card information, on which they charged thousands of dollars in rental and shipping costs. The next day, the big expensive device could be sent to Santa Barbara.

Problem: who did we know who was trained to use the device? Sadly, no one.

So, we connected Abe Powell, the volunteer leader of the Bucket Brigade, with a device expert over the phone, and Abe got a tutorial on how to use it.

The next few days, our team and Abe were using this big, ride-on-mower-looking device, trying to find the missing children. We learned that because the mudslide tore through so much land, unsettling layers of existing ground and depositing rocks, boulders, and damaged pieces of homes as they washed away, this technology was not going to be of use to us. Although sadly this system did not work, at least we'd added a scientific method to our search.

Our team had been searching for over 18 months. We'd had multiple search dogs covering different areas; we'd tried ground-penetrating radar. A local expert and neighbor, Jordan, located archived maps to show areas where old, buried wells existed in the flow path. After securing the county permits, we even dug up a couple of the wells whose covers had blown off to check if Jack or Lydia had been caught in one of them. Our mantra was "no stone unturned," and we methodically crossed off areas we'd searched on our debris flow map. Coming up with a cleared area advanced the search, as it narrowed our focus.

CHAPTER 29

A SURPRISE, A HEARTTHROB, AND A BASEBALL JERSEY

BY LATE FALL 2019, the team's efforts were ebbing and flowing, based on any new clue or finding that directed us to search a specific area. My urgency to find Jack's remains was becoming more tempered. I clearly felt that shift and I wasn't as frantic. I had heard clearly from Catherine and others that Jack had said, "I will be found!" I knew I had to surrender to God's time, not mine. This was a new feeling for me. I was feeling less attachment to the outcome, yet I continued to follow the leads. Early on, I felt such impatience and when people said, "All in God's time," I'd get pissed. How could a loving God be dragging this out, if He or She had a say in the matter? Now, experiencing all that I had gone through, I surrendered to this notion, and it gave me some peace.

A few months later, I received a phone call. The gentleman on the other end of the phone told me that he worked with the movie and TV actor Rob Lowe. He explained that Rob wanted to interview Lauren and me for a documentary.

I responded, "I'm not interested in talking about the mudslide; I'm focused on the search for our missing children — one being my son, Jack."

"Okay, let me run this by Rob and I'll get back to you," he said.

I didn't think much more about it until two days later when he called to say, "Rob wants to talk with you and help with the search."

I thought, *I'll take all the help I can get*. We had 110 acres to search.

A few weeks later, the teenage heartthrob of the '80s and '90s, and currently a popular and talented actor and producer, walked through my front door, ready to help walk the creek with us. Though he was both handsome and talented, what I admired most was that he was a compassionate and kind neighbor. He lived in Montecito, and understood that this disaster was a community disaster. He wanted to help in any way he could. So, that afternoon, we walked into the open space, and Rob climbed down into the creek bed to work.

I handed him a pickaxe. Rob picked at the debris flow mud that was a cement-like, hard layer of soil. Sherri and Ann enjoyed the handsome scenery, conversation, and search support.

At one point, Rob asked me, "Kim, why do you keep looking after all this time?"

"Because we keep finding Cantin things that reveal themselves. And if we find these things, we may find my son and Lydia. We're using search dogs, we've tried ground radar, and my intuition tells me his remains are out here somewhere. I strongly feel that he did not go to the ocean," I said, as I dug my shovel into debris a few feet from Rob.

Rob pickaxed an area of debris built up on the side of the creek. Immediately we heard him yell, "I found something!"

He carefully dug out some poker chips that were Dave's, and then, next to them, a clump of Dave's silk ties, now muddy and torn. I felt so sad seeing the damaged red silk tie in the clump he found, as that was my favorite tie of my late husband's.

Rob's eyes widened as he discovered Dave's things that had been in the mud for 18 months.

We made our way down the dry creek, talking as we went. Rob dug on the south side of the creek even when I had suggested we work on the north side. A few minutes later, he noticed something else.

"I think this is a piece of T-shirt material," he said as he gently pulled out the clump of material. After he shook dirt off it, Rob said "It's a Red Sox T-Shirt!"

"That's Dave's! Is it large or extra-large?" I asked, with a heightened anticipation.

"Extra-large," Rob said.

"Then that's Dave's!" I said, as I took it from Rob. It was like a long-lost treasure. After losing everything, this muddy and torn T-shirt pulled at my heart. It meant I'd at least have something of

Actor Rob Lowe with Sherri, Ann, and Kim, as they searched. Dave's Red Sox jersey was found that day.

Dave's that he enjoyed wearing. Baseball was Dave's sport; he was in an adult league baseball team on weekends, and it was his way to stay active and enjoy a fun team sport. The Red Sox were his team, and he'd worn this jersey with pride. Of all the items we could have found of his, this was a meaningful gem that reminded me of my sweet husband and his infectious smile. I was eager to get it home and wash it. After handing me the dirt-ridden jersey, Rob said, "Now I get it... I get why you are still looking!" And he encouraged us to keep at it. Rob got to experience firsthand how many of our things were still hidden just a few inches underneath the mud and debris and he deduced what that could mean in terms of our search effort.

My life was so different. Who would have ever imagined handsome, charming Rob Lowe crawling down into a dry creek with me and my friends, in search of my son's remains? All I could feel was gratitude. He was a kind neighbor who showed up to help after the community tragedy. Almost a year later, I watched his documentary, *Madness in the Hills*. His film did a phenomenal job of documenting the human impact of the community disaster, and it also accurately portrayed the search for the missing children.

CHAPTER 30

A BIRTHDAY CELEBRATED

IN NOVEMBER, to recognize Jack's second birthday that he was not physically with us, I invited a few of his friends out to dinner with Lauren and me. Lauren loved being around Jack's friends. I sensed that she got a little bit of her brother back in spirit, when she was around them. It reminded her of earlier days as the younger sister, hanging around when Jack's buddies were over. Now, she had a bunch of older kids who were keen on watching out for her. Casmali, one of Jack's best friends, always tried to show up for Lauren at key events, which warmed my heart. I knew our going to dinner with his friends would have made Jack very happy.

Coming home from dinner after hearing some fun stories that the friends remembered about Jack, Lauren proceeded to tell me in the car, "Mom, Jack was no saint. Folks know about his community service and his Eagle project, but he could be a real brat. I remember him chasing me around the yard once, and using me as target practice with his new bow and arrow."

"What!? I never heard about that," I said.

Lauren's story made me remember a short video one of Jack's friends took with their camera while Jack was in a high school computer class. Jack was expert with the computer, and was in a school academy that taught multimedia and design with the computer. He also had a sense of humor. Certain classes were held in computer labs. In this particular video, Jack was quickly moving from his computer desk to another part of the classroom, trying to contain his laughter as he held a computer mouse and cord in his hand. On the video you can hear an attractive female student who'd been seated next to him yelling at him. "Jack! Don't you dare, what are you doing!" Nearby students watching were chuckling at Jack's silly prank.

Apparently, as a joke, Jack would change the computer cords so he could control the mouse of the unsuspecting female student sitting next to him. Casually, he'd be moving the mouse cursor around on the other student's computer and, knowing Jack, probably even altering a bit of their assignment before the student would realize something was wrong with her computer. As Jack heard his classmate start freaking out that something was wrong with her computer, he couldn't help but laugh. He was no saint, but he was funny. I appreciated Lauren reminding me about some of his antics.

Although it was emotionally tough to set up events to celebrate Jack's and Dave's birthdays that first year, I found it helpful in my healing process. It was a way for me to know that they were not forgotten, as I tried to adapt to my new life. I was able to connect with their friends that now I did not get to see very often. Many of the friends who attended said the gatherings were very helpful for them, as well. I realized that so much attention was given to Lauren and me, yet Dave's and Jack's friends were suffering, too. Having friends together for their would-have-been birthdays helped us all.

CHAPTER 31

ANTHROPOLOGY AND LIPOSUCTION

TWO YEARS after the mudslide, while sitting in my kitchen, my cell phone rang. It was Catherine. We hadn't chatted for over a month, not since we saw each other at the two-year mudslide anniversary community event in early January. I was happy to hear her voice. In the conversation, she told me that the purpose of her call was to share with me an overwhelming feeling she'd recently had.

"Kim", she said, "you need to talk to a detective about the search."

A detective? I thought. *Well, I know a detective.* An old buddy from my teen years had recently retired as a top, big-city detective.

"I'll call my buddy Jake," I told Catherine as we finished our call.

Over two years of experiences related to such clues had made me a believer. I did not challenge or dismiss Catherine's intuition. Her message was just another step of my journey in the search for Jack's remains, and in my healing journey.

I called Jake, and told him what we'd done thus far over the past two years related to the search: the excavators, the search dogs, the digging, the ground-penetrating radar, the meaningful finds, the camera-scoping of drains, the mapping and logging of the information, the search of old buried wells.

After listening intently, Jake said, "Kim, I think you need an anthropologist. In fact, you may want to reach out to your local university and see if they have a forensic anthropologist."

I'd never heard of that type of person or profession.

Jake and I finished our chat. I hung up the phone and googled the email address of the University of California, Santa Barbara (UCSB) Anthropology Department. It was ranked in the top 10 anthropology departments in the country. The university was only a 20-minute drive from Montecito.

On January 31, 2020, sitting at my desk in my home office, I drafted an email to the Anthropology Department, explaining who I was, and asking to speak with a forensic anthropologist.

Within 24 hours, I saw a message from an associate professor of anthropology and the director of the P.L. Walker Bioarcheology and Forensic Bone Lab at UCSB, Dr. Danielle Kurin. In her email, Dr. Kurin expressed that she was interested in helping me, and would be willing to meet my search team next week.

The energy was certainly moving on the "get an anthropologist involved" front.

Six days later, on February 6th, gathered in my living room were the members of my search team (Grant, Ann, Sherri, Rick, Catherine) along with the professor. She had just returned from an extensive period where she'd led archaeological excavation work in Peru. Dr. Kurin had not been in Santa Barbara during the mudslide. Our team gave her a comprehensive overview, and we watched with new hope as she leaned in, eager to lend support, science, and technology to the effort.

Just a short drive away was a forensic biological anthropology lab, filled with students eager to learn and apply anthropology techniques, high-end technology equipment, and scientific methods that could help in our search. We were all thrilled.

That little nudge from Catherine must have had some special inspiration. It was amazing, the speed at which we found a local anthropology department and secured a forensic and bioarchaelogical anthropologist who would lead a student volunteer team.

Getting up from the couch to leave, Rick shook his head with a smile and said, "Wow, where were these guys two years ago?" As everyone left my house that afternoon, Catherine and I said to each other in wonder, "Thanks, Jack!" Maybe part of this journey was about connecting people from Search and Rescue with the forensic lab. Not only might it help us now as we searched for Jack and Lydia, but this connection created the possibility of helping many more people in the future. The UCSB Forensic Anthropology Lab was taking a leading role in the search. I was even more hopeful when Professor Kurin strived to make the search a 4-unit course at the university. She said the students were humbled and honored to work on such a meaningful project.

In a few weeks, the team went out to dig and take soil samples at various locations. The professor secured a grant to have historical human remains canines (forensic "grave" dogs) come in to search the area. These dogs were trained to find the scent of human bones that had been buried for an extensive period; in fact, these types of specially trained dogs, I heard, had gone to look on a deserted island in the South Pacific for the remains of Amelia Earhart in 2017. We'd had many search dogs come searching; it was estimated that over two thousand dog search hours had already gone into the search for our needles in the haystack. I appreciated these specially trained forensic dogs and their handlers travelling to help, yet this time, two years out, I was more reserved in my expectations for a positive outcome.

Months earlier, I had met a nice couple from Arizona, Jay and Jenn, who had tragically lost their teenage son, Austin, in a jeep accident. They had learned about Jack all the way in Arizona, and were touched that both of our sons, Austin and Jack, were Boy Scouts.

Austin had been working on his Eagle project. A mutual friend introduced us, and I was struck by their kindness. Jay, by trade, was an expert in river dynamics and landscaping. Unbeknownst to me, from his computer in his Arizona office, he studied the mudslide topography and tried to ascertain where eddies could have formed, and/or pockets and catchments created by the flow, where Jack or baby Lydia could have been trapped. To my surprise, on Memorial Day weekend, Jay and Jenn, people I had never met in person, loaded up their car and drove over 450 miles from Arizona to Montecito. This mom and dad felt compelled to walk the area and show me areas that Jay thought might be potential pockets that we should search. I was in awe of their kindness, a stranger applying his expertise to help me. The acts of human kindness I experienced after the tragedy were nurturing to me.

After their trip to Montecito, I kept Jay abreast of any search updates. I told him that a university anthropology team was engaged, and told him about the elite trained canine forensic dogs that were scheduled to come search. Bless this kind soul; I'd soon learn that Jay researched to see if there was any clinical data on how to create the best soil conditions for the canine search dogs. He scoured the clinical data to understand if we wanted a hot, dry day, or if it would be better to have the dogs sniff in moist soil or dry soil.

After his research, Jay called to let me know he'd found a university clinical paper written. He shared the name of the paper's author.

After dialing the number of the university, within minutes I was speaking with the scientist and author of the paper. I explained that we wanted to know how best to prep the soil for the dogs. This expert gave me some tips, and at the end he strongly recommended we "test" the dogs' abilities on a human training aid before they started working the search area. He explained that I'd want to be certain that the dogs would pick up human scent.

"So how do I do that?" I asked.

"Well, if you can get a 1- to 5-year-old human bone and hide it 30 feet away upwind from the dog, you'll see if the dog finds the bone — and, if the dog is any good, they should find it within three minutes."

Thinking about his recommendation, I replied, "If I had a 1- to 5-year-old human bone, I'd be arrested! What other options do I have?"

"Well, you could hide some human liposuction — you know, the fat they take from people who want to get their fat removed from their bellies."

Hmmm ... That was something I thought I could possibly make happen, I thought.

Dave and I had worked at an aesthetics company years back. As coincidence would have it, Dave was the marketing lead for the company's liposuction products. Through this role, he had developed good relationships with some California plastic surgeons. I thought, *I could call a plastic surgeon Dave had worked with, to see if he'd save me some lipo (fat) after one of his procedures. I could then do what the scientist suggested, and put it in a mason jar with a clean make-up sponge, to use as the dog training/test-aid.*

It sounded simple enough to me.

I thanked the scientist for his advice, and called a plastic surgeon Dave had known. Unfortunately, the plastic surgeon explained that my rather odd request was an ethical violation; he could not give me someone's post-procedure lipo due to privacy reasons. Sorry that he couldn't help, the surgeon gave me his condolences.

I was disappointed, but as I'd learned from my earlier career in sales, *Never take the first 'no' as gospel. There has to be a legitimate way,* I thought. And I certainly was not giving up this easily.

So, I called a local plastic surgeon; I did not know him personally, but I had heard he was a great guy. I asked the receptionist if I could speak with him on the phone, since I had a very unusual request.

The surgeon called me back, and I went through my spiel. "I'm the mother of the missing boy, Jack, killed in the mudslide. We have an elite team of canine forensic dogs coming into town next week, and we are working with a UCSB Anthropology team... and I need some lipo."

I shared the recommendation from the expert regarding a training-aid to test the dogs before they got started. "I just need a half cup of human liposuction." I informed him that the professor and her team were certified to handle Class B Biohazard material properly, so that any concern about the bio-hazardous nature of the material would be addressed.

On the other end of the phone, came a painfully long silence. The plastic surgeon and was taking it all in.

Definitely, mine was an out-of-the-ordinary call. Because he was local, he knew of the devastating mudslide, the magnitude of this community tragedy, and the sadness so many people felt about the two missing children. He was familiar with Jack's name and story.

"Can you come in Friday? I could pop you up on a table and take some lipo from you. Do you think you have enough fat to give?" he asked.

"Ah, um. Sure," I muttered, thinking, *Boy, do I.*

And, so I went.

The next day, I drove to his office, climbed up on his procedure table, and lifted my shirt to expose my stomach. For the next twenty minutes, he liposuctioned about half a cup of fat by entering through my belly button.

A nurse held my hand, trying to distract me as my hands started to sweat from the pain. As we had discussed, he used a few needles of a painkiller injected to numb the area, rather than the more traditional way of stronger anesthesia. I knew we needed the sample, so I was not going to wimp out.

That doctor and staff were a great example of human kindness in action. They, like others, used their expertise to help with the search and to support me.

Back at home, I put the sample, properly packed, in our second fridge, which was in the laundry room, to keep until the professor could transfer it into the lab's dehydrator.

When Lauren came home, I said, "Hey Lauren, just stay out of the laundry room refrigerator for a while, please."

"Okay, but why?" she asked

I pulled up my shirt and displayed my abdomen covered in white bandage gauze and tape. Her eyes bugged out of her head.

"What happened!?" she asked with concern.

"I got some fat removed to test the dogs with," I replied. "Don't worry, sweetie, it will be fine. I'll just be black and blue for the next ten days or so as it heals."

"Gross!" she exclaimed, probably thinking I'd lost a few of my marbles. She avoided the laundry room refrigerator for a long, long while.

Any parent would move mountains for their child. Digging in the mud, walking the creek, observing search dogs sniff, and engaging with an anthropology team, all fit the bill. But stomach liposuction had never entered the realm of possibility, until now.

When the six forensic dogs arrived, we tested them with the training-aid on my property. Each dog performed perfectly; their noses picked up on human remains scent. Now officially tested on site, the dogs were ready to search for Jack and Lydia's remains.

On that day, 989 days since the mudslide, I did not hold out much hope that they would find anything. But I was certainly willing to let them try.

I had sobbed and cried for the loss of my husband and son for nearly three years. When working to guide the search, I focused on keeping it together. I knew if I wept or was hysterical, I'd have less success in coordinating the people, agencies, and businesses that had their own way of aiding in the search. I had to be level-headed to get the support from so many people and agencies.

That morning, I mentally prepared myself. The search thus far had been an emotional rollercoaster. We had spent hundreds of hours searching, although we'd found key items and randomly received clues that moved us closer to finding our hoped-for outcome. Yet, I had to be realistic. Thus far we'd come up empty-handed.

This day, we had six dogs and six handlers who planned to work in four marked areas.

The anthropology team showed up in their orange safety vests, prepared with landscape flags to mark areas, and GPS coordinate markers. Property owners had been made aware and gave us access permission. A fire department captain came to observe as his team prepped the soil for the dogs. A few from my search team also joined. A neighbor allowed us to set up a folding table on her property, and graciously offered one of her restrooms so everyone involved could work comfortably throughout the day.

It was my understanding that the dogs could only work while the ground temperature stayed below 100 degrees. It was now September — typically the warmest month of the year in California. Fortunately, this day was overcast and cool. *Perfect climate for the search*, I thought.

During the search, all six of the dogs alerted in one general area.

The area was scattered with boulders. As stated earlier, I had been told that if one dog alerted in an area, then it meant there was roughly a 30% probability of human remains there. If two dogs alerted, there was a 60% probability; and if three dogs alerted, it meant a 90% probability. To our surprise, *six* dogs had given an alert.

What we also knew was that scent could travel. So, there was a possibility that the human remains might not be directly under the specific alert location, but somewhere nearby.

Everyone was surprised. We'd searched for so long, we had resigned ourselves that the dogs may not get a scent. In a couple of other areas close by, a few of the dogs gave alerts, too. One was near a big boulder on the edge of the creek, where the superhero costume had been found.

After the dogs alerted, Ann used her excavator, and a fire department captain stayed with the team, watching each entry of the excavator bin scraping back the soil. Meanwhile, the anthropology team took soil samples and marked the GPS locations of each alert.

During the excavation, someone noticed what looked like part of a black-and-white snake in the side of the mud pit we were clearing. The team stopped, and carefully rehomed a five-foot-long Kingsnake. The professor noted, "Snakes symbolize death."

We concluded that day not finding human remains, but we were more hopeful about this general area. Once evaluated at the lab the soil samples would help us refine our search. Ann and our team needed to move soil. The car-sized boulders near the creek would be moved next, so we could search underneath them.

Surprisingly, I didn't feel dejected from this effort.

Instead, I was bolstered by the support from my team, the Montecito Fire Department personnel who helped prep the area, the dogs from the Institute of Canine Forensics, their handlers, the new scientific efforts of the UCSB Anthropology team, the students, and the neighbors who gave us access to their property. I continually witnessed the best in humanity; each person working to do his or her part to help find our children.

During this search, COVID and social distancing hit; thus, we had to wear masks and keep six feet away from one another. I wanted to hug each person who helped, but for now it had to be an elbow bump or an air hug.

Despite COVID shutdowns, the professor continued her efforts by engaging with other university scientists to gather data on the flow. Her team also designed a tissue decomposition study using locally sourced pig remains to better understand how soil composition and chemistry were affected by decays, so that work was in place to continue the science related to the search.

The professor updated our team on the methods they were using. They were curing the soil samples, and in five months they'd be able to compare over 100 soil samples with soil contents of a proxy. This would help them understand in which area the team should proceed with a careful archeological dig. As she gave us the update, she told us about the forensic work at Fresh Kills Landfill, one of the sites used as a sorting ground for the debris and miniscule human bone fragments from September 11, 2001, when planes had crashed into New York City's Twin Towers and into the Pentagon. She recalled that the largest piece of human bone found at the Pentagon crash site was about a six-inch piece of femur. She told our team this example as an analogy: she felt that the force of the mudslide and being caught in one of the swirling eddies was akin to a plane crash. Jack, she felt, must have gotten caught in an eddy, and his body may have been pushed down by the force; that was why we had not yet recovered him, unlike the other victims. At this point, we had to patiently wait until the soil was cured and ready for examination.

CHAPTER 32

CONSISTENTLY CLEAR MESSAGES AND COVID LOCKDOWN

I CONTINUED to look for my son's remains, and I'd met several intuitives who were trying to help find Jack's location and provide me peace. From the readings or messages, I understood that Dave and Jack were alive and well in a space we just couldn't see. Catherine did a few writings for me. She had been a communications major at UC Santa Barbara years ago, and admitted her surprise when, in her late twenties, she learned she had a unique communication ability. Nearing the three-year anniversary of the tragedy, Catherine called to ask if I wanted a writing done. She would write what she heard, and then read it back to me. At this point, I was not interested in another reading, but I did go through prior writings to see some of the key messages. Through them all, Jack was definite that he would be found.

Some of the readings I re-read said:

May 2018

Me: "Are you near the white house?"

Jack: "I don't know."

Me: "Are you near the tennis courts?"

Jack: "I don't know. I was bending over, then BAM, I was hit. I tried to understand what was happening to me, but BAM, I was picking it (computer) up. I had everything on it . . . shorted out."

Me: "Is there anything you see around your body?"

Jack: "It's like God covered me. I'm trying, but I don't know where because I don't see with eyes like you. I didn't go far, I know that."

August 2018

Jack: "I'm still trying to let you know. Don't worry. I will turn up eventually. I wish I could make it happen, but it doesn't work like that. I'm sorry. I'm not able to know where that shell is now. It's not me, Mom. It's a shell."

September 2018

9/10 Jack: "Soon now Mom — Pieces of me returned to you, I love you, I'm trying my best."

December 2018

Jack: "I never want to be a martyr of the missing or a poster image for the lost but not forgotten. I will be found by my heart, the me God created never died. Just the shell I was borrowing. Now I see when I am and can be a source for touchpoints that light up in people. Love — touchpoints, beautiful, the full color spectrum that reaches in all directions. I'd rather be a touchpoint hero to inspire others to love and be closer."

January 2020
Jack: "I know I will be found. I know it—but it's taking so much earth time. I don't know where I am. I can't see the old me anymore because that is not me. I'm me... I wish I could help, like "X" marks the spot. For you it is only "Y." I don't know my location, or I'd tell you so you could grab a shovel and go... I will be found, Mom. Don't let them tell you that I got scooped and dumped. I know I didn't. I can't tell you where the body is buried, but it's not gone. And it's in God's time and we don't have to like it. I will be found."

I was fascinated by the multiple times Jack said he would be found, almost in a matter-of-fact sort of way. I believed him. These messages, along with the clues along the way, became the needed push that enabled me to persist in searching for Jack, and to be open to the various clues and discoveries. I was willing to pull on the thread of something so unknown to me, and to be open to the possibility of how it may help us in the search.

Life moved forward.

Lauren was a rising senior in high school, and the COVID pandemic was sweeping the globe, locking us in our homes. We only would venture out with face masks and hand sanitizer to help mitigate the chance of getting the virus. It was a challenging and isolating time. The world was suffering, and so many people were dying from this highly contagious virus. My daughter, along with most of the rest of the students worldwide, could not go to school. The isolation of being at home with only a Zoom call for class made the entire year and a half feel fearful and lonely. A couple times a week, Lauren and I would go for a walk along the beach or in the neighborhood. Sometimes to quell the boredom, Lauren would bring out the bag of tiles of the Bananagrams game. As we played, we conversed about how we were doing. Lauren always won.

"Lauren! You keep beating me. You're so good at this game," I said once, about 30 minutes into our game time together.

"It's because you never start over during the game with your tiles. You don't try to make new words once you make your initial words," she said.

"Yep, you're right. You scrap the tile-build you made mid-game, and start over making all new words; and you win. You are more strategic than me with this game," I said.

A confident smile formed, and then she responded coyly, "I know."

After we lost Dave and Jack, Lauren needed a friend or two to stay over with her most of the time. The distraction of having friends over helped her to not feel alone. I liked that she enjoyed that, but it also meant a house filled with different people, and made me less able to grieve openly. However, the COVID lockdown made it so that it was just the two of us. We slowed down our pace, and we each had more time to grieve. We adjusted to being a two-person household with two goofy and affectionate doodle pups. I also felt frustrated that COVID slowed our search. To me, it was like one massive test of patience. Patience while searching for my son's remains, then even more patience when COVID lockdowns delayed the search efforts. I'm not a naturally patient person, but I was forced to be patient. I worried that the effort to look for Jack and Lydia was waning. And with each day in the elements, the potential of finding less degraded remains was drastically diminishing.

Lauren filled out her college applications, wrote her college essays, searched online for colleges to visit once they opened again, and secured letters of recommendation. The process was unbelievably daunting. Also, while hunkering down at home, Lauren and I lifted out my sewing machine from its storage box. We placed it on a small table, and started sewing face masks to donate to first responders during the shortages. This was something we both enjoyed doing together, and it felt good to try to help.

Like everyone else, the UC Santa Barbara team was impacted by the COVID lockdown. The professor worked remotely from the East Coast, and her students took classes remotely. As places started to open and vaccines became available, the team's efforts nudged forward in the search. Behind the scenes, the forensic anthropology team reviewed coroner reports, assessed the flow patterns in Montecito, and cured soil samples in a freezer so they could test them for any essence of Jack or Lydia's physical remains. They applied a space-age-looking device to detect an item's elemental composition — a phaser-type gun called a portable X-ray fluorescence spectrometer. This device could, when pointed at a chocolate chip cookie, for instance, tell exactly how much flour, sugar, vanilla, and butter was in it. If pointed at fish in the market, this device could detect the mercury levels in the fish's flesh. Used in soil or an item that they assessed might be bone, it could reveal the chemical composition that might align with elements found in human remains. This $50,000 piece of equipment was instrumental in the progress of the search.

At their lab 20 minutes away, they used high-tech scientific technology, including X-ray fluorescence, fluoride ion selective electrode dating, standard and polarized microscopy, and forensic biogeochemistry. In addition, they used spectrometric and spectroscopic approaches. When I learned this, I became more hopeful that we'd find Jack's remains.

During a team update, the professor shared some somber news. We had asked her about her assessment regarding the missing two-year-old. She announced that children her age had bone that was more like soft cartilage rather than hard calcium. As a result, Lydia's remains, she believed, would have become "one" with the earth, decomposing at a much faster rate than an adult or teen. This upset all of us. The professor met with the toddler's mother to deliver this sad news. I learned that based on her beliefs, the news may have given her some peace.

As to leading the search effort, I started to take a back seat and trusted the university team to lead with their science. That was a big shift for me, and one that I needed. It was now over three years since I had lost my son and husband. Lauren and I tried to lead as normal a life as we could, without them.

One day in April, I opened a letter from the county. A similar letter had been sent to all the property owners in my neighborhood, to notify us that in a month, the county would tear up the median close to our properties to replace the damaged storm drains from the mudslide. It was a courteous and informative update for most, but it triggered me to spring into action. I wanted to ensure that the workers who'd be tearing up the median — the same median where I had been found — would be extra cautious in their repair efforts, and look for potential human remains.

Once home, I called the county office and spoke to the person who authored the letter. I explained that the university team was assisting in the search, and we needed all workers to be aware of the potential of human remains, and that student spotters would be on-site. The county team was very responsive, and said they'd let us know when the work was scheduled to take place. They were targeting just a few weeks from now, in May.

CHAPTER 33

MEMORIAL DAYS

FITTINGLY ENOUGH, around Memorial Day 2021 was when we'd discover something important in the search. And it had been on Memorial Day weekend 2020 that Jay and Jenn drove from Arizona to point out where Jay thought catchment areas could have built up.

Summer 2020 was quiet and lonelier with the shutdown affecting the world. We kept up with our counseling appointments, but they had converted to Zoom meetings, which were not the same. With the shutdown, psychologists and mental health professionals were in even more demand and sadly one of Lauren's trusted counselors moved away. Despite the counselor giving us advance notice, Lauren and I felt abandoned. I wondered when life would let us catch a break.

Lauren took ownership of ordering the vegetables, eggs, and fruit that would be delivered weekly to our front door. This service helped reduce time at a crowded grocery store, and the chance of contracting the virus. Summer meant more focus on college applications, and Lauren worked diligently on them. At her young age, she had no idea what she wanted to major in. Psychology seemed interesting, and she liked the schools that did not require an incoming freshman to immediately declare a major. As fall approached, we learned that her senior year would start out remotely with classes on Zoom. I told her that the school may return to normal once the vaccine was readily available. I reminded her that indeed this situation was not ideal, but at least she was not a senior the year before, as sadly those students missed graduation and all the traditions of senior year, including homecoming and prom. Scrambling for a positive spin, I also told Lauren that she'd have great stories to tell her grandchildren one day about living through a global pandemic. I also realized that she needed to vent.

Soon senior year was in full swing. By October, Lauren had hit the "send" button for all of her college applications. It was now wait and see; a vulnerable time for many teens. It was daunting for Lauren to put herself out into the world in such a way, and wonder who may or may not accept her application.

That November, Jack would have been twenty years old. I couldn't help but think about what his life would have been like. He would have been in college, with new friends and a chosen major. I was angry that my son had lost out on 60 or more years of living.

Around that time, Lauren started to complain of toothaches, and I realized that I needed to schedule an appointment to get her wisdom teeth extracted. Ouch. Like most teens, she was not looking forward to it, but after years of wearing braces, she knew she couldn't wait any longer. The wisdom teeth were trying to emerge, and they would move the other teeth that had been straightened. Lauren told me that she remembered Jack lying on the couch after his wisdom teeth extraction. As she said this, I recalled that Jack, still groggy with the painkillers, shook each of the nurses' and doctor's hands as he thanked them before we left.

The day of Lauren's extraction, she came home afterward and diligently iced her cheeks, then rested in her room. At 4:00 p.m., I asked

Lauren if she would come out to the kitchen with me near the computer. She was unaware that her top choice university, Stanford, was emailing out early decision notices in a half hour. She had thought the announcements were coming the following Monday. Groggily, Lauren walked into the kitchen, her face puffy. As she hit the "click here" button on the site, a cascade of digital confetti appeared on the computer screen.

"Lauren! You got accepted!" I exclaimed.

She was stunned. She was overjoyed.

With a gauze-in-mouth muffled voice, she quickly called a few people to tell them her happy news. One of her first calls was to Andy, her Montecito Fire Department rescuer. He was overjoyed for her. It was a happy afternoon, and I was glad to see that all of Lauren's hard work had paid off with an acceptance from her dream school. That afternoon, I had a hopeful feeling that I had not felt in a long, long time. The idea of Lauren attending her dream school gave me hope for happiness in her future. That early decision also let her relax a bit and enjoy the rest of senior year.

By late March 2021, as the new quarter started, we got the good news that the kids could return to in-person classes. I knew this would be good for Lauren, as she was energized by being around people. To my surprise, she signed up for a class on small-scale gardening. Although she did not enjoy the early 7:00 a.m. start time, she flourished learning about gardening and working in the soil. Due to COVID protocols, the class had the students make their gardens in their yards at home instead of using the school's raised garden bed area. I watched Lauren bent over tending her garden, her hands immersed as she worked in the soil. She was breathing the same smell she'd endured smelling when buried alive, yet now she was setting the stage for pea seedlings to grow. This was progress, indeed. I realized that I was more present in the moment, observing how my baby girl was doing. Before, when I had a big job, a full family, and a house to manage, I was distracted by trying to keep all the balls in the air. Today, as I looked from my window down at Lauren gardening, I appreciated being witness to progress in my daughter's healing.

Before I knew it, it was coming up on Memorial Day 2021. Thinking back on the past two holidays, I was curious what this Memorial Day might have in store for us, as it related to the ongoing but slowed search for Jack's remains. At times with the search, there would be periods of slowness, and other times it felt as if in some way the energy was moving again, advancing us forward. This energy-moving time revealed itself in new communications that folks sent to me, new or scheduled city efforts clearing areas, or simply advances with the university team's effort. As in each year prior, I prayed this year would be the year we'd find Jack.

Randomly, a couple weeks earlier, a dear friend called excitedly to tell me about an intuitive she'd met with, who she found was "spot on" in what she'd sensed. I was thrilled for her, but by this time, I felt that I didn't need any more intuitives in my life. My friend was so enthused about this person's talent, she suggested that I call her to see if she could help with locating Jack's remains. Somewhat hesitant, and skeptical that this would lead me anywhere new, regardless, I placed the call. Based on her insights, I asked if she would walk around the debris flow area with me.

In late April 2021, I met LeAnn on a corner near my damaged lot. She was how my friend described her.

As we walked, she told me her thoughts. "He's in four different areas," she said.

If I had heard that description right after he was lost, I would have collapsed.

Over three and a half years later, I still felt the gaping emptiness and sadness about losing my son, knowing that his body had been most likely hit by boulders, and that he'd suffered unimaginable pain while being taken down in the mud. Now, however, I was able to hear this, and not be incapacitated by grief. We had searched for so long, thinking many times that we might have found Jack's remains, and were disappointed each time. Maybe his remains *were* in different areas, and this could be the clue Catherine had received early on about an archipelago. Maybe that clue about a "scattering of like things" referred to Jack's bones.

"Yellow, Kim, is important," LeAnn said, as we walked along the edge of the creek. I never mentioned to her anything about where search dogs had alerted before, or even areas where the team had found our items. I was trying to be as neutral as possible as she walked the area with me. By a bridge, we had a good view of the sidewall of the now-dry creek. Yellow wildflowers, like canyon sunflowers, were growing in the area where the Halloween costume had been found.

Walking further, we came across a debris pile near an embankment that was a mixture of boulders and dirt. The pile had an array of yellow and white wildflowers all over it.

"There is something here," the intuitive said matter-of-factly. She added, "It is probably part of an arm."

In other locations during our walk, I was astounded that she identified the areas where the dogs had alerted and where we had had found items. After walking with LeAnn, I immediately called Catherine to ask whether she could also walk by the same debris piles and embankment. I hoped Catherine would sense something there, as well. Catherine, ever gracious, agreed to come walk the area. As she walked near the debris piles that were covered with wildflowers, she heard, *I will be found . . . pieces of me.* Although when we were out walking the search areas, Jack often said, "I will be found," this was the first time he had said, "pieces of me."

I felt as if the search was moving forward again. I had a new area to investigate based on the intuitives' messages.

Sitting on a boulder nearby, I reflected on our efforts thus far.

Since Jack and Dave had been killed, I had met with half a dozen people with intuitive abilities. I was looking for my son's remains in what felt like an impossible mission. I was open to anything that could help us. We had implemented all the science possible, via UC Santa Barbara's world-renowned anthropology lab. The professor who led our effort was a global expert on human remains identification and analysis, and had just written a book, *The Bioarchaeology of Disaster: How Catastrophes Change Our Skeletons*. I had rented a ground-penetrating radar device from Canada, although that hadn't helped. Also, highly trained search and recovery canines had been deployed over the area, logging over two thousand hours of canine and handler searching. I had walked almost every inch of the flow path from my house, climbed down into a dry creek bed, poked into hillsides, requested property owners' permission to search their lots, and had spotted large excavators as boulders, debris, and tons of dirt were moved. I had driven 45 miles to check out a hauled-away debris pile located on a private ranch. In conversations with local workers, I learned of other piles on private ranches where mud and debris had not been checked, and had already been hauled away. It was a stunning realization of the lack of documented coordinated effort while clearing, despite two beautiful children who'd gone missing in this very area. It was outrageous.

Around the same time, I received my first COVID vaccine. The COVID lockdown was slowly lifting for our town and the world.

Looking at my calendar in my office, I noted that the following week was the scheduled storm drain repair at the triangular median. I had this marked on my calendar so I could meet with the crew and invite the university team to observe the excavation. For this repair, the workers requested I wear a high-visibility vest and hard hat as a safety measure, so I went to the hardware store to get these items.

On May 11th, I pulled up in my car around 8:00 a.m. and parked by my damaged lot. Two construction workers were standing in the middle of the median talking. I thought, *Great! I'll park, introduce myself, and let them know the team from UCSB will be here to spot while they excavate.*

I did think it strange to see only two workers, though. I wondered where the big earth-moving excavators were. I approached the two workers and introduced myself.

They told me, "Kim, we are only *planning* the work today. The excavation starts in two days, *not* today."

"Oh no!" I exclaimed.

In the distance, Professor Kurin and a couple students walked toward us with buckets of equipment. One of the students had driven over 90 minutes from Los Angeles to help spot.

My heart sank.

I was so grateful for these university helpers, and now I feared that I had wasted their valuable time. Frustration filled me. Coordinating the activities and relying on what the planners told me about the scheduled work wasn't easy, or always reliable.

I had to pivot.

I wanted these university experts and resources to be utilized today. I immediately thought about that yellow-flowered debris pile; the one where Catherine had heard Jack say, "I will be found . . . pieces of me," and LeAnn had said, "There is something there."

"Professor Kurin," I asked, "would you guys work that one debris pile while you're in Montecito today? I have a feeling that it may not have been properly searched."

"Of course!" she said, and off they went.

I called Rick to check his availability, and whether his search dog MacGyver could come sniff while the students dug through the debris. "I'll be out of town, but let me call Shirley to see if she can come out from Burbank tomorrow with her dog Keegan."

"Great, thank you!" Knowing that the anthropology team was working the debris pile, I headed home.

Once home, Rick called to tell me Shirley would make the drive in the next few days to have Keegan sniff the debris pile. I was happy that things were coming together, despite the unexpected snafu regarding the date to dig up the median wells.

In the afternoon, I ran to pick up my pups from their daycare play place, and thought about what I'd make Lauren for dinner. Lauren loved a chicken dish with artichoke hearts, olives, chickpeas, and turmeric that I made in a cast iron pot; as it simmered, the ingredients blended. As I opened the can of chickpeas, a text rang out on my phone. Hands messy from food preparation, I saw that it was Professor Kurin, texting an update on their day. I washed my hands so I could call her back.

"Hi Danielle, how was your day?"

"Hey Kim, it was good." She paused, took a deep breath, and said, "We found bone."

In disbelief, I grabbed a chair in my kitchen, and listened intensely.

We'd been looking for over three years. "Do you think it's Jack? What size, what bone?" My mind was racing.

"I'm confident it is bone. They are small pieces," she softly informed me.

After waiting so long, I was cautiously hopeful that we had found what we'd been looking for. My heart broke to learn that part of Jack's remains were in little pieces, which indicated that he had suffered a traumatic and violent death. Although I knew that this was probably the case, hearing about "small pieces of bone" hit me hard.

After I hung up, I scrolled through my phone contact list and found the sheriff's cell phone number. When he answered, I told him the university team had found bone, and asked what I needed to do with his office for next steps. He said that in the morning, a detective would ring me to bring in the bones, and he would take a DNA swab from me. I wanted the bones treated with great care, as they might be all I had left of my son. He assured me they would be handled with care. I asked the professor to bring me the bones, so I could comply with the sheriff's direction.

That evening, I told Lauren about the findings. I wanted to protect her from sad news, but believed that she should know the truth. I always prefaced any discussion with her regarding Jack by asking, "Lauren, do you want to know about where we are in the search? Do you want to hear the details?" She always wanted to be kept informed. Hearing this news, she recognized the magnitude of their finding part of Jack's remains. Sadness emanated from her, and her eyes expressed grief. With her trauma, her brain had trained itself to hold too much of the grief inside. In a few moments, she took a breath, and I sensed that she was mentally trying to compartmentalize it all.

I wanted to regulate my emotions until we received the analysis. I experienced a mix of emotions, including relief and profound sadness. Anger resurfaced when I thought again about how I had lost him far too soon. My mind raced. I wanted to know who made the final evacuation decisions, and why the town was not evacuated down to the freeway, as I understood the Fire Chiefs had advised. I thought about how Jack lost his future experiences with college, dating, marriage, children, career, vacations, everything. I would miss those milestones with him. I knew that the loss and grief would reappear for me during all of the milestones in my life, like Lauren's graduation, or moving her into the dorms, or her finding a life partner, marrying, and perhaps having children of her own. Then I felt overwhelming gratitude to those who had helped in searching for Jack. Everything was being stirred up in me, at a time when I was trying to keep calm and get the analysis.

Shirley, the search and rescue handler, and her dog Keegan, came to work in the target area. Keegan stopped chewing on some tall grass and officially started to work. She then immediately alerted the pile that was covered in yellow and white wildflowers. Keegan continued

Search dog Keegan alerting to human remains on the pile

to alert the pile throughout that morning, even when she was taken away and brought back from a different direction, which meant that she could smell human remains. I believed that the professor and the students had found pieces of Jack's skeleton, and possibly might find more, and/or important artifacts, as they continued to dig.

The university team meticulously and carefully dug through the pile with tiny brushes. Keegan had accurately identified a few more bone fragments by alerting to the scent of human remains, as more bone was found in the debris.

I had known from the beginning that Jack did not flow out to the ocean. I somehow knew that he was still on land. I had thought that if I knew he had been buried by the creek under a canopy of majestic coastal live oaks, I could live with that. Or, if Jack had gone to sea, that would also be a beautiful final resting place.

But I couldn't bear the thought that his remains might be under a debris pile among twisted chain link fences, carpet remnants, and shower tiles; or worse, in the elements where animals could get to them. That was totally unacceptable to me.

Sadly, we found parts of Jack in such a pile.

The search team had also found a piece of his cotton underwear near a broken pale-yellow tile from his bathroom shower. The bones were found around carpet fragments from our home. Per the archeological dig process, I'd have to wait for the experts' final reports that would come after the debris pile had been meticulously searched. It was very slow, methodical work. The discovery of Jack's remains occurred around Memorial Day, 2021.

The university team carefully dug through the piles, following appropriate protocols. One evening, a student came to my door to drop off a bouquet of flowers that they had collected from the top of the debris pile. Her message was, *Life finds a way*. This pile was unique in that it was covered in glorious yellow and white flowers. To myself, I thought, *Love found a way*.

It was a kind gesture from the university team.

I felt pensive apprehension as the days progressed, and I looked forward to hearing the research team's final assessments as they prepared their report. It was yet another test of my patience, which continued to be a lesson I had to learn since the mudslide.

This period occurred during the end of Lauren's senior year. I was determined to make my brain switch gears to engage happily and fully in her end-of-year milestone events. I felt like an air-filled beach ball, pushed down into the deep end of a pool. Like a ball that wanted to burst out of the water exploding high in the air, but unable to because a restraining hand was holding it down. I had to wait longer to learn it if was truly our miraculous and tragic find.

Yellow flowers covering the debris pile
where some bone was found

Despite our miraculous discovery, routine town activities continued as planned. In June, I received a letter from the Montecito Fire Department. I read about "weed abatement and fire prevention safety," along with a specific notice to me regarding my damaged property. A fire department inspector determined that my lot needed some weed clearing to be compliant with fire season. *Weird, I thought. I had just had a lot of weeds whacked three weeks ago, but I guess more weeds sprouted up.* This was a distracting task during a time when I was holding my breath, as the professor and her team continued to dig through the debris pile in hopes of finding more remains of my son.

Yellow flowers from Jack's pile were given to Kim from a few of the student volunteers.

Typically, I only checked my PO box every other week, and thus the weed abatement request letter was dated almost two weeks ago. The letter said that the following day, my property would be inspected again to ensure compliance with fire prevention guidelines.

Tomorrow! Yikes!

I quickly called my gardener to ask if he could clear the lot before the next day's re-inspection. He could, so I drove over to unlock the gate for him. As I was pulling out of the lane, I realized that not only my lot, but all areas in Montecito were being inspected and cleared, including the debris piles where Jack's remains were being recovered.

Oh no!

This was the moment where I stopped holding it together, and almost fell apart. I went from zero to eighty miles per hour in my mind.

I urgently called the fire captain listed in the letter, and frantically asked him whether the other mudslide areas were going to be cleared. He responded, "Yes, all areas are being inspected." My voice trembled and my emotions were unmanageable. I blurted out, "There is one area you cannot touch; I want no one to touch it!"

I tried to explain, but I lost my composure and started sobbing uncontrollably.

"You have to come to me right now and I'll explain!" I implored. I can't imagine what the fire captain thought, hearing someone so upset about a weed abatement letter.

The captain agreed to meet me where I sat in my car, not far from my damaged lot. Feeling desperate and impatient, I called the main line of the Montecito Fire Department and told the receptionist, "I need Andy, Ben, Jeff, Garet, or Kevin to meet me right now — it's about Jack." I rattled off the names of the firefighters whom I knew, who had rescued Lauren and me. At that moment, I needed help from familiar faces and people I trusted, and who knew my history. I was terrified that a landscaping crew would clear and haul away the very debris pile that might hold more remains of my son.

"Kim, those guys aren't working today, but a captain is on his way now," the receptionist said as she tried to comfort me. I hung up the phone and waited on the side of the road near the creek, then I frantically called Allison, who lived nearby.

"Allison!" I choked out between sobs. "I need you now! Please come."

"Sure, where are you, honey? I'm on my way," she reassured me.

Allison delayed taking her daughter to volleyball practice. She dropped everything she was doing and ran out her front door, turned the corner onto the street, and ran toward me.

A few minutes later, the fire trucks drove down the road. As they parked, I saw Allison sprinting toward me. Her warm, kindhearted energy and her knowledge of the history of our search effort gave me comfort.

Three years of grief and agony were welling up in me, preventing me from answering the questions the firefighters were asking. Allison told them why I was upset, and I handed her my phone so she could put in the captain's cell number if I needed it. My hands were trembling. I could not see straight.

"I don't want any weed clearing or anything touched in this area until the team finishes in two weeks," I managed to communicate between sobs.

"Well, Mrs. Cantin, what if we cleared weeds, but did not remove any dirt from the pile?" the captain innocently asked.

His question agitated me so much that I blurted out, "NOTHING! Please, please, keep everyone away! I can't have ANYTHING touched!"

At this point, I was ready to throw my body on the pile to protect as much of it as possible. I needed to ensure that no one went near this area.

"Okay, sure, Mrs. Cantin. We'll tape off this area and place pylons around it with a sign that says, 'Do not touch or move anything.' We'll list the fire department's contact information, if anyone has questions. Will that work for you?" the captain asked.

"Yes, perfect, thank you so much," I replied, beginning to calm down.

They taped off the area, and left signage so the landscape crews would not clear the area.

After I had released some of my stored-up emotions, I felt a bit better. I was so grateful to the Montecito Fire Department team, and to Allison.

The discovery of Jack's remains came just as Lauren was about to go off to college. Lauren would see her brother laid to rest, and I hoped she could have some closure and peace that her brother had been found. Even so, it was horrifying to learn that he had suffered in his death, and I knew it would be difficult for her to leave home and adjust to this knowledge.

I started planning a graveside burial for the distant future when our family would be in town. My sister and brother-in-law would be flying in from Europe. I drove to the cemetery to secure a date for Jack's burial, and to give them a copy of Jack's death certificate. I wanted to have the ceremony before Lauren left for college, so we could grieve and mourn together.

I had hoped to feel some closure once Jack's remains were found. For me, it would be a relief, to know that a part of him was properly laid to rest next to his father. I'd have a place to go, where I could visit and know where some of his remains were. I had tried my best for my son. A burial would help me accept even these few bones as enough. And it would help me heal in my grief journey a little more. I sensed that after the burial I would not feel compelled to search anymore. It was my hoped-for element of closure.

The students who had found Jack's remains shared how meaningful this project was for them. They had been learning about anthropology, and now they had helped find my missing son, and Lauren's brother. The professor shared with me that when they first discovered a bone, the students all teared up, knowing it was my son. These students were not lacking in compassion, they understood the importance of what they had discovered. It was a miracle that they had found even a small part of Jack.

Many others before them had simply resigned themselves to believing Jack had been swept into the ocean. That was the convenient belief for them. Later, I read in the professor's 50-page final report that based on their assessment, it was highly unlikely Jack would have ever made it to the ocean. This was concluded because of the location and dispersal of personal items from his room and the house, and because he was inside the house when the disaster hit, which slowed movement as the house was being torn apart. My husband, who was outside when the flow hit, was found at the beach, but he didn't have any water in his lungs. A research team checked that the flow hit at low tide, which made it less likely that *anyone* would go out to sea. Another victim was recovered on the beach, as well.

A few weeks later, our core team joined the call with the professor. Her extensive report documented the analysis, science, and various technologies used. She had deployed anthroscopic, microscopic, and biogeochemical testing on the fragments, and found them to be likely human bone. A renowned expert globally known for her analysis of human skeletons, I knew she was the right expert for the job. During her analysis, she conferred with other experts for their assessments, to ensure that she accessed all the resources available to analyze the findings. In the presentation, she shared carpet remnants from my house that the bones were found among. The carpet worked almost like netting, collecting and holding some of the bones. The pieces were small, and had been buried in acidic soil that included arsenic, lead, and other toxins that came from garages and home contents that had been washed away. She referred to the soil from the mudslide as a "chemical soup." She surmised that the toxic soil leached the collagen from the bones, leaving behind dry, brittle calcified elements. In such conditions, the professor was not convinced that DNA analysis would yield a conclusive result, but even if it did, the bone fragment would be destroyed in the process. These were bones I'd spent over three years searching for.

During this time, the professor reached out to global experts to get their opinions on DNA technology options, and she was in communication with the detective and coroner at the sheriff's department. My goal was to preserve Jack's remains so I could bury them next to his father's. The professor was able to determine that one bone was diagnostic in nature, in that it had a growth plate from someone who was 17 to 18 years old. Jack was 17. She could also deduce that the remains belonged to someone with a height between 5'9" to 6'1". Jack was 5'11". She did chemical analysis to confirm that the bones were not ancient remains, but those from a recent event. No other person lost in the mudslide had been around 17 years old, and 5'11". When she finished presenting her analysis, she determined, "Based on a reasonable degree of scientific certainty, there is a preponderance of evidence that the human remains, and associated artifacts are consistent with those of Jack Cantin." She went on to say, "With 90% certainty, the remains are those of Jack Cantin."

Almost 1,300 days had passed since the mudslide. Thirteen hundred days of being made to wait, facing delays and continuing to follow various threads with various resources and efforts to finally get something found. I felt an odd sort of relief, mingled with my sadness at the finality of knowing that Jack was gone forever.

CHAPTER 34

MIRACULOUS

AS NOTED, the professor's extensive report concluded that the remains were most probably Jack's. My son, in pieces. This was a heartbreaking tragedy. I thanked the team for finding him, and knew I'd be forever grateful to each of them.

Back at home, I sat in my bedroom chair and just breathed. The enormity of finding Jack, the sorrow I felt, and the relief I experienced in response to finding part of my son, was almost too much for me to handle. Now I could bury him with dignity.

Later that day, when I was at the mortuary, I realized that over three years ago in 2018, my friend Stacey had helped me pick out a casket for Dave. I remember how surreal it was to choose a casket in which to bury him. At that time, I was also recovering from the physical trauma I had experienced in the mudslide, which made even climbing three steps to the casket showroom a daunting effort. Now, I had physically healed, and was able to walk in unassisted. This time, I went alone. I wanted privacy and quiet as I processed the magnitude of our loss.

I selected the same casket model that I had bought for Dave, and I thought about what we could place in the casket along with Jack's remains. After dinner, when Lauren was still in the kitchen chatting with me, I asked, "Lauren, is there anything special you'd like to put in the casket for Jack?"

Saying nothing for a few moments, she pondered the question thoughtfully.

"I want to put in the Stitch plush toy, and I know we are putting in the lightsaber," she said.

"Sounds perfect," I said. As I started to load the dishwasher, I continued, "Lauren, I'm going to ask some of Jack's friends if they'd like to write a little note to Jack to tuck in the casket as well. If you feel you want to write a note, just let me know, and we can add that too if you'd like."

"I'll think about it." She grabbed her notebook and headed to her room to start her homework.

She had told me that she often felt numb about it all. I worried and wondered when the numbness might wear off. And when it did, would she have the support to get through it all? Someone told me that the mind can only handle so much at each developmental stage. She was only 14 when this happened to her. Now, it was three years later.

This must be so tough on her, I thought.

I planned to have his remains wrapped in a quilt I had made that had a heart silhouette of our family. Last, I would include an orange crocheted throw that his grandmother had made for him. She had asked it to be laid by his feet; sadly, the condition of Jack's few remains would not allow us that much specificity, but the throw made with love and tears would go in.

We still had to await the sheriff's procedures and processes, including an amended death certificate from "missing" to a cause of death such as "blunt force trauma." With an amended death certificate, I would be able to finally secure a burial permit.

One afternoon, I looked through some of Catherine's clues from 2018 and 2019. She was getting messages and writing them down as early as three days after the mudslide—before I even knew her.

On January 12, 2018, Catherine's clues included:

Fractured femur
Appendages found
Pieces of me

In 2019: "*Look for a foot bone that could be mistaken for a rock*"

In May 2021, the bones found included:

One fractured femur
Toe bone. (An appendage)
Ankle bone that indeed looked like a rock
"Pieces" were found

I heard from community members and from members of the fire department that everyone was relieved and grateful that Jack had been found. A first responder shared that healing could begin, once the news of Jack's remains began to circulate. The mudslide was a community tragedy, and the community healed a little bit more after Jack was found. The journey involved a combination of science, methodical search, tenacity, technology, compassionate helpers, and at times, following the thread of intuitive clues that got us to the needle-in-a-haystack discovery.

No one thing was the answer. Just as the tragedy was a community tragedy, the search was a community search. It involved members of the community, neighbors who had become friends, and volunteers from the local university, as well as first responders and those with communication abilities much greater than my own. Being open, aware, and receptive to how help was being offered made the difference.

PART 5
CRACKED OPEN

"Changes"
—David Bowie

CHAPTER 35

WHISPERS

THE PAST THREE and a half years had been grueling and painful. Like others who have endured loss and tragedy, I noticed and questioned the coincidences that had occurred during our search for Jack. "Whispers" was the word I used for interesting events or occurrences that made me wonder if they were hints or a foretelling of things to come.

In late November 2017, I had had an overwhelming sense that I needed to have a family portrait taken. Thinking back on those family photos, I am so glad that we had our pictures taken because weeks later, Dave, Jack, and Chester were killed in the mudslide. I wonder whether something in the universe gave me a nudge. Whatever it was, I am forever grateful that I have pictures of my family together.

The open space near the trail had a special place in my heart as I remembered the happy times we had while taking our family photos. Two years after the mudslide, I asked my friend who photographed us to walk me to where she had taken our family pictures. Her husband offered to show me the locations, since she was working that day.

We strolled the path to the area where she had taken our pictures on the boulders, and then to the location of the downed tree.

I shook my head in disbelief. Remarkably, this was the same area where the cadaver search dogs had alerted in the search for my son's remains, and where we found the "Dave" train engine. It was also the location where Lauren's teacher's aide shared that she had experienced a weird feeling by a tree with a big burl at the base of the trunk; and where intuitive Suzanne sensed something.

These coincidences felt connected.

And I know that some people believe that in life, there are no coincidences.

A few months before he was killed, Dave had scheduled an appointment with our home insurance broker to update our homeowners, life, and auto insurance. I learned later that some other victims had, as well.

The summer before Dave died, he fell in the driveway as he missed his footing on a cement step while chatting with our gardener. He had fallen on his wedding ring finger — the same one he'd broken in baseball as a youth. His finger swelled dangerously while on a business flight, and upon landing, he drove himself to the nearest urgent care. The only option was to cut off his wedding ring. He brought back the pieces of his engraved wedding ring and we tucked it away in a drawer; I had hoped one day to make it into another piece of jewelry I could wear. Three months later, Dave mentioned that he'd had a vivid dream the night before of his late brother, Michael. In the dream, Dave's brother told him to replace the wedding ring. Dave illustrated how his brother pointed to Dave's ring finger, firmly telling him to "Get it replaced!"

After Dave told me about his dream, he said, "Kim, I know we don't feel financially flush right now, but I think we need to replace my wedding ring." Dave had never shared any details about his dreams during our 20-year marriage, except for this one. Later that day, we drove to the jewelry store to order an exact replica of his damaged wedding ring. We had the same inscription inserted inside it: "Eternal Love," along with the date of our wedding. We had the same inscription engraved inside both of our wedding rings.

After the mudslide, I'd realized what a gift Dave's dream had been, because the ring is one of the two belongings that I have from Dave.

It was while I was in the hospital healing from my injuries that the sheriff's officer who told me about Dave's death visited my room to give me a plastic bag with Dave's replacement wedding ring inside. I wear Dave's wedding ring on a necklace when I want to feel closer to him. It is symbolic of our everlasting love, and I am reminded of the vivid dream he had that prompted him to get a replacement.

Eighteen months after Jack died, Lauren and I were invited to the middle school that she and her brother had attended. The administrators invited the high school seniors as a mini-reunion. The headmaster handed each student an envelope that was meant to be a time capsule of papers, poems, fun quizzes, and work that each student had collected for themselves three years ago, when they were in middle school. They had gathered these important artifacts and sealed the envelope with their name attached. Lauren and I were invited to receive Jack's time capsule envelope. Among the items in the envelope was a poem Jack had selected. He'd read this poem, his favorite, in his world history class in 9th grade. It's titled "Flowers" and is from *The Dhammapada: The Sayings of the Buddha*. An excerpt spoke to me and his sister:

> Death overtakes the man
> Who gathers flowers
> When with distracted mind and thirsty senses
> He searches in vain for happiness
> In the pleasures of the world.
> Death fetches him away
> As a flood carries off a sleeping village.
> Death overcomes him . . . .

When I read the poem Jack had chosen, I couldn't help but see a similarity in how he died. A flood *had* carried off our sleeping village. It hit around 3:30 a.m., when most of us were asleep. It killed 23 people and injured over 150 more. And death had fetched Jack away.

It was remarkable that Jack had chosen a poem that later echoed how he had died.

I recalled a woman's words that were shared with me a year before the tragedy. I had strolled into a local store in town that had spiritual books and artifacts. I was looking for a set of Tibetan brass bell chimes to give Jack as a graduation gift. Many of his middle school trip campfires began with the headmaster using these bells to chime once, which worked effectively and serenely to quiet the group down and get them ready for a meaningful campfire discussion. While at the store, I saw that they had a person doing readings. Not one for doing this kind of thing, I surprised myself and, on a whim, asked for a reading. During the reading, the lady said to me, "Kim, you will experience loss in the next year." I sighed as I logically assumed it meant one of my aging parents, or that maybe Dave's parents might pass, and that would be the loss that we would experience. I never thought too much about it until a year later after losing half of my precious family, our dog, and our home: unimaginable loss.

After his death, someone pointed out to me the quote Jack had had on his Instagram, weeks before he was killed. It seemed prophetic.

> Don't cry because it is over.
> Smile because it happened.
> —Dr. Seuss

What whisper did his soul know about what was going to happen?

I had spent a lifetime being busy and feeling driven to prove myself successful. I strove to be a super wife, a super mom, a successful career woman, and an engaged community member. I spent a lot of time in my head, reacting—instead of in my heart, feeling. And, I would have said that I'd been happy in the world.

I'd had it all, I thought naively. Now stripped bare, I felt a deep gratitude that my life and the life of my daughter had been miraculously spared. I thanked the first responders and God for that. Some people asked me if I was mad at God for not intervening and preventing the tragedy. I'd heard that anger toward God is a common occurrence after a tragic experience and death. Curiously, I did not feel that at all. I was heartbroken and immensely sad, but I never had that anger toward a higher power; I had more gratitude and wonder as to how on earth my daughter and I survived in the flow. My experience seemed complex; I was facing devastating loss, yet I felt profound wonder and gratitude. My daughter miraculously rose out of a twenty-foot-deep entombment, like a powerful phoenix rising. She is stronger than she ever imagined. When I decorated her childhood bedroom, I hung a sign my aunt had designed. The sign messaged something to the effect that my daughter was strong and powerful. This focal point in her childhood bedroom could not have been more fitting for the strength Lauren exhibited struggling to stay alive while buried under the mud.

After losing Jack and Dave, I felt changed.

Part of the change is due to my shock, but now I am more fully present, and I live more in the moment. I continue to survive by focusing on each moment at any given time. I am profoundly different than I was before losing my son and husband. I am more spiritual and open to believing people with intuitive capabilities. So much of my life, I lived in a rational, precise, and scientific business world. Now, through the events I had experienced, I have changed. I feel much more. Now, I am aware of love coming to and through me more than ever before. I'm more present in the moment. Losing my son and husband, and meeting so many people who supported Lauren and me through our loss and during our search, opened me up to seeing and feeling more deeply.

I had been cracked open through our unfathomable tragedy. My life might be described as resembling the "art of precious scars," as in the Kintsugi art form.

I look different now too. For most of my adult life I had highlighted my hair blond. That is the hair color the kids knew. Jack had often asked that I switch to my natural hair color, which was more akin to his and Lauren's. So one November day after the slide, near Jack's birthday, I asked my hairdresser to color it my natural color. After the chestnut hair dye was applied, I quickly took a picture and texted it to Lauren in class with the caption "twins." She was shocked, but laughed. It was a big change, but it felt right and was easier to manage. As an unexpected perk, it allowed me more anonymity in town; I was not as easily recognized from the slide media coverage.

Like many who experience sudden loss, I have read a lot of books to learn about the afterlife and what happens after we die. Up until I lost my son and husband, my beliefs were more conventional, consisting of what I learned as a child and in Sunday School. Heaven, as I imagined it, was a spectacular place with big pearly gates, angels with wings, and unparalleled joy. After the tragedy, a neighborhood friend and fellow school parent, who had intuitive abilities, called me to say, "Kim, both Dave and Jack are in pure joy," and "they are all around you." This was a comforting idea. While I was distraught and inconsolable about losing my husband and son, her message gave me some peace when hearing that they both were in pure joy. Who wouldn't want that for their loved ones? Hearing they were "okay" in this different way, was comforting.

I now have a more expanded view of heaven. I still believe it is magnificent and full of pure joy, but I don't think of heaven as a place just "up there." I feel that heaven is everywhere all around us in some invisible, mysterious way, as are the souls of those we love. And I'm convinced that we are all connected through love. The debris flow items found, just when I needed them the most, and the many inexplicable events I experienced after the mudslide, make me believe that we are more than just our physical bodies.

Various books and podcasts discuss that some people who are about to transition, or those who have had a near-death experience, often describe vivid visions with deceased relatives or friends appearing in their dreams. Hospice workers who tend to patients who are about to die report this as well. Perhaps as these visits present a welcoming entry into the eternal realm, they make thoughts of leaving this world less sad or frightening. Or perhaps they are clues that one's life is about to end. Dave's vivid dream of his late brother, Michael, may well have been a coincidence, or maybe it was a hint that Dave would soon be with his brother.

The things that I experienced both a short time before and for years after losing part of my family illuminated for me that there are things bigger than ourselves working in our lives. There is an interconnectedness that seems utterly profound.

CHAPTER 36

GRIEF: AN "AND" CONVERSATION

IN JUNE 2022, my small duffel bag was packed as I prepared to drive up to the Bay Area to pick Lauren up from Stanford University. I was not dreading the six-hour trip. Driving the central California coast was scenic: farmland, ranches, famed coastal beach towns like Pismo Beach and Morro Bay. Large signs and grand entrances graced the wineries that had sprung up along the route. This stretch of 250 miles from Santa Barbara to Palo Alto was a straight shot for the most part. I liked that. Now, more than ever, I liked simplicity.

I knew I'd need every inch of my car to pack Lauren's dorm stuff, and I was looking forward to having her home for the summer. Freshman year could be the most challenging year for any student, given the big life transition to college and living away from home. For Lauren, it must have been that and more. As she packed for school, she took with her all the trauma she'd endured while buried alive, and the grief she stored that was still waiting until she was ready to let it out.

With six hours driving ahead of me, I'd have lots of time to reflect on our year; to reflect on the last four and a half years.

Driving through the Gaviota tunnel, I'd officially leave Southern California and enter Central California. I took a deep breath as I entered the tunnel. Each time my family would go through this short mountain tunnel, I'd enthusiastically call out, *"Hold your breath and make a wish!"* That memory was a fun goofy moment that I think about each time I drive through the tunnel.

The drive triggered a lot of memories.

As I drove Route 101 near the town of Arroyo Grande, I noticed the exit we'd take to the Lopez Lake campground, to join a dear high school friend and her family for a summer week of camping. At another part of the freeway, I recalled when our bikes fell off the tent-camper and we had to retrieve them on the side of the road. We were so lucky no one got hurt.

I smiled when I thought about staying back with Jack from a day of jet-skiing on the lake because he had an ear infection. That sunny day, he and I strolled into town and headed to the ice cream parlor. Jack got two scoops. With ice cream cones in hand, we crossed the street, where I got my first "how to quilt" book and starter fabric kit at a cute quilting shop. Little did I know, that visit to the quilt store would be the start of a hobby that I would fully enjoy and embrace. I thanked Jack for that.

Today on my drive, I could smile because my heart was grateful for those memories, despite a few tears welling up. I'd learned that grief never went away, but for me it was shifting into gratefulness for the adventures and the depth of love I'd experienced. I felt the full array of emotions; sadness, love, and appreciation.

Ten minutes later, I saw the exit sign for the famed Madonna Inn hotel and restaurant. This unique hotel was known for individually themed guest rooms, with one appropriately called the "Cave Room." That room was booked year-round, and its décor and rock walls made it seem like one was really sleeping in a cave. For Lauren and me, this hotel was the stopping point for a lunch or sometimes an overnight stay as I drove her to her weeklong summer camp.

After I parked my car, I entered the coffee shop and took a seat at the copper-covered counter for a quick bite. Today, I simply enjoyed watching the other guests. I noted that difference in me. When I first walked into that restaurant in Lake Arrowhead a few months after the tragedy, I was struck by my loneliness. I felt so alone, and I'd sadly look at the other guests enjoying dinner with their spouses and families. Today, as I sat at the dining counter, I overheard a conversation that an eight-year-old boy was having with his mother. Frank Sinatra's famed "Fly Me to the Moon" was playing over the restaurant speaker. The boy exclaimed loudly, "Mom, I like this music they're playing!" The 30-something couple next to me chuckled, saying, "What eight-year-old says that?" I looked at them and said, "Isn't that terrific?"

I was in the moment. I was fully present and able to appreciate what was happening around me. The shock had worn off. In this case, I delighted in hearing the joy that an eight-year-old found in music that clearly was not of his generation. This sense of being present mirrored the way in which I have changed since the tragedy. And in this case, I saw it as a positive shift.

This trip even felt markedly different than the same one in September. Nine months ago, I was driving Lauren to school without my family, feeling the enormity of the loss and the responsibility. Lauren's milestone of starting college was missed by Dave and Jack. But today driving to pick her up after her freshman year, I simply felt more present.

This *was* my life now. I could feel the happiness and anticipation of seeing Lauren after ten long weeks.

I feel the gratitude, *and* I feel the sadness when I remember the memories along the 101 that my family had shared. I doubt the hole will ever be filled, yet I know I'm adapting.

During this drive, I thought about the notion of adapting. I'd read various articles and books speaking to the importance of adaptability. Life shifted, and unexpected things happened in our lives. It would always be that way. I was striving to be less attached to the outcome. I think because I'm less attached to a specific outcome, I can simply be more present. Maybe this is a silver lining.

I have changed. I have a wisdom that I never asked for; the wisdom of profound grief. And grief makes us human. It is part of the human experience.

Through it all, I was fileted open. Somehow this journey's path enabled me to be open to follow various threads — even the alternative ones that became a part of the search effort for Jack. If we had *only* relied on the science, or the canine search dogs, or the ground-penetrating radar, or the methodical approach to clearing the debris piles and plotting the results on the map, I doubt we would have found what we found. A combination of it all led to the final discovery. The interconnectedness of it all made it happen. Maybe that is what I have learned: no one thing is the silver bullet. There is value to being open and observant to things that present themselves.

Various clues kept the team engaged searching, and it was an intuitive clue that prompted us to clear the pile we'd been missing all along. I certainly don't know how it all works, but I can't deny what this journey has illustrated for me, or the synchronicities we experienced. What I do believe is that we are more than our physical bodies.

We each can make a huge difference for one another by engaging like so many in my community did. Using one's talents to help another in their time of need made a huge healing difference for my daughter and me as we navigated the unimaginable. I was witness to a community who engaged to help, and who stayed to help — long after the immediacy of the tragedy. That was a profound gift for me and Lauren.

I pulled on every thread available to me to try to find closure and find some of Jack's remains. Listening to my intuition, I knew he was not swept to the ocean. This was validated even more when we found multiple areas that were never checked or properly searched. I listened to Jack's message that Catherine kept hearing: "I will be found." And I chose to believe him because the fabric of Jack's character included honesty.

So, how have I evolved? Well, for sure, I have more patience. That was forced on me. I had to wait 1,218 days for some of Jack's remains to be found. I learned patience and felt a peace knowing it would happen — one day. Oddly, during those long three years of searching, somehow, I learned to have less attachment to the outcome. Sadly, not all of Jack was found. Yet, I had a newfound peace; what we did find could be enough for me. Less attachment to a specific outcome or thing created more peace and calm in me. I certainly recognize that in my new home. The furnishings are simply functional for me — I'm much less invested in them. They work, they look fine, and I'm not too attached to them. Appreciating people and experiences, and being present and aware in life, are my focus now.

The six-hour drive was over. As my car pulled up to the curb in front of my daughter's dorm building, I saw a group of six or so students walking with Lauren, each with a smile. Each student had a box, or a duffel bag. One had a guitar, and another was carrying a large plastic bin. *What's this?* I thought as Lauren approached me.

"Mom, my friends each carried some of my stuff down from my room," she said with appreciation. "It would have taken me at least ten trips to get it all down three flights of stairs."

"Wow! Thank you!" I exclaimed to the students.

The impact of helping another person makes a huge difference.

I'm taking what I've learned with me on the rest of my journey.

CHAPTER 37

WHY ME?

WHY NOT ME?
I believe that each of us are on earth to evolve toward love. A month after I lost my son and husband, I called a colleague from my days in a medical device company. We had attended UCLA together. She had been a kinesiology major, and I had majored in political science. Kristin had been in the sorority house next to mine, both located across from campus. After graduation, our paths crossed often when she joined the same medical device company. Kristin was selected to take my position as a sales representative after my promotion. She was assigned to one of my key former accounts, UCLA Medical Center. I knew she'd work hard for all my former customers, many of whom I'd come to consider dear colleagues and friends. After a few years, when I saw Kristin at the corporate headquarters, I noticed she had changed. She no longer dressed in a conservative corporate, navy-blue suit; instead, she was dressed more like Fleetwood Mac's Stevie Nicks, circa the *Rumors* album. Kristin was changing. She decided to leave a career where she had spent many years in the world of Western

medicine—studying kinesiology at UCLA and working for a Fortune 500 company with world-renowned surgeons—to become an evolutionary astrologer.

"A what?" I exclaimed, totally perplexed when she told me of her plan.

She explained why evolutionary astrology inspired her. She was clear about her move into this new-age, spiritual area that was different from her conventional past. Years later I spoke to her on the phone soon after the disaster, letting her know about Dave's and Jack's deaths. It was at that time she introduced me to the metaphor of Kintsugi. As she shared her condolences, Kristin said with conviction, "Kim, this is not the first lifetime you've lived when your family has died. I sense in a past life you carried your family on your back like a warrior after they were killed."

Wow! This is getting weird, I thought.

Kristin explained that sometimes souls experience similar tragedies as they reincarnate. She added that if someone had an addiction in a past life, that event might recur in a subsequent life. I was stunned by Kristin's message.

"Kristin, oh my God, please tell me some good news. I can't imagine experiencing losing my family so tragically and early, ever again. How do I *not* sign up for *that* again?"

She reiterated to me that Kintsugi was an example for my life and my possible metamorphosis that could happen in response to my loss. Once broken and repaired with gold lacquer, an item could be considered more beautiful. Said differently, something broken and scarred could be put back together and repaired one day.

What a phone call. I went to lie down and relax after that mind-blowing conversation.

A year later, an intuitive helping with my search for Jack said, "You've lost family members tragically early in prior lives," but she assured me with, "No, it won't happen again to you."

"Why not?" I asked.

She said, "Because in your past lives, you could not move on after your family's death. You could not find peace. This time, you will find your way to peace and acceptance. You will be able to carry on with the rest of your life. That's one of the things you are supposed to learn and teach others who have experienced similar tragedy."

In our phone call, my friend Kristin had gone on to tell me that you must reenter the fracture in order to heal it. She said this occurs so the soul is re-submerged in the emotional waters that must flow in order to grow, versus remaining frozen from old trauma.

It was interesting to hear the similar messages. I would not stay incapacitated by grief; somehow, I would be able to attain peace and move forward in life. Dave and Jack would want Lauren and me to thrive and be happy. I know that because I would want *them* to thrive if the tables were turned. I also know this because of the generosity of their souls; each of them would want us to be happy. Brilliantly happy, one day.

I am wiser about the experience of grief.

I've learned firsthand about the emptiness in my heart when I think about losing Dave, Jack, and Chester. I will feel like I'm doing okay, but then I'll feel like I've been hit in the chest with an overwhelming wave of sadness.

The waves roll in at unexpected times. What I know for certain, is that I have been cracked open.

I've witnessed events I cannot explain: The ultrasound of Jack in my belly was found 409 days after the mudslide, wedged between two rocks, in the elements, by the cliffs at Butterfly Beach on Valentine's Day, and in perfect condition. The pictures of Jack or Dave that people sent to me on special occasions when I needed it the most. When our search team felt dejected and began losing hope, it was then we'd find a special item revealed in the mud, which would give us the jolt we needed to continue.

The special quilt with the silhouette of Dave and Jack's first scuba dive, tattered yet with the silhouette appliqué still on the fabric is another example. About two and a half years after the mudslide, six canine forensic search dogs alerted on the same location, helping the university anthropology department target that soil for testing. The items revealed and experiences that defied logic kept my hope alive and my spirits bolstered. Through it all, I began to heal through my search efforts. And, as with grief, the search and process was not linear.

I like to think that Dave and Jack are around Lauren and me all the time; simply at a frequency I can't see. I imagine them as two guardian angels watching over us. I celebrate their lives, and I am grateful for the love we shared. I honor their lives by how I live out mine.

CHAPTER 38

FINDING JACK, PIECES OF LOVE

THE SEARCH for Jack was how I expressed love for my child. The search for Jack opened hearts. The intuitives told me that Jack had communicated that he would be found, and I believed them.

I am grateful that Catherine urged me to talk to a detective, and that I was willing to follow this thread of advice. Days later, this act manifested in a full engagement of a local university professor, a bioarcheologist, who offered to create a class for students to apply their science and technology to support the search effort. Through this, the university lab and the forensic and bioarchaeological professor had an introduction with the Santa Barbara Search and Rescue team. I'm hopeful that the two groups will collaborate even sooner in the event of another disaster, potentially helping more people. Maybe, just maybe, together they can employ the technology and forensic and bioarchaeological skills to see if they can find the remains of victims still unrecovered from the 2005 La Conchita mudslide. It would give the anthropology students a learning environment nearby, and may just help some of the survivors get more closure.

The professor designed new scientific techniques in her efforts. Now these new protocols may be a study design that helps research in other parts of the world when tragedy hits.

The "lipo" I had harvested created training aids for the search dogs. Wouldn't it be amazing if that training resource helps a dog to successfully locate another missing person for their family?

My journey through grief was agonizing, and continues to leave an unhealable hole in my heart. Because Jack was listed as missing, he was not one of the 21 immediately confirmed victims who had their pictures posted with a few sentences about their lives, for viewers to read and see. Instead, because Jack was one of the two missing children, the community learned perhaps more about him and his life than they would have otherwise. We got to hear about the love he gave in his short life. The community learned that Jack co-created and led a youth community service group, and this touched their hearts. The city created a Jack Cantin Youth Volunteer Award. Now a youth under 21 who leads in community efforts can receive this award, presented to them by the mayor. I hope that because of this award, even more local teens will be inspired to volunteer and give back to their community.

The Boy Scouts of America in the Pacific Coast District created the Jack Cantin Memorial Scout of the Year Award. Jack had earned the ranks of Eagle Scout and Eagle Scout with Palms (honors) when he was 15. The Boy Scouts recognized the impact Jack had had in his short life with Scouts, and how he refurbished an entire basketball recess area at a local elementary school. At his middle school, they dedicated a new flagpole to Jack with a plaque at the base that reads, "He gave more than he got," citing a quote from Lord Baden Powell, the founder of the scouting movement.

The community learned of Jack's kindness, philanthropy, and his sense of humor that was a gift to us all. Through this, love was revealed through all the people in the community and beyond who helped and prayed for us in our time of need.

Like my treasured Kintsugi-repaired green pig that I proudly display with its gold scars, Lauren and I are also healing. The metaphorical "gold adhesive" that binds us back together is made up of the love of friends, family, and community members who contributed their individual touches that work to repair our broken hearts.

The combination of science, people's effort, and the clues that were given to me, like a beautifully pieced-together quilt, weaved together and resulted in this hoped-for outcome. I'm glad I was willing and open to follow all the threads of this intricate and beautiful search quilt.

I know I would have crumbled if my son were found while I was lying in the hospital injured and in shock. Since the search took over three years, I was more prepared for the outcome and in a way, less attached to it. The search journey was so unbelievable. I was in a better place, knowing that Dave and Jack exist in full joy.

I plan to honor the lives of my husband and my son by striving to give others love, just as I received it in response to my loss.

PART 6
EPILOGUE

"I'm Still Standing"
—Elton John

YEARS LATER

ON A SUNNY DECEMBER eighteen months after Jack's bones were first recovered, Lauren and I packed the car with the items that we wanted to place into his casket. Unbelievably, it took that long to finally get permission to bury the remains next to his father at the cemetery. Along with the priest, only Lauren and I were there for the burial to attain closure. It seemed intimate and private, with just the two of us laying Jack to rest. In my car that morning, we hung the navy blue suit, orange tie (his favorite color), and white shirt that my friend had purchased almost five years ago—soon after the tragedy, when we thought Jack's body would imminently be recovered.

As we walked into the funeral home, the beautiful mahogany wood casket lay open, exposing a serene, white-pillowed satin interior. I broke down crying when I saw the casket. Seeing it made losing Jack even more real. I certainly knew that he was gone, but my reaction was one of profound sadness at the permanent loss of a 17-year-old who had so much more living to do. Feelings of relief were mixed with my tears. Finally, Jack would get the burial he deserved, and that we needed.

That morning, Lauren said she wanted to help dress the inside of the casket, and lay the suit in place. "He was so big," she softly said between the tears, as she delicately placed the suit, shirt, and tie in the casket, as if a body was inside the suit. Before she did that, I had draped in the quilt I had made for this occasion. Stitched onto it was a silhouette of our family. My mother had crocheted an orange throw, which Mom wanted placed near his feet. After Lauren had arranged some items, I placed the throw at the foot of the casket, where typically the feet would be. Jack's favorite childhood toy was a Stitch plush doll. Lovingly, Lauren placed the doll inside, and wrapped an arm of the suit jacket around it. Then, we laid in an amazing lightsaber that was given to us by a kind, compassionate soul who learned that Jack was a huge Star Wars fan. Jack would have loved that.

A few days prior, I had purchased a beautiful wooden box to hold the bones that had been recovered, so they could be in this special box inside the casket. To my surprise, Lauren said that she wanted to see the bones.

"Lauren, if you see them, you can't unsee them," I cautioned her. "Don't you want to remember your brother just with his great big smile?"

"No, Mom, I want to see them. I never got to see Dad, and I wanted to; it would have helped me know it was real."

I had read a few books about different cultures, and many encourage those living to sit with and see the body of the deceased, realizing how important that can be in the closure and grief process. Listening to her request, I decided to let her see the bones.

Lauren wailed and cried, which was monumental. Her crying was so significant because for years she had told me she felt numb, and that she could not get to the emotion of the grief. Today, she was able to express her grief through crying and sobbing, and I sensed that it was cathartic. I was relieved to hear the pain move out of her, almost as an overfilled balloon gets untied and gradually releases its air.

As we did some final casket preparations, I tucked in the letters that some of Jack's friends had written to him. We felt good about how we prepared the casket, and we got ready to travel to the cemetery.

I did not anticipate how profound this process would be for me and for Lauren in our healing journey. The ritual of a casket burial helped me to appreciate the power of cultural traditions and rites of passage. I certainly did not have a conventional route to this outcome, yet I was glad it finally happened.

Lauren and I followed the hearse to the cemetery, and met the priest at the plot. With all the publicity about the tragedy, it felt perfect that today it was just Lauren and me. After the prayers, we watched the casket go into the ground next to my late husband's plot. Although December, this day was a spectacularly beautiful clear, warm, and sunny day.

Finally laid to rest almost five years after the tragedy

"I'm glad this chapter is done. It went on too long," Lauren said after the casket was in place. I hoped that this meant she would be able to have more closure. I knew that I had always wanted Jack to be buried, and not left in debris. Going through this process made me realize how emotionally important it was to me. Being able to bury the bone fragments helped to give me and my family some much-needed comfort. I am aware that in the future, as homes are being rebuilt or creeks widened, there is a chance we might find more of his remains. If we do, we will get those tucked into the casket as well, and we will be grateful for the find. I choose to focus on where his soul lives now, and I believe that he is in pure joy, along with my husband.

Like the yellow flowers that illustrated a beauty where there should be none, I choose to look for the positive.

I recently got word that every scout in Dave's original troop earned the top rank of Eagle Scout. Only a small percentage of scouts nationally ever make the rank of Eagle. Now 100% of Dave's original troop of 13 earned this highest rank. They are fine young men who give back to their communities and are strong leaders. Not only that, but as Montecito's Troop 33 continues to expand in size, it warms my heart to see the legacy my husband left with the troop, through the young men that he mentored. Many of the scouts' parents tell me that Dave played an important role in their sons' lives, and that makes me very proud.

Love found a way.

IN MEMORY

Faviola Benitez Calderon, 28
Jonathan Benitez, 10
Kailly Benitez, 3
Joseph Francis Bleckel, 87
Martín Cabrera-Muñoz, 48
David Cantin, 49
John "Jack" Cantin, 17
Morgan Corey, 25
Sawyer Corey, 12
Peter Fleurat, 73
Josephine "Josie" Gower, 69
John McManigal, 61
Alice Mitchell, 78
James Mitchell, 89
Caroline Montgomery, 22
Mark Montgomery, 54
Marilyn Ramos, 27
Rebecca Riskin, 61
Roy Rohter, 84
Peerawat "Pasta" Sutthithepa, 6
Pinit "Oom" Sutthithepa, 30
Lydia Sutthithepa, 2
Richard Loring Taylor, 79

Cory Iverson, 32,
firefighter killed in the Thomas Fire, December 14, 2017

And, in gratitude and loving memory of search
dog extraordinaire, who never gave up,
"MacGyver" Stein (June 14, 2022. Eight years old.)

ACKNOWLEDGMENTS

LYING IN the hospital bed injured, I felt a profound gratefulness to God for sparing my life and that of my daughter. After the journey of writing this book and recalling all of the amazing, sometimes inexplicable occurrences during the search for Jack and Lydia, I am even more grateful and filled with awe.

My heartfelt thanks goes out to everyone who helped and supported me in my endeavor to tell my story and write my first book.

To my amazing daughter, Lauren, who supported this work and was willing to share her experience to help others. There is no one I love and adore more. Your bravery, courage, wisdom, and kindness continue to inspire me. We alone have the shared experience in our family of four, as well as our unimaginable tragedy and its aftermath. I wish for you continued healing; I am encouraged as I watch you strive to create for yourself a life of joy and meaning.

To Jack and Dave. For trying to help from your new residence, and for helping me feel your love.

To my extended family. Thank you for your continued support and for loving Lauren and me. I love you each tremendously.

The Sacred Search Team — Rick Stein, MacGyver (RIP), Ann Burgard, Sherri Ball, Grant Dyruff, Catherine Weissenberg, Allison and Jacques Marcillac, Shirley Smith and Keegan — my deepest appreciation. This book could have never happened without each of you. There would not have been this sacred search team story. Without you, the search would have never advanced nor achieved the final outcome. Over three years you engaged with me to look for the missing kids. Not only did your efforts advance the search, but they also gave me the support I needed in my grief to work toward healing. Through your efforts going out with me, I got to witness true kindness, compassion, and generosity of spirit. Each of you played a part in supporting me, so that I did not give up hope. And I learned how important hope is. To Jake Jaakola, thank you for your expertise and advice. If it had not been for you, we would not have gotten to the point to seek out a forensic bioarcheologist and university team, which unearthed the miraculous discovery. And, in each of you, I gained new treasured friends.

To the first responders that heroically rescued Lauren and me — I am forever grateful: Andy Rupp, Ben Hauser, Jeff Villareal, Garet Blake, Kevin Taylor, Pat McElroy, and every one of the heroic first responders who engaged to help. And to those with unique intuitive talents, and who used those to try to help find the missing children, including Suzanne, Catherine, Marisa, LeAnn, Jan, Deb, Karee, and the other kind souls. You each gave with generosity of spirit, aiming to use your talents to help a grieving mother. Your efforts and clues helped us refine the search area, and gave me hope.

There are more people than can be mentioned who each helped post-tragedy and throughout the search, and I appreciate each one of you. Montecito Fire for prepping the soil for the canine historical human remains effort, and who always engages to support the community. To Das Williams/Lisa Valencia Sherratt, who responded to my request to inquire as to where the county hauled-away debris went, and who coordinated a cross-departmental meeting at the Fire House. To all the kind neighbors (too many to name) who went out of their way to provide me with support, graciousness, and compassion, by granting me and the team permission to search on properties, offering a meal or simply access to use their facilities when we were out long days searching. And of course, "popping up" whenever I seemed to need search support, Noel Strogoff and her three sweet-hearted children who invited Jack into their lives as a topic of conversation. To Abe Powell and the Santa Barbara Bucket Brigade, who helped clear the mud-ridden areas while searching for the missing kids; and to general contractor Darrell Becker who carefully searched as he cleared damaged lots. Appreciation to the Santa Barbara Search and Rescue canine division's search dogs and handlers, including Anne Marie and Riley: a profound thank you for each of your efforts. For the dog handlers that came from Southern California to search — thank you. Your volunteer efforts are vital to any community. To the university professor, Dr. Kurin, and her student volunteers, who came out to use their expertise and science to try to help a grieving mother, and the community, find the remains of her late son. I was witness to your tireless effort, professionalism, technology, science, and compassion.

To Anna who gave of herself so graciously to support Lauren post tragedy and encouraged her faith. Many community members, neighbors, dear friends, the Charity League ladies, the Teens on the Scene teens and parents, the Middle School community, to name a few. To Cottage Hospital for great medical care and for establishing the "How We Heal" group for the survivors of the mudslide, led by Layla Farinpour. The group you created should be a model used in every community, as it was instrumental toward healing and support. To all the non-profits who engaged to help after the disaster, such as Unity Shoppe and Direct Relief; you make a positive difference in lives. To everyone else who helped in the search or in the tragedy's aftermath whom I have not named here — thank you.

For reading and commenting on my early manuscript efforts, I thank Sherri Ball, Anne Bakstad, Kathleen Cantin, Marie Cantin, Joe, Noreen, and Ellie Chenoweth, Brian Gardener, Stacey Michaels, Kathy Miller, Nella Miller, Pam Neumann, Fiona Stone, Doug Stone, Catherine Weissenberg, and Kim Wise. You each gave me valuable feedback that I took to heart as I shaped the story, as I felt it needed to be told. To my dear friend Lydia Martinez, who cheerfully said "yes!" to my request to help me early on. Friends from college, I knew with your expertise teaching English and knowing me well, that you'd provide sage advice. You helped shape my early draft by making corrections to grammar, suggesting modifications to sentence and paragraph structure, and with skillfully posed helpful questions that prompted me toward more meaningful content development. Your ability to laugh and find humor in all things — even when directed toward me — makes me smile and makes me treasure you even more.

I am so grateful to my editor, Leslie Wells: I'm so thrilled you agreed to work with me and my project, despite this being my first book. Your extensive background editing over 49 bestsellers made it an honor to work with you. Your beautiful editing and vision helped shape my book even more into the story I felt it needed to be. I appreciated your encouragement. Your willingness to review my draft jacket summaries, or book cover options, and to respond to my other novice questions is so valued and appreciated. You helped make the process easy, whichever country I was in while we worked. To Julie Simpson and your skillful fine-toothed comb, ensuring we caught as much as possible in the layout before we called it "pencils down," thank you.

For reading my finished manuscript, I thank Kenny Loggins, Suzanne Giesemann, Catherine Weissenberg, Rob Lowe, Jean Harding-Miller, Don Fergussen, Marsha Prudden, Leslie Zemeckis, Anne Bakstad, Kim Wise, Layla Farinpour, Michael Stamos, Sue Grau, and Dr. Gayle Beebe—I am humbled by your continued generosity of heart.

Taking on this endeavor, I simply had no idea the number of people involved to bring a book to market. Thank you, Precocity Press, for publishing my words. Thank you to my supportive and insightful book shepherd and designer, Susan Shankin, who was a continual source of encouragement and who took the extra step to seek out Luisa Millicent, an artist, to manifest a book cover that I envisioned.

Dea Shandera-Hunter, I appreciate your interest in my book and your integrity and authenticity while working media outreach and publicity, so that the book can land in front of the eyes that most need to see it, and can reach those who may benefit in some way from hearing this story of hope. Darcy Hughes, Dream Work Marketing, thank you for being my right hand as you helped envision the needed website and the promotional aspects. Jonathan Kirsch, my copyright attorney, you made the process manageable; I appreciate that you guided me in what I needed to do to properly prepare the book so it complies with all legal requirements. To Ryan Stonerock for graciously reviewing parts of the manuscript to ensure it messaged in the way I intended. To all the helpers not mentioned in the above, my sincere thank you.

CREDITS

1. "Flowers" from *The Dhammapada: The Sayings of the Buddha* by Thomas Byrom, translation copyright © 1976 by Thomas Byrom. Used by permission of Vintage Books, an imprint of the Knopf Doubleday Publishing Group, a division of Penguin Random House LLC. All rights.

2. "I Dreamed a Dream," from *Les Misérables*. Songwriters: Jean-Marc Natel, Herbert Kretzmer, Claude-Michel Schönberg, Alain Boublil. Lyrics Chappelle Music, Inc.

3. Selections from the writings of Catherine A. Weissenberg, copyright 2022 by Catherine A. Weissenberg.

4. Selection of rescue images provided by photographer Tom Piozet, copyright 2018 by Tom Piozet.

5. Photo of Lauren Cantin onstage, ONE805 Kick-Ash Bash 2018. Copyright ONE805.org, permission by Richard Weston Smith, President and Co-Founder.

6. Photo of Lauren Cantin singing at Teens Sing for Santa Barbara by Steve Kennedy, copyright 2018 by Steve Kennedy.

7. Image copyright on search dog images JC Corliss secured 11-28-2022.

ABOUT THE AUTHOR

KIM CANTIN was living the American Dream in Montecito, California, along with her loving husband, two great kids, and their goofy dog — until the early morning of January 9, 2018, when catastrophe struck in the form of a natural disaster.

She met her husband Dave when they both worked at Johnson & Johnson. Having enjoyed a 20-year career in sales and marketing leadership, working for a Fortune 500 medical device company, she later started her own successful marketing consulting firm so that she could have more work and family balance. She also worked as a senior director of marketing for Teleflex Urology. In her spare time, Kim volunteered in the community and was involved in her children's activities.

Kim still resides in the Santa Barbara, California area. When she isn't spending time with her daughter, friends, or family, she is with her two pups.

Where Yellow Flowers Bloom is her first book.

For more information visit KimCantin.com.

www.ingramcontent.com/pod-product-compliance
Lightning Source LLC
LaVergne TN
LVHW091548070526
838199LV00024B/579/J